BIG ASIAN ENERGY

BIG ASIAN ENERGY

An Unapologetic Guide for
Breaking Barriers to Leadership and Success

JOHN WANG

Tiny
Reparations
Books

An imprint of Penguin Random House LLC
1745 Broadway, New York, NY 10019
penguinrandomhouse.com

Illustrations by Victoria Black

Low-context to high-context countries charts on pp. 182 and 185 from *The Culture Map* by Erin Meyer,
copyright © 2014. Reprinted by permission of PublicAffairs, an imprint of Hachette Book Group, Inc.

Parenting style chart on pp. 87–88 by Dr. Shimi Kang, MD, author of *The Dolphin Way*.

LIBRARY OF CONGRESS CATALOGING-IN-PUBLICATION DATA
Names: Wang, John (Leadership coach), author.
Title: Big Asian energy : an unapologetic guide for breaking
barriers to leadership and success / John Wang.
Description: [New York] : Tiny Reparations Books, [2025]
Identifiers: LCCN 2024042794 (print) | LCCN 2024042795 (ebook) |
ISBN 9780593475430 (hardcover) | ISBN 9780593475447 (epub)
Subjects: LCSH: Leadership. | Asian American businesspeople. | Success in business.
Classification: LCC HD57.7 .W3556 2025 (print) | LCC HD57.7 (ebook) |
DDC 658.4/092—dc23/eng/20250217
LC record available at https://lccn.loc.gov/2024042794
LC ebook record available at https://lccn.loc.gov/2024042795

Printed in the United States of America
1st Printing

BOOK DESIGN BY KRISTIN DEL ROSARIO

To my mom and dad:
Some say that writing a book is like birthing a child,
so now you can't complain I haven't
given you any grandkids yet.

CONTENTS

BIG
ASIAN
ENERGY

Welcome to a New Generation of Asians

There has never been a better time to be *Asian*, especially in the Western world.

The last few years have brought a flurry of wins: Michelle Yeoh became the first Asian to win the Academy Award for Best Actress; both *Parasite* and *Everything Everywhere All at Once* won Best Picture Oscars; *Crazy Rich Asians* became the highest-grossing romantic comedy in a decade; Marvel's *Shang-Chi and the Legend of the Ten Rings* broke box office records; and K-pop groups BTS and BLACKPINK topped the Billboard music charts and became the top-selling acts in the world. Everywhere I look, there seems to be more Asian representation in Western mainstream media.

I still remember the excitement I felt, going to the movie theater with friends to watch *Crazy Rich Asians* and *Shang-Chi* on their opening weekends. It felt momentous. For the first time, we weren't just stereotypes, fetishes, or sidekicks. We were romantic leads and superheroes. When *Everything Everywhere All at Once* followed, we were excited to see more relatable stories come alive—somewhere between the ridiculousness of a raccoon chef and people kung fu fighting with floppy rubber marital aids was a deep and heartfelt story about the nuances of Asian American families, immigrant struggles, and intergenerational trauma. The theater felt electric with the air of change, and it seemed as if the possibilities were endless. With greater representation in art, in business, in tech, in politics—including Kamala Harris, the first Asian American presidential candidate—it felt like we had finally arrived.

These were hard-won achievements for Asian representation, but it also seemed that underneath the glam and glitz of progress, there were subtler, deeper problems and struggles that were swept under the rug. Our stereotypes may have evolved, but they have not disappeared. The old, underlying perceptions of who we are, and the gates that have previously locked us out, remain as impenetrable as ever.

For example, studies conducted by Ascend Foundation and MIT Sloan School of Management have shown the "bamboo ceiling" is still prevalent. The phrase was coined to describe how Asian American employees, particularly those from East Asian backgrounds, are vastly underrepresented in positions of leadership, such as among executives, CEOs, and board members. We are less likely to be promoted into management positions. We are seen as good workers but not as good leaders. And more and more, despite the pushes of diversity initiatives, studies show that Asian job applicants who hide their race on résumés still get *twice* the callback rate of those who don't.

There remains this elusive impression that Asians are hardworking and nice, but are also shy. Many are told they lack leadership or strong communication skills. These misconceptions also impact us outside the workplace, including in our social groups and even in our dating prospects.

Many of our deeper struggles have gone unspoken or unnoticed in mainstream media. Research studies show that only 22 percent of Asian Americans say they feel that they belong and are accepted in the US. Asian American students are experiencing a higher rate of impostor syndrome and struggle with self-confidence or self-criticism more than any other racial group. But when the topic is brought up, many of us feel uncomfortable complaining about it, as we don't want to be seen as complaining or as victims. For a long time, I tried to stay far away from even being identified as "Asian," because it feels like it puts me into a box, which I desperately wanted to avoid.

That's the problem with the "model minority" stereotype. We're often put into boxes by others that we struggle to get out of. We are told that working hard, keeping our head down, and not making waves will lead to success. And when we're then passed over for jobs, promotions, or other goals, we're told to stop complaining or that our problems aren't serious enough. Often, when the issues Asian Americans face are brought up, the dominant narrative dismisses our concerns. Some might enforce the stereotype, saying, "Oh, that's just who they are; Asians don't speak up." Ignoring the fact that being treated like perpetual foreigners might be why we might not speak up to begin with. Or that even our pointing out the fact that we've been put into a box, based solely on how we look, feels to us that we're causing trouble or being unreasonable. And after a while, we've come to believe and accept it.

In my own journey, I've seen and heard so many of these types of experiences, firsthand. As a leadership coach and workshop facilitator, I've spent the last fifteen years working with hundreds of Asian clients and students from a variety of backgrounds. Some were professionals at Fortune 500 companies like Google, American Express, Goldman Sachs, and Apple, while others included health care workers, firefighters, stay-at-home parents, or seven-figure entrepreneurs. I've also held workshops and spoken at colleges, public organizations, TEDx, and corporations such as McKinsey. The people I've worked with often have diverse backgrounds: most had been living in North America for years, many were second-, third-, or even fourth-generation immigrants, and many are mixed race. And while I never intended to *exclusively* work with Asian diaspora, and they rarely brought up race as being a major topic when they approached me, discussions around culture, family, and societal expectations were usually common.

In fact, some of the patterns that were being brought up appeared so commonly that I often felt that I was staring into a mirror when my clients told me their stories, as I have lived through so many of variations of it myself. For example, while many of them were overachievers, most confessed feeling that their accomplishments were never quite enough. Others felt stuck in people pleasing patterns where they self-sacrificed to help everyone else around them but felt guilty about receiving or claiming credit for their hard work. Some simply struggled with guilt in saying no, or discomfort over asserting themselves, or feeling overwhelmed with fear of disappointing or upsetting others. Many of them were carrying the weight of their families' expectations on their shoulders, feeling stuck, burned out, overwhelmed in secret—not wanting to burden others by asking for or even accepting help.

These are struggles I've experienced my whole life. I've tried to fit into the archetype of a hardworking, quiet, self-sacrificing worker and have caught myself unnecessarily over-apologizing or caretaking others out of habit. I saw these patterns emerge from a wide range of people with different backgrounds. In our parents' homes, many of us were taught to be good, not make waves or cause trouble. Out in the world, some of us confronted misconceptions of who we were because of our culture or appearance. We're seen as nice, polite, smart, or even *cute*, but rarely as powerful, fearless, or decisive. And no matter how many generations our families have been here, there's an underlying pressure of trying to fulfill our parents' expectations of us as well as society's. While no two people will have the exact same upbringing, heritage, or family values, many of us encounter the same challenges again and again when we're attempting to break out of those roles.

However, when I started doing research on what books, resources, and training were out there to help us overcome these struggles, I found most of the advice was framed only by a white or Western lens. Regardless of whether it was career advice, leadership advice, or even relationship advice, the books were largely written by authors who couldn't speak to the nuances of our cultural experiences. They couldn't understand why values like humility and harmony—often referred to as *collectivist* cultural values, as opposed to Western *individualistic* cultural values—were so important to us. They couldn't grasp why their advice of "just speak up more" doesn't always work for us. Or why saying no or turning down requests, especially from our parents, can feel impossibly guilt-inducing. Or even why the social expectations of assimilation could impact how Asians are viewed as dating prospects, as interviewees, and as potential leaders.

We have different problems and need solutions that honor who we are as a diverse collective. And we need tailored advice that doesn't reduce us to a label.

To find the solutions, I started compiling all the studies I could find on issues that obstruct our success. I discovered studies that show how we may have faced a different type of conditioning that affects everything from how to communicate, to how we lead, and even to how we handle our mental health.

When I started talking about these issues on social media, the response was overwhelming. In a mere few weeks, my videos on these topics racked up over 25 million views, and thousands of people reflected on how my videos resonated with them. On TikTok, I had over 240,000 followers from places like the US, Canada, Europe, Asia, and Australia. These experiences were felt deeply across Asian diaspora around the world.

I also started a podcast interviewing successful Asian Americans from a variety of backgrounds, from CEOs and psychologists to film directors and celebrities. They spoke to me about how they broke through their respective ceilings in their own industries. The main topic we came back to was: How do we create tools that are *just for us*, where the answer isn't simply "be more like the white leaders you see"?

The answers to overcoming these issues can be found here. This book is divided into three parts.

The first part of the book is a guide to our inner work. We'll examine how cultural values like collectivism and humility might cause us to hold unreasonably high standards for when we should speak up. Or how growing up with academic or career pressures from our parents might result in feeling like we need to work harder or sacrifice to be enough. Or whether being seen as perpetual foreigners or being taught to not speak up to be accepted might cause us to take on patterns of self-censorship. This section is all about finding the possible patterns we play out, and removing any limiting beliefs that might be holding us back.

The second part of the book is a practical guide on the social skills to be more assertive and confident in our communication and leadership, without seeming arrogant or domineering. The tangible techniques based on the framework of compassionate assertiveness cover everything from exactly what to say to get people's attention and respect, to how to incorporate our core cultural values of harmony and collective success into our leadership styles.

Finally, the third part of the book is about strengthening our community. In it, we'll touch on some of the more common potential barriers to true belonging, including discrimination, for those of us across the Asian diaspora, as well as how to bridge generational gaps and how to improve our relationships within our families and our communities. This part of the book will also touch on larger social issues of race and the invisible struggles we may face. The purpose here is to help you identify when stereotypes, microaggressions, or subtle racism might get in your way, and strategies for overcoming them in our own professional, personal, and even romantic lives. Because although the challenges we face may be external, the power to make a change must come from us.

• • •

There's a lot to unpack here. Even today, I'm writing to you from a place of continued learning and discovery. I'm not here to be anyone's guru, because only you can find the right path for you. But throughout the book, I will give you real-world success stories, research studies, and proven tools and exercises to help you embody your own inborn strengths. I've seen how these concepts and tools can lead to profound transformations in people's lives. They've gained the confidence and clarity they needed to break through the areas where they may have felt stuck—in careers, in relationships, or in life generally. And in doing so, they became leaders, inspiring others to reach the same heights.

That's the goal of this book: to empower a new generation of future leaders. People who will break through the ceilings in their own fields and showcase the true strength of who we are, becoming the next generation's mentors, teachers, and trailblazers.

Let's get started.

PART ONE

· · · · ·

BIG
ASIAN
ENERGY

Sometimes, the biggest challenges we face aren't about working harder or doing more but about breaking through our internal blocks.

Maybe we hold ourselves back from speaking up during a meeting, not because we're shy but because we hold high standards for what we consider worthy enough to share, and we don't want to be a bother.

Maybe we hesitate to say no when being asked to do work that's outside of our job description because we want to seem like a team player, or because we feel guilty for turning others down.

Maybe we downplay our achievements or turn down compliments, even when they were hard-earned, because we feel arrogant in accepting recognition.

Or maybe we talk ourselves out of opportunities, promotions, or even speaking with that super-cute person across the room because we've decided at some point that we aren't good enough.

These types of self-sabotaging behaviors are usually driven unconsciously. Sometimes, they come out as habits or patterns, like being overly apologetic or unnecessarily self-deprecating when we're talking to others, because we want to be liked or accepted. Or we don't want to be a burden or inconvenience, or to bother others with our problems, so we try to avoid accepting help.

At other times, these patterns might show up internally, causing us to obsessively overanalyze tiny details of past conversations to decipher if there was something we did wrong.

We end up spending hours fighting with these diminishment thoughts nagging at us that we're secretly impostors who don't deserve recognition and success, belittling our accomplishments, and mocking our goals and dreams.

How exhausting.

Studies have shown that while these experiences have affected people from every race and culture, they seem to happen more often, and more intensely, for Asians than for other groups. Perhaps this is related to the fact that we come from cultures that prioritize respect and humility, and we are taught that self-promotion is shameful and selfish. Or perhaps this is because we're mistaken as outsiders and have been taught that hiding our background or true beliefs is the only way to belong and thrive in a Western environment.

Being Asian is awesome, but we are not a monolith. Out of a global population of some 4.3 billion people who live in the Asia-Pacific, there's just no way to contain us in a single identity. We all have multitudes of cultures and experiences that make us who we are.

At our core, we are all undeniably unique, with talents and potential that have been waiting to be unleashed. And this first part of the book is all about helping you connect with that unstoppable version of you.

The chapters ahead will explore various patterns that show up in our lives and impede our success. These include studies and stories that show why we might censor ourselves, doubt ourselves, or stay in toxic relationships that hold us back. We'll explore how these patterns might form and where they might have come from. Additionally, you'll learn exercises and tools to help you break free from any self-sabotaging patterns or limiting beliefs that keep you from taking action or getting what you deserve.

Because once we break through our internal ceilings and can tap into that unapologetic *I've-got-this* version of ourselves, we can own any room we walk into without saying a word.

The journey starts within, and it starts right here.

But first, let's dispel some myths about us.

1

Asian Confidence Hits Different

Daniel isn't shy, and he's tired of people thinking he is.

He is a second-generation Korean American, and often feels that people assume his more soft-spoken demeanor or vibe of polite friendliness reflects a lack of confidence or assertiveness.

"My boss thinks I'm too quiet at meetings, but I didn't think it was necessary to always hog the spotlight. I'd rather say it in an email after the meeting so I'm not inconveniencing everyone else or wasting their time. But as a result, I often felt like I was working more than others, yet getting less recognition for my work because I'm not speaking up enough."

Daniel asked his boss why he was getting skipped over for a promotion at work, even though he felt that his white coworkers who did get promotions didn't work as hard, or didn't have the same seniority. His boss said he was a great worker, but wasn't sure if he had the "leadership presence" or confidence they were looking for. And like so many Asian Americans, he was tired of the myth that Asians aren't confident.

"I didn't want to make a big fuss about it, but it's not that I'm shy or not confident. I just don't like to be boastful or to always be talking about myself. It's really frustrating because I feel like they want me to play this character, and it's just not who I am."

Despite being born in California, Daniel described his upbringing by his Asian parents as traditional. He was always taught to be humble, to keep his head down and work hard to meet their expectations, which is what he strives for. "My parents were pretty strict, and they did push me to focus on academics rather than stuff like making friends or socializing. I'm grateful for them and the sacrifices they made, but now I wonder what would have happened if I had the same kind of swagger the popular kids did."

He sighed, then admitted: "It's not just at work either. I feel this way in my social life as well. My girlfriend has mentioned I'm too nice and easygoing. I think she secretly wants me to be more dominant and aggressive, but I don't know how. I'm just a simple guy, and don't want to be an asshole to people just to gain respect."

"Sure." I nodded. "What if there's nothing wrong with the way you are, but you're just misunderstood? What if the truth is: confidence simply looks different for you?"

When people talk about confidence here, they usually picture someone bold, extroverted, or loud-spoken. Growing up, most of the movies I watched had action heroes like Indiana Jones, Tony Stark, Captain Kirk, or Katniss Everdeen. They exuded a self-assuredness that bordered on cocky, which was different from how Asians were portrayed (or entirely left out) in those same movies.

And I noticed when I turned to the heroes from Asian media, they act differently. They're more reserved, humble, and understated. Their heroism is usually reflected in their quiet sacrifice and perseverance, rather than their brashness. In *Crazy Rich Asians*, for example, when the billionaire male lead surprises his girlfriend with a first-class flight, she asks if he's rich. He answers with a humble and embarrassed smile: "Oh, we're comfortable." I laughed because it was something I've heard so often from Asian clients, who worked hard to downplay their successes in front of others, out of humility. We don't self-promote our accomplishments.

In Asian cultures, true confidence doesn't need to flaunt. The heroes aren't often going around challenging everyone to a fight. They are simply going about their lives undercover, as hidden dragons, until the situation calls for them to step up and unleash their true capabilities to the surprise and awe of everyone around.

The embodiment of confidence in Asian stories seems more humble and subtle. In fact, those who are always trying to show off their power or wealth are usually seen as villains or comedic side characters. Studies on Asian cultures show that humility or modesty aren't meant to underplay personal strengths. Instead, this reserve is seen as a sign of respect to the community.

Viewed through that lens, confidence is not about the display or performance. Your true confidence can come from your acceptance of your own strengths, without feeling a need to show your superiority to others. You don't have to be the person talking over others or cutting them off. You can be the one who simply maintains a reserved stance most of the time, but when you do decide to speak, everyone immediately quiets down and listens. The effect is felt. Confidence can look like many things—quiet and unassuming, but powerful in the ways that matter.

Yet external expectations often lead us to genuinely believe we're not enough. We're assumed to be meek instead of confidently reserved. We're perceived as not having accomplishments, simply because we aren't loudly promoting them. When we're repeatedly boxed in by these expectations by the people around us, it can be easy to question ourselves. So how do we begin the tough process of becoming more confident and breaking through our own internal limitations first?

Many of my clients struggle with this first hurdle, and it's an understandable frustration. They often feel they must puff up their chest or be more extroverted to be seen as strong among their white peers, who misinterpret their humility as weakness. "In my culture, being humble is really important. It shows respect to your elders and your peers," Daniel continued. "We were taught to put others first."

I agreed—being considerate is absolutely a great virtue. I then pointed out that the definition of confidence or strength looks different across cultures. In the United States, confidence tends to be portrayed as being loud, domineering, and aggressive. I asked Daniel to list examples of figures in Asian cultures he'd consider to be confident and powerful. He wrote down names such as Bruce Lee, Lucy Liu, Michelle Yeoh, Kumail Nanjiani, Sandra Oh, Ken Watanabe, Manny Jacinto, Iman Vellani, and Seo Kang Joon.

Once we had this list of names, we started examining what features were universal across both Asian and Western cultures. We came up with the following values of what almost every culture sees as being strong, confident, and empowered, regardless of their race or gender:

1. They don't need external validation.
2. They have integrity and are willing to stand up for what they believe in.
3. They are willing to make difficult decisions, have difficult conversations, and do difficult things.
4. They have the capacity to be assertive and direct in their communication.
5. They can fully accept themselves, faults and all, and can also be seen for their strengths, without sacrificing humility.
6. They take ownership and responsibility for their own lives rather than externalize blame.
7. They have the grace and courage to seek out help when needed.
8. They are capable of leading, even if they don't fight for leadership at every turn.

Suddenly, the picture seemed much more universal. These Asian characters we admired were not perfect, but they were also not people-pleasing. They can put others first without putting themselves last.

When we started listing what was universally seen as the opposite of being strong, confident, and powerful, the following answers seemed obvious as well:

1. They're people-pleasing or self-diminishing.
2. They work hard but never give themselves credit, or they feel like they're constantly not doing enough.
3. They struggle to speak up for themselves and avoid any confrontation, usually through passive aggression or "being nice."
4. They are always caretaking other people's needs, even when their own needs are neglected or their lives are a mess.
5. They obsess over how other people view them, and project a false veneer of being happy or successful, but struggle in secret.
6. They burn themselves out doing things for others, and feel guilty for saying no.
7. They're indecisive or often flip-flop between decisions.
8. They often censor themselves instead of being direct about what they want.

Daniel stared at this list for a second, and confessed, "I think I fit almost all of these." He paused, then quietly asked, "What's wrong with me? Why am I like this?"

I said, "There's nothing wrong with you. These are just behavioral patterns you've learned at some point in your life. We've all grown up with different types of conditioning that help us fit in and survive in the environments we're in. The conditioning isn't *bad* or *good*, it's just a matter of figuring out if they're still helpful for you."

I walked over to the whiteboard and drew three circles, layered within each other. In the inner circle, I wrote "True Self"; in the middle circle, "Family Conditioning"; and finally in the outer circle, "Social Conditioning."

Then I said, "At the core of who we are is our true selves. It's the most authentic, confident, and empowered version of us. Over time, we are given family and cultural roles and conditioning that taught us who we are supposed to be in those positions. And finally, we leave our homes and go into the world, where we experience social conditioning, such as pressures to assimilate or to adapt to a different culture to belong."

I pointed to the outer ring: "Each of these layers represent conditioning that has helped us to adapt, survive, or thrive. Kind of like learning a new language. For Asians, especially those of us who live in non-Asian countries, the clash between our Asian family conditioning and the outer Western conditioning can create some confusion, because they aren't always the same. At the same time, some layers of our conditioning may no longer be serving us. That's what we're looking for."

Finally, I added, "It's really not about how to look or seem more confident, but about finding the source of who *you* truly are, and unapologetically owning it in the world. That's what true confidence is."

A few months later, I heard back from Daniel. Over coffee, he excitedly told me that his life had transformed. He was able to negotiate a promotion at his company that not only paid him more but also allowed him to take charge on a project he had wanted to lead for years. He also said that his relationship improved, and that his girlfriend had even complimented him on how much more confident and assertive he seemed. But what truly surprised him was the fact that even his parents noticed the change and started praising him in front of others.

"Of course," I said, "and that version of yourself was always there. You just needed to unlearn some unhelpful habits."

"Who Do You Mean by Asians, Anyway?"

Asians aren't a monolithic group. That would be impossible since Asia currently covers some 4.7 billion people. That's 60 percent of the world's population, including some fifty-five individual countries and states. There is simply no way to ever try to generalize or even categorize that many different types of human beings. Which is why even throughout this book, nothing I'll say will ever intend to suggest "this is something that all Asians do or are." That'd be silly.

Yet, in regions like North America, Europe, Australia, South America, and Africa, the word *Asian* seems to focus only on a few select racial stereotypes. For example, South Asians (from countries like India or Pakistan) in North America might feel left out of conversations when a racial identifier like *Asian* is brought up, because the term here tends to refer to East Asians. Interestingly, this is often flipped in countries like the United Kingdom, where *Asian* is usually more closely linked to India and Pakistan due to the larger population in the UK.

Among all these countries, there is a vast collection of diverse ethnicities, religions, lifestyles, languages, and nuances. But for the most part, anthropologists and sociologists have found the one thing that connects us is that the majority of Asian cultures are more *collectivist* than *individualistic*.

In most collectivist cultures, the core values prioritize the duty you have toward your family and community, whereases individualist cultures hold that you have a duty and responsibility to look after yourself. For example, there is usually an expectation in individualist cultures for children to move out of their family homes when they reach adulthood, as opposed to the Asian expectation for them to stay in the family home and continue to care for their parents in their senior age. That's because in collectivist cultures, our duty might include making sure that the family's goals are kept in mind over our individual goals.

Roughly speaking, across most studies on collectivist cultures, some common core values that appear are:

Harmony: Family and community harmony is a major focus. This value stresses the importance of social duty and the expectation for everyone to play out the roles assigned to them. Being nonconfrontational so as to avoid burdening others is often part of the social expectations of maintaining harmony.

Hard Work: There is a strong emphasis on working hard to provide not just for ourselves but also for our family and community. One needs to self-sacrifice and prioritize academic or workplace achievement over personal enjoyment. This value is not merely a reflection of one's personal abilities; it is a reflection of one's ability to contribute to the family and to society.

Humility: Being humble and modest is highly valued in collectivist cultures. This isn't simply about being less prideful or arrogant, but the recognition that our successes are often at the sacrifices and hard work of those who have supported us along the way, especially our parents and family.

Honor: Each individual is seen as an extension of their family. When a person is pressured into a certain social position or gender role, their ability to embody this role is seen as a reflection of family honor or "face." Since you are an extension of your family, how you show up is also a reflection of your family's status.

Hierarchy: Filial piety is promoted as an important value. This involves respecting and obeying the desires of your elders, parents, or members of authority in the community. Children are expected to care for their parents in old age. Multigenerational households are much more common in collectivist cultures.

These are all great values and are deeply embedded in the fabric of the culture I grew up in. Of *course* it was normal for me to be at home practicing piano instead of going to watch a movie with friends on the weekend. I needed to work hard, not just for my own sense of accomplishment or personal fulfillment, but so that I could live up to the sacrifices my parents made for me.

In a really subtle way, the expectation to achieve and behave well in front of others seemed universal, in the same way the desire to succeed is universal. Maybe your parents never forced you to study hard or go into a field they want, but the pressure was still there as they had made sacrifices for you. To be a good child means one day repaying their sacrifices, so how could you *not* return the favor by also making sacrifices?

Fortunately, most Asian parents now realize there are detrimental mental health impacts of corporal punishment or intense focus on competition. Many are shifting to focus on their children's wellness, critical thinking, and creativity. But while the methods may have changed, we see that the core motivations and expectations have not. Studies have shown these values get passed down regardless of wealth and circumstance, and stick around long after someone immigrates to another country or environment. Even when other cultural experiences like music or food tastes have shifted, these core familial values can linger, even four to five generations after immigration.

No matter what we currently watch, listen to, or eat, we still carry elements of our familial values from years of teachings, beyond what our parents have directly told us is allowed or not. These values seep through the little messages, stories, and conditioning that shape how we see our world.

For example:

- If we read stories as children about heroes who never boasted but kept their true strengths a humble secret, we may feel differently about how we show up in the world than those who grew up with stories about brave knights on white horses who conquer foreign lands, rescue princesses, and slay bad guys.

- If we were taught that working hard, keeping our head down, getting into a good college and a good job is what it means to be a good son, a good daughter, and a good member of the community, we may feel differently about choosing "selfish" career paths that are more in line with our sense of purpose than with our duty.

- If we were taught that sharing our vulnerability through anger or sadness is a loss of self-control or even a betrayal of our family's honor, we may feel differently about being seen authentically than someone who was taught that being vulnerable is an act of courage and strength.

And of course, for every one of the experiences I've listed, there are millions more who have felt differently. We're a vastly diverse group with diverse experiences. Someone from a traditional South Asian family living in Australia is probably going to have an entirely different experience than a third-generation East Asian person growing up in the Bronx.

But no matter who we are or where we're from, we are the result of the familial or community values we were raised with. Those values can come from our parents or from our friends, our classmates, or the countries in which we live. They exist in stories, in social media, in the hidden rules of how we socialize, date, find work, and live.

Which brings me to the next layer of conditioning—our families and upbringing.

The Rebel Cry of the Tiger Child

Family upbringing is another form of conditioning that might affect us as adults. And it's impossible to discuss family dynamics without calling attention to experiences shared by many Asian kids, sometimes referred to as "Tiger parenting." These often include stories of being told to pursue certain career paths, experiences with cram schools, or even, for those with gentle and supportive parents, growing up feeling like they're somehow letting down their parents by choosing their own path.

Many of the most famous Asian comedians, including Lilly Singh, Russell Peters, or Steven He from the "emotional damage" memes, have all cracked occasional jokes about their parents on stage and in social media. Often, the jokes are around how Asian parents will focus on education and career and will ban things like dating or learning social skills with friends, only to suddenly expect a wedding and grandchildren as soon as the kids become adults.

In 2011, author Amy Chua wrote a shocking book, *Battle Hymn of the Tiger Mother,* as well as an accompanying article in *The Wall Street Journal* titled "Why Chinese Mothers are Superior." On the jacket, Chua describes her book: "This is a story about a mother and two daughters. This was supposed to be a story of how Chinese parents are better at raising kids than Western ones. But instead, it's about a bitter clash of cultures and a fleeting taste of glory."

Both the article and the book detailed the common beliefs of a demanding, strict disciplinarian "tiger" mother. Chua describes calling her children "garbage," "cowardly," and "pathetic." She also refused to allow her children bathroom breaks, water, or food whenever they struggled to perfect a piano piece. Chua referred to a study of forty-eight Chinese immigrant mothers who all "believe their child can be 'the best' student" and "if children did not excel in school, then there was 'a problem' in the household and the parents 'were not doing their job.'"

The book pissed off everyone, everywhere, all at once.

Scores of parents online were infuriated at Chua's mistreatment of her children, expressing how the descriptions of her parenting style bordered on child abuse. David Brooks of *The New York Times* called Amy Chua "a wimp" for overprotecting her children from "managing status rivalries, negotiating group dynamics, understanding social norms," etc. Education experts and psychologists penned lengthy essays critiquing her ideology. The press was damning, to the point where she later came out and explained that many of the book's stories were hyperbolic and how she would "never burn the stuffed animals of my children."

This "bitter clash of cultures" is an important point to be made. In the culture Chua describes, a child is an extension of the parent and is expected to fulfill the roles of the child in the family. For example, this might include the expectation to provide financially for your parents in their old age or to marry only a person whom your family approves of.

• • •

As a child of Asian parents, though, I wasn't shocked. I was amused. Because Chua was describing a common theme in the childhood of so many of my Asian friends. I sent the article to a group chat of friends who discussed stuff like this often.

One of my friends laughed. "They call *this* strict parenting? Where's the plastic slipper smacking you in the head?"

The others cracked up in agreement. "She is talking about grounding her kids. I was never grounded—I was never allowed out of the house!"

This was then, naturally, followed by a forty-five-minute "Who had it worse?" parental gripe competition. We reveled in our respective punishment descriptions, such as getting whacked on the knuckles for missing piano notes, being told to copy down poems 200–300 times, or attending cram classes with endless homework. All trotted out in a parade of ever-escalating parental sins.

However, the stereotype of "All Asian parents are like this" is just that—a stereotype. Obviously, not *ALL* Asian parents are tiger parents, and there are some studies showing it's not even a majority. For example, a self-reporting study of Chinese American parents and their children found that only some 37 percent of parents classify their own parenting styles as either "tiger parenting" or "harsh parenting."

But even if this concept applied to only a percentage, it's still worth addressing, especially because the impact of "tiger parenting" is not about corporal punishment or yelling at your kids. It's really about instilling heavy familial expectations and pressures, and the lesson that the pursuit of who we are or what we love could be deemed wrong or even a betrayal of our parents' sacrifices. And this effect could be felt even by those whose parents never once raised their voices to issue harsh criticism.

Many of my clients who professed having wonderfully loving and encouraging parents still felt deeply pressured to perform, pressured to fulfill familial duties, or pressured to pursue certain career paths such as STEM, medicine, or law. These career paths not only hit all those collectivist cultural values, such as honor and achievement, but also validated the sacrifices our parents made in our upbringing, especially if they were immigrants who chose to leave behind their home countries so we could have a brighter future.

This doesn't necessarily mean those paths didn't benefit us. Many of us might come back as successful adults, grateful for the pressures that helped us achieve success. But that doesn't change how these experiences have long-term impacts on our self-esteem, and the ways we feel we need to continuously chase after bigger and bigger milestones, even when they no longer fulfill us.

There's a saying that goes: "The voice you talk to your children with is the voice they will hear in their heads for the rest of their lives." These are some of the deepest forms of conditioning we can grow up with. Regardless of what kind of parents you have—supportive, loving, and encouraging or "tough love" tiger parents—they make an impact on your life, and understanding how and why is our first step to discovering who we are at our core.

Side note: if you're expecting this book to be filled with woe-is-me stories blaming my Asian mom for being strict and trying to turn me into a sad robot obsessed with overachievement, that's not where I'm going with this. Blame is typically black-and-white; it ignores all the incredible things my parents have given me, and most importantly, ignores the simple truth that my parents are *human*, as all parents are. There's no blame here, but there needs to be an understanding of how these experiences can and have affected us.

The Stereotype of the "Cold" Asians

A common thing I've heard from many students and clients is that they want to strengthen their social skills. Some point to the fact that their parents, being immigrants from an entirely different culture, couldn't teach them how to socialize in a Western environment. Others talked about how they focused most of their time on academics, so they didn't have the time to learn more advanced social skills. But there was a third group that I often felt most sympathetic toward—those who grew up in environments where they were socially rejected at school or work, simply because they were Asian.

In 2002, a group of social psychologists from Princeton, UCLA, and Lawrence University, including famed psychologist Dr. Amy Cuddy, examined social stereotypes of different groups of people.

In the study, they examined individuals in various settings and realized that, effectively, whenever we meet someone, we instinctively categorize them by *two things*. That's it. The decision can happen instantaneously and then solidifies over time, and it becomes who we see them as. It's why first impressions are so important.

The two units we judge everyone by? Competence and warmth.

When these two elements are combined and we meet someone who is highly socially competent and has high social value, and at the same time is warm and caring toward us, we automatically and unconsciously view them as being charismatic.

The study wasn't just about social likability, however. In the research, the psychologists developed the Stereotype Content Model and analyzed common stereotypes across multiple groups. They discovered that Asians, Jews, and the rich are viewed similarly: we're all viewed as being "high competence, low warmth."

COMPETENCE

		Low competence	High competence
WARMTH	**High warmth**	*Pity* Low status, Not competitive (Elderly, disabled, housewives)	*Admiration* High status, Not competitive (Close allies, in-group)
	Low warmth	*Contempt* Low status, Competitive (Poor people, welfare recipients)	*Envy* High status, Competitive (Asians, Jews, rich people)

Asians are seen as being intelligent and capable, yet also highly competitive and having low warmth. This is where stereotypes of "model minorities" and "perpetual foreigners" are really visible, as both view us as capable or smart but without the sense of emotional closeness.

• • •

When I first read the study, I was a bit offended by the stereotype. Most Asian people I know are warm, kind, and caring people. In my travels through Asia, people's kindness and hospitality were over the top. I've been invited to strangers' homes, fed ridiculous amounts of food by people I'd barely met, and even was invited to an Indian wedding simply because I was walking by. In Indonesia, it's common practice to leave an empty table at a wedding in case someone just drops by. How can that be considered "low warmth"?

And if we know that we're not actually cold, distant, or polished, then why does this stereotype exist?

Just Be Yourself. No, Not Like That.

When we're growing up, we don't learn to act based only on what we're taught in childhood. We also learn it from our social environment, such as in the friend groups we might develop at school, in clubs, or at work. And we learn different social conditioning depending on the environment. Many Asian clients I've worked with are extremely charismatic, warm, extroverted, and outspoken when they are among their Asian friends, family, or peers, but then they changed their demeanor when they were at work or around their white peers, a practice often known as "code switching."

In one instance, I was tasked to give a presentation with a cofacilitator who was of Asian descent. The night before, we had dinner at a karaoke bar, and he proceeded to rock the entire house so hard the whole place was cheering for him. Yet when we were presenting the next morning, I noticed he was sitting quietly in the back, passively waiting and listening to me with a smile. It was a Dr. Jekyll and Mr. Hyde moment, and during the first break, I pulled him aside and asked why he seemed more quiet and reserved compared to his performance the night before.

His answer was simple—yesterday, he was among friends, so he had the freedom to do and speak as he wished. But he had always learned to not be too loud or expressive around superiors at work or in more formal contexts. Even though I wasn't his boss, I was the one who had brought him in, and he was respecting my leadership by not speaking up until I directed him to step in.

The irony of this whole scenario struck me. So many Asian people I know are *taught* to be quiet because, as part of the model minority identity, speaking up or being too visible felt to them like they were breaking the social rules. Yet, they're also faulted for not speaking up enough and thus being "cold" or distant. We're damned if we do and damned if we don't. When you are part of a visible minority, acceptance is earned only through assimilation. We are reminded in little ways of how our culture, our appearance, our food, our music, or even our names are foreign, even when we are not. It's hard to explain this to those who have never experienced it, but there's a reason why we constantly get asked questions like:

"Where are you from?"

"Oh, I'm from New York."

"No, I mean, where are you *really* from?"—even if we were born here, and so were our parents and grandparents.

There's also a reason that when people think "immigrant," they tend to think of someone like us, while our white immigrant friends from Ireland or Australia, who moved here the exact same year, are seen as "expats," or are unquestionably *normal*.

Because there is "normal," and then there's *you*.

I rarely feel outright rejected from places, but sometimes I still feel like the awkward kid standing in the middle of the cafeteria trying to decide whether I should sit with the Asians or the white kids. Being Asian among other Asians feels subtly different from being Asian among white people, simply because our normalcy won't be questioned.

A couple of years ago, *The New York Times* published an article titled "Applying to College, and Trying to Appear 'Less Asian.'"

It caught my attention because it discussed the already open secret I think many Asian Americans have known: when it comes to getting into a top school, being Asian is a bit of a disadvantage. Applicants of Asian descent consistently receive a lower "personal rating" for traits like self-confidence and likability—regardless of the similarities of their profiles to other races. A 2018 *Times* article had reported how Harvard's own internal investigation showed bias against Asian American applicants, and how an external analysis of more than 160,000 student records exposed how "Harvard consistently rated Asian-American applicants lower than others on traits like 'positive personality,' likability, courage, kindness and being 'widely respected.'" These personality scores "significantly dragged down their chances of being admitted."

This isn't even a recent phenomenon. In the Princeton Review test prep guide *Cracking College Admissions* published in 2004, students of Asian descent were already being taught to "conceal their racial identity" for the best chances of success. College admission consultants long advised students to avoid activities that were considered "too stereotypically Asian," such as competitive chess, piano, or Indian classical instruments like the venu flute.

Yet, due to the number of Asian applicants overall and how many of them have high academic abilities, Asian kids are either seen as overrepresented in higher education or at least we do not "count" as a minority. One Washington State public school district announced they would be removing Asians as a racial category in their reports on equity and achievement, and categorizing them in the same group as the white students instead. Asian influencers immediately flooded social media with reaction videos mocking the news that we were suddenly being considered white, not because we were wholly accepted by the white community but because it's useful when we're pitted against other races.

Many of these schools justify the suppression of Asian admittance by saying affirmative action for other ethnic groups is necessary to support greater diversity. And many in the Asian American community strongly support affirmative action. Though I can't think of any who feel that scoring Asians as lacking personality or warmth is the best way to support other minorities.

Helping underrepresented groups like Black, Latine, and Indigenous students is always a good thing, but many of these schools are at the same time choosing to pit Asian students against other minority groups.

When Asian students are advised to hide their backgrounds when applying to schools, this leaves students with a subtle message if they do get in: *Have you thought about being less . . . you? Sure, you want a connection with your heritage and to learn the Indian flute, but what about the bass guitar instead? Sure, you spent years practicing calligraphy, but isn't environmentally conscious graffiti art cooler? And when you trauma-dump about the challenges you overcome as a new immigrant, let's not repeat those cliché stories about smelly lunches or the racism your father faced; let's not be* those *Asians.*

This goes far beyond academic consequences. We also face these same issues at work.

As I entered the workplace, "being myself" also meant learning different social rules of communication at work. As Asians, we're often categorized as being smart at things like math, or we're considered such hard workers that we're assumed to be happy to work through weekends. We're also stereotyped as introverted or quiet, leading others to tell us we need to "just speak up more!" When in reality, managers and bosses would actually benefit from *listening* more.

While studies show that Asian Americans are the most likely group to join employee diversity groups, they still don't feel supported. In my conversations with Fortune 500 corporate HR representatives, including organizers of diversity, equity, and inclusion (DEI) initiatives and events, many of them would complain to me quietly that Asians were largely ignored in their initiatives. The leader of an Asian Employee Resource Group of a major Fortune 500 company mentioned how, despite nearly 30 percent of their entire workforce in the US being Asian, they struggled to get any funding compared with other groups. The general feeling is: "Asians seem to be doing fine, and they don't complain, so executives avoid talking about any issues."

However, a 2022 study by Bain & Company revealed Asian workers feel the least included or the least sense of belonging at work, with only 16 percent of Asian men and 20 percent of Asian women feeling included in their workplace. Feeling marginalized leads to lower workplace satisfaction, higher turnover rate, and a barrage of negative stereotypes.

The more I spoke to people, the more I realized a common thread seemed to emerge. Underneath our cultural differences, our similarities differentiate us from the majority, and it shows up in the roles we have learned to take on to fit into society, our culture, and our families. In these environments, we are taught to "be ourselves" but are also shamed when that "self" isn't what the Asian culture expects or values.

This has resulted in phenomena like the "bamboo ceiling," where many Asian Americans, especially East Asians, find it hard to get promotions into leadership positions despite Asian Americans being well represented in the professional workforce. While they represent 13 percent of working professionals across the US, they also represent only 3 percent in executive and leadership positions.

The AAAIM (Association of Asian American Investment Managers) conducted a study in which they surveyed a general population of investment managers. In the survey results, 93 percent of respondents agreed that Asian employees are considered to be diligent workers, 85 percent thought Asians are good with numbers, and more than 75 percent of respondents felt Asian and AAPI (Asian American and Pacific Islanders) are associated with being "smart and thorough."

However, almost 70 percent of respondents also believed AAPI members are not perceived as good leaders, and almost 40 percent of respondents felt they weren't considered "good managers or strategic thinkers."

. . .

We're bombarded left and right with conflicting messages about how to be ourselves, be it in front of our Asian families, college admissions officers, workplaces, or friend circles. But how can we be ourselves, let alone confident in ourselves, if we're not accepted?

We're hitting roadblock after roadblock trying to fit in everywhere, yet when these stereotypes directly affect how much we make, our career options, or our social lives, it seems like a pursuit that will never end.

Over time, the things we were told, the values we learned, and the ways we adapted to fit in can all solidify into behavior patterns and habits.

The good news is, since our behaviors and habits are learned, we can also learn new, more useful ones. We need to understand how these expectations show up and *why* they show up, so we can learn how to manage them. And as we go over the next few chapters, we'll dive into more specific types of conditioning that show up, and explore ways to change them.

Starting with the seven most common patterns that might show up.

2

Meet the
Seven Patterns

When I was six, I heard a story about a secret statue. It went
something like this:

In ancient Thailand, there was a giant Buddha statue
made of pure, solid gold. It was a prized possession of the temple, and
the villagers loved it dearly.

One day, the monks got word that foreign invaders were attacking
their city. They realized if the statue was discovered, it would likely be
stolen and sold off in pieces. Its magnificent size and weight made it too
difficult to move in such a short time, but one of the monks came up
with a brilliant idea: they would cover it in clay and make it look ordinary, hiding it in plain sight.

The invaders arrived and, having mistaken the statue as one of
many hundreds of unexceptional stucco-covered Buddha statues in the
temple, ignored it and moved on. The monks who protected the statue
perished during the invasion, taking its secret with them to their graves.

For two hundred years, the statue was left forgotten, hibernating
under a tin shack roof in a neglected pagoda.

Eventually, kings and rulers came and went, and the country re-
turned to peace. The old, now decrepit temple was deemed in dire need

of reconstruction, and demolition workers were tasked to clear out the ancient rubbish. However, just as the workers tried to lift the unassuming statue, the thick rope pulleys snapped, causing the statue to crash to the ground below. A loud crack rang out as the terra-cotta coverings of the golden Buddha broke open, shocking workers nearby who stood in awe of its dazzling, golden statue.

The coolest thing about this fable, though? It's *a true story*.

Named Phra Phuttha Maha Suwan Patimakorn, the actual statue is listed in the Guinness Book of World Records as the world's largest gold Buddha statue, and it is estimated to be over 700 years old. It was plastered over during the Burmese invasion around the 1760s and rediscovered in 1954, hidden under a simple tin roof and forgotten for 200 years. Made out of a massive 5.5 tons of 18-karat gold, it is now worth more than a quarter of a billion dollars, and still can be seen at Wat Traimit in Bangkok today.

What I've always loved about this story is that it so perfectly represents the struggles of so many people I've met over the years, myself included. We get the sense that we have a greater purpose or potential—if only we could figure out how to reach it. And just like the golden Buddha, there's a chance that to get to it, you'll have to crack through a few layers of clay as well.

Our Role Selves and Our Real Selves

Imagine for a moment that when you were a baby just learning how to speak, your parents handed you a script. On the first page of the script is the title and description of who they expect you to be. Kind of like the role an actor takes on in a film or TV show:

● Maybe your role is "The Smart One." And in the descriptions, it reads: "Your role is to always study hard and to get a great job so you can take care of us when we get older."

- Maybe your role is "The Caring One." The description reads: "Your role is to take care of your brothers and sisters, so Mom and Dad can go to work and make money."

- Maybe your role is "The Presentable One." Your script says: "Your role is to look great and to speak eloquently, so that other people will appreciate and admire our family."

Whatever the role is, most of us were given one. Sometimes we were told directly, but at other times, they're silently taught through conditional approval. For example, every time you helped out with your parents' work, they'd compliment you on what a good son or daughter you were. They don't necessarily have to punish you when you're *not* performing those roles, but you would receive positive attention *especially* when you did.

Sometimes, these roles don't come just from our parents. They are also influenced by our environment, such as our siblings, our teachers, or peers. For example, you may have been given the role of "The Responsible One," wherein you were expected to be a perfect little adult who was praised for taking care of your messy, irresponsible younger sibling. Or you were yelled at when your little twerp of a younger brother made a mess in the kitchen because you weren't watching him. So now, even as an adult, you might feel guilty whenever you aren't making sure everyone in your family is taken care of, as if you're letting someone down.

Sometimes the role we're tasked to play might even be a seemingly negative one. You might have been given the role of "The Trouble-maker" or "The Rebel," wherein you were always the black sheep of the family in comparison to "The Golden Child," meaning all your faults were always magnified so your sibling's successes shone brighter. This might mean that later on, you might feel this immense and invisible pressure to appear to have your life together, even if you're not quite sure who's really watching or grading you.

These role selves are then taken up and are usually further developed unconsciously. They shape our understanding of who we need to be—to be accepted, to be good enough, and to belong. Belonging can be such a strong desire when we're young, and many of us found belonging by fitting into what was expected of us. Even if it meant we had to give up a little part of ourselves in exchange. We might hide what we really feel, what we really want, and what we really value, because if our silence is the price to be exchanged for love, that seemed perfectly reasonable.

But our real selves don't go away just because we're not allowing ourselves to be who we are. When our real self gets ignored for too long, it feels like we're stuck in a rut. Maybe it's a job we've been in that we secretly feel stifled by. Maybe it's a relationship we kind of secretly hope the other person would help us end. It feels emotionally draining, and we don't know why we're so tired. We distract ourselves from it with social media, with more work, with mindless television that we keep on in the background even though we're not even watching anymore.

In order to stay in our role selves, we end up suffocating the needs of our real selves. Sometimes that desire is to be creative, or to pursue something we're passionate about, or even just to take a break from work. When that happens, we feel guilty because we feel we're being irresponsible.

Over the years, especially those of us who are visible minorities, we may also develop Social Role Selves—whether we're "Asian enough," or meeting assimilation expectations of being "Western enough." Underneath that, we also have our Familial Role Selves, like "a good daughter/ a good son," based on whatever values our parents raised us with. And underneath all that, is who we actually are—the version of us who's fully comfortable in our own skin, pursuing our deepest callings, and remains blissfully unbothered by what anyone else thinks of us.

These roles we take on are like the layers of clothing we put on. Sometimes, they're easy to take off—like the roles we're expected to

SOCIAL ROLE SELF
(SOCIAL ADAPTIVE CONDITIONING)

- HOW I SHOULD APPEAR TO BELONG OR SUCCEED
- CODE SWITCHING TO FIT IN
- CONDITIONAL ACCEPTANCE
- PRESSURES TO PRESENT AS POLISHED/PERFECT
- PERPETUAL FOREIGNER SYNDROME
- MODEL MINORITY EXPECTATIONS
- NOT SPEAKING UP OR SELF-CENSORING
- IMPOSTER SYNDROME
- VALIDATION-SEEKING
- OVERGIVING/CARETAKING
- WAITING FOR PERMISSION
- "NICE GUY / NICE GIRL"
- SOCIAL INVISIBILITY

FAMILY ROLE SELF
(CULTURAL/PARENTAL CONDITIONING)

- I NEED TO DO/BE MORE TO BE ENOUGH OR WORTHY
- GOLDEN CHILD/BLACK SHEEP
- FEELING LIKE A BURDEN
- EXPECTATION TO BE THE PARENT
- EMOTIONAL INVALIDATION
- SELF-SACRIFICING
- PLAYING FAMILY THERAPIST/ SECRET KEEPER
- CARETAKER ROLES

TRUE SELF

- UNAPOLOGETIC SELF-ACCEPTANCE
- COMPASSIONATE ASSERTIVENESS
- PRIDE IN SELF, HERITAGE & IDENTITY
- PERFECTLY IMPERFECT

play at social gatherings, where we put on a polite smile when we tell people that we're doing fine or great, even if inside we're secretly thinking *Oh my god, my life is a dumpster fire please send help.*

Often, when I talk about this, people ask: "Isn't this just doing what we're supposed to do to succeed? Why isn't this just us making rational decisions to belong or to get what we want?"

In response, I'd say that issues arise when our role selves are activated even when it *doesn't make sense*, like instinctively or reflexively agreeing to take on a project, even though it doesn't help our career, because a part of us feels that we *should*.

Our role selves can sabotage our true selves, such as when our perfectionism can render us paralyzed, or when we feel too guilty to ask for what we want, or when we agree to something even when we feel overwhelmed. Unlike the personality traits we were born with or developed, our role selves show up as learned habits and *behavior patterns*.

We all have patterns, and most of them are invisible to us, like mindless habits we do before realizing, except on a larger scale. Most adaptive patterns were created to help us get what we want.

If you ever noticed, you often dive into relationships with people who seem really exciting at first, but then they stop responding to your texts after a few dates; that might be caused by a pattern.

As they say, if you find a bad apple, you might be unlucky, but if you've been picking a whole bushel of bad apples, maybe it's time to get some therapy instead of wasting all your time picking crappy apples. (Okay, this isn't a real saying, but you get what I mean.)

For example, I have a habit of unnecessarily overexplaining my decisions when I'm talking to friends. If you were to ask me about a pair of jeans I recently bought, I might go into a long speech about how I previously had another cheaper pair of jeans I had loved since childhood but one day I discovered they had a permanent stain, how I attempted to resuscitate the pants as if they were a fellow soldier dying on the battlefield, and how distraught I was when I finally had to give the jeans to Goodwill before heading to the mall to buy a new pair.

Dude. I just asked you where you got them. I didn't need their life story.

I've gotten a bit better about keeping these monologues under control over the years, especially around polite company who don't know me well enough to tell me to shut the hell up. But it took me a while to realize the reason I did it was because, growing up, my parents valued frugality, and I always felt guilty making any purchases they would deem unnecessary or frivolous (which was basically . . . everything). It's probably also why I have a drawer filled with plastic bags from the 1990s. As such, I feel compelled to have to justify or explain my decisions, even though no one asked.

Not all patterns are problematic. In fact, useful patterns are superpowers, like having a sixth sense when your friend is secretly struggling with something despite saying "I'm fine" over and over again. That sensitivity can be powerful and useful for tending to friends and family during tough days.

The Seven Patterns

Throughout my career, I've noticed there are seven major types of clients who keep showing up. Despite the fact that they may have completely different jobs, backgrounds, upbringing, and challenges, they all clustered around the same sets of patterns of behavior. And I started giving them nicknames.

These include the Achiever, who is driven so strongly to be always overachieving, always doing more, always expecting themselves to hit the next big goal, that they often end up either burning out from feeling never good enough or struggling with impostor syndrome, inner criticism, or even perfection paralysis.

Or the Fixer, who is often focused on healing and fixing others' problems, who rushes to support or sacrifice themselves for everyone around them, but does not allow themselves to receive even the slightest help or recognition.

Or the Chameleon, who can adapt themselves to fit the needs or expectations of everyone around them. But as such, rarely gets recognized for their actual, unique selves, who they've often hidden deep inside.

Or the Charmer, who focuses on appearing positive, entertaining, or likable, but also ends up alienating themselves from real, in-depth relationships because the only version of themselves they allow to be seen is a performative self.

Or the Invisible One, who stays out of harm's way by not speaking up or risking conflict, but ends up being forgotten and overlooked over time as they've shied away from the spotlight.

Or the Commander, who often feels obligated to take charge and give direction, believing they must carry the massive responsibility of everything going well, or they have failed the expectations of everyone around them.

Or finally, the Rebel, who often reactively rejects or rebels against any external pressures or expectations from others, but often ends up alienating themselves, or sacrificing the closeness and belonging that they may still secretly desire.

Each of these patterns is there to serve a purpose. They were learned or emerged to help us get something we felt we needed. They may have started as adaptive strategies but ended up becoming such a habitual part of who we are that it becomes difficult to see whether we are doing something out of a genuine desire or doing it out of that old habitual pattern.

None of these are *Asian-specific* patterns. Variations of each of them, and many more, exist in people from every race and cultural background. In fact, they exist in *everyone*, because we're all just humans at the end of the day.

But over time, I've started to track these patterns so much and so commonly that I realized it was faster for us to recognize when and how they take control of our decision-making: for example, when we begrudgingly agree to a coworker wanting to dump extra work on our plate, is it because we genuinely want to be of service or is it the Fixer coming out to make sure they will like us? And if so, that might still be a relevant strategy, but is it still serving us?

With that said, let's explore each of these in a bit more detail, including the unspoken rules that often accompany them.

ACHIEVER

The importance of academic or work achievement, especially over-achievement, is by no means foreign to us. Regardless of whether it's external or internal, high expectations can result in our becoming habitual Achievers throughout our lives.

COMMON ACHIEVER TRAITS

- **Toxic Perfectionism:** Achievers often become the perfectionists of the group. They're usually highly capable and ambitious (though they might refuse to accept either label out of humbleness), which sometimes can lead to burnout as they strive to reach their full potential. I've often heard clients say that if only they'd worked harder, tried more things, or sacrificed more, then all their problems would be solved.

- **All-or-Nothing Thinking:** They can either be totally extraordinary or feel like a complete failure, with little middle ground. Achievers strive to overcome challenges, and they believe the more they strive and struggle, the more worthy they are.

- **Prone to Burnout:** Achievers are particularly prone to burnout because they often feel like the only time they can rest without guilt is when they are no longer *able* to continue. They can't have an extraordinary career while being in an ordinary relationship—there's a frenzied pressure to hit high standards in EVERY area, much like the circus act of spinning plates.

UNSPOKEN ACHIEVER RULE: *"I don't deserve recognition unless it's been earned and externally given."*

FIXER

The Fixers are in the caretaking, protecting, and rescuing patterns. Fixers can be genuinely helpful, nurturing individuals, especially with people they care about, such as friends and family. But they are often self-sacrificial. They value being helpful to others because this identity gives them a sense of deeper purpose and self-worth. If not careful, Fixers end up being "nice guy/nice girls" who unconsciously become overly giving as a strategy to be more likable or acceptable.

COMMON FIXER TRAITS

- **Non-Confrontational:** Fixers are rarely confrontational and may agree to something that they don't want to do, out of a sense of duty.

- **Self-Abandoning:** Fixers highlight the needs of others over their own, and might even be uncomfortable accepting help when it's offered. While they regularly support others, they don't feel that they can ask for support. When asked about their struggles, Fixers tend to deflect and focus attention back on the asker.

- **Minimizing or Self-Dismissive:** Fixers often minimize their own needs or contributions, while feeling responsible for those around them. This sometimes also leads to taking responsibility for things they have no control over, or apologizing for them, such as: "I'm sorry the sun is so bright today!" (True story.)

UNSPOKEN FIXER RULE: *"As long as I'm in service to others, then I'll always be safe and accepted."*

CHAMELEON

The Chameleons are great at adapting and fitting into almost any group they arrive at, be it a regatta gala or an underground rap battle. I find many Asian diaspora who grew up in non-Asian environments learn to become a Chameleon in order to assimilate to their surroundings and fit in. Additionally, Asian collectivist cultures play a major role in creating Chameleon habits, since communal harmony is so highly valued. We're often taught to adapt to complex social rules as children when spending time with our parents' friends and community.

COMMON CHAMELEON TRAITS

- **Shape-shifting:** They often develop an uncanny ability to read the energy and feelings of those around them and mold themselves to mirror exactly what the other person is or what the other person needs to be. Chameleons in social settings are easygoing and infinitely forgiving, and can go with what everyone else wants.

- **Peacekeeping:** Chameleons are often able to sense when conflict is brewing between others, but they're rarely the ones getting caught in the middle of it. As a matter of fact, Chameleons are excellent at facilitating harmony and going along with others around them.

- **Indecisiveness:** Chameleons are often good at seeing all sides and are so "easygoing" they struggle to make decisions, from simple ones like where they would prefer to go for dinner to major things like what career path to commit to.

UNSPOKEN CHAMELEON RULE: *"If I can fit in anywhere, I'll always find a place to belong, to be safe, and to be liked."*

CHARMER

The Charmer is the ultimate performer, the life of the party, and a master of keeping people entertained. They emanate charisma wherever they go and draw your attention when they walk into the room. Charmers were praised or conditioned to keep their happy, positive selves seen, and their "unacceptable" sadness or anger hidden.

COMMON CHARMER TRAITS

- **Charismatic:** Charmers are highly charismatic and are great entertainers, storytellers, and performers. They have exceptionally high emotional intelligence and can "read the room" with high degrees of accuracy. Charmers are great at navigating social situations and know when to drop a perfect story or a joke. You can't help but *like* Charmers, even if you aren't fully sure if you know them.

- **Masked Self-Identity:** In some cases, Charmers put on a performative act because they feel they're expected to. However, in doing so, they also are hiding emotional vulnerability and avoiding deep emotional engagements with others. Charmers will often try to crack a joke or make light of a situation, or of themselves, to deflect attention from themselves or avoid "serious" moments and discussions. As such, there is a preference to stay on the "positive" side of conversations.

- **Polished Social Performance:** Charmers can, sometimes, look too polished and perfect to others. They seem to be always doing fine, they seem energetic and gregarious. But on deeper exploration, the Charmer might in fact be going through tough times. Charmers typically feel like they don't want to burden others with their emotional truth, or they are afraid if others discover how "messy" they are, people would dislike them.

    UNSPOKEN CHARMER RULE: *"People might not accept the real me, but so long as the show continues, I'm loved and respected."*

INVISIBLE ONE

The Invisible One keeps themselves safe by staying quiet in the background. By staying quiet, they are a burden to no one, offend no one, challenge no one, and as such, avoid being judged or abandoned. Some may be waiting for others to acknowledge them or come to their aid. In some cases, the Invisible Ones may spend years waiting for someone to recognize their value, to call on them, to give them the opportunity to shine. In other cases, they might tell themselves they are only preparing and strategizing, and may even have imagined what they'd do if a crisis ever appears where they will undoubtedly shine. They may find themselves waiting for something that'll never come. Unlike the Chameleons, who will adapt themselves to others to still be seen and accepted, the Invisible One remains quietly on the sidelines as an observer. In a group setting, they will be found awaiting permission and instruction—to speak, to question, and to be themselves.

COMMON INVISIBLE ONE TRAITS

- **Self-Censoring or Deflecting with Humor:** An Invisible One rarely talks about what is happening in their own life, their family, or at home, even with close friends. Or they can communicate about themselves only through self-effacing jokes or self-deprecation.

- **Disproportionate Shame or Self-Criticism:** They often feel extreme or disproportionate anxiety, criticism, or guilt after insignificant mistakes, including small social faux pas. They can obsess about a single, often insignificant social interaction for days or weeks, replaying the situation in their mind while self-criticizing.

- **Self-Isolating:** Despite desiring connection, Invisible Ones often withdraw from social connection. Receiving attention from others, even positive attention or personal questions, can feel burdensome and exposing.

UNSPOKEN INVISIBLE ONE RULE: *"If I'm not seen, I can't be criticized or judged."*

COMMANDER

The Commander is the micromanager of the group. In collectivist cultures, the "most responsible" child is often expected to take on some household management roles, such as making sure the younger siblings are properly taken care of or playing translator for immigrant parents. Whether they were praised for their capabilities or for how mature they were, this can often result in a mindset in which their value comes from being able to micromanage everyone around them. They're told things like "She's such a good daughter, she's like a little adult." Or "I never need to worry when she's around."

COMMON COMMANDER TRAITS

- **Self-Sacrificing:** Commanders often feel that they're responsible for others, regardless of whether or not they asked for or even accepted their help. Commanders will often jump in to manage other people's lives, give unsolicited relationship advice, or even do things for others because they can't stand seeing someone doing it at a different standard than their own.

- **Controlling:** Since they feel their capabilities and standards are higher, Commanders often believe they need to take control because, "If I don't do it, it'll never get done, or it won't get done properly." (Commanders are often matched up with Chameleons or Charmers, the one who is always in control, and the other always happy to give up control to keep the peace.)

- **Isolated in Doing All the Work:** Commanders who cannot delegate often feel they're alone or isolated in having to take on the work for others, especially family. Because they mean well, they often feel that other people don't understand or appreciate how much work and energy they put in to keep things running smoothly.

UNSPOKEN COMMANDER RULE: *"If I can take care of everything and everyone, I'll have served my duty and obligations and I'll be good enough."*

REBEL

The Rebel is the challenger of the group, preferring to play by their own rules rather than conform to the crowd. If they were seen as being the troublemaker of the family, Rebels who didn't find belonging at home may decide to chart their own path, out of necessity. They often feel a strong resistance against anyone telling them what to do. For those who grew up in environments without many other Asians, this can also be a survival strategy to remain true to who they are in an environment where they do not feel accepted.

COMMON REBEL TRAITS

- **Enjoys Challenging the Norm:** True to their name, Rebels seek to challenge traditional hierarchy or rules. Rebels typically don't lack assertiveness or confidence, and in fact revel in creating provocation and ruffling a few feathers. They don't fear taking the road not taken. In fact, it's the only road worthy of them.

- **Individualistic:** Rebels tend to go where the crowd does not. This, again, is often seen as a counterreaction to the collectivistic or hierarchical values commonly found in Asian cultures. By defining success in their own terms, Rebels find greater freedom to self-express. If well directed, many Rebels end up becoming innovators, cultural icons, and some of the most interesting creatives you'll ever meet.

- **Resists Any Attempt to Control or Conform:** Rebels hate being told what to do, even in casual scenarios, and will resist any external control or suggestion unless from someone they deeply respect. They tend to have high standards for who they're willing to follow and, typically, will only seek to follow other Rebels.

UNSPOKEN REBEL RULE: *"People will eventually reject me anyway; if I reject them first, I won't get hurt."*

When I mapped out these archetypes, I realized they fit well into three main preferences, which are assertiveness, competence, and empathy. Here's what it looks like, visually:

Over the course of the next few chapters, we'll take a look at some of these patterns in greater detail, as well as *where* they come from and how they might show up in your life experiences.

The purpose here is not to categorize ourselves but to see how these patterns might have impacted us. Because more often than not, I find that people can readily see how these patterns are helpful to them,

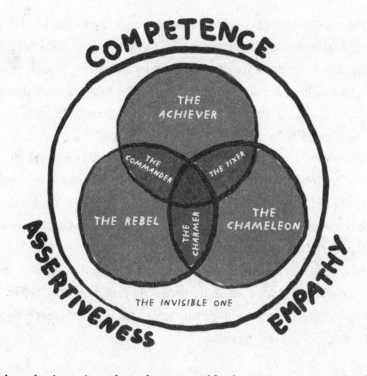

yet they don't notice when they are self-sabotaging as a result of the patterns.

Self-sabotage can look like any behavior that makes it harder for us to get what we want.

For example, I know of someone who was going into a salary negotiation with her boss and had smartly spent hours preparing for the meeting by finding comparable salaries, compiling all her best work and setting up exactly what she wanted to say.

Then, as soon as she went into the meeting and started her spiel, she noticed her boss's hesitation and immediately said, "Oh, but, you know, I'm not, like, here to try to negotiate or anything." And proceed to semi-apologize for the very thing she came in to do.

When I heard that story, I couldn't help but sympathize from the bottom of my soul. Why would she decide to reject herself even though she had prepared so much and knew that she was just asking for her fair compensation? Why would she give up her power like that?

There are many ways we self-sabotage on a day-to-day level. Sometimes, it might happen when we self-diminish, or minimize how important our hard work and contributions have been. Sometimes, we self-reject, talking ourselves out of opportunities that we are more than worthy of claiming, saying "Oh, I'm not good enough for that job" or "Oh, he'll never be interested in someone like me."

These forms of self-sabotage can be both invisible and deadly, killing our dreams before they've had a chance to take form, and killing our motivation before we build momentum.

It sounds kind of silly because . . . who would want to make their lives harder? And *why do we keep doing it?*

As we dive deeper into some of these patterns and where they might have come from, I invite you to explore if they've shown up in your life, and if so, if there are ways they may have kept you from reaching your goals or fulfilling your potential.

• • •

Take a moment and try this journaling exercise, and see if you've noticed any of these self-sabotaging patterns before:

Journaling: The Seven Deadly Sins of Self-Sabotage

Over the years, I've met countless highly intelligent, hardworking people who have spent their entire lives feeling underrecognized and undervalued, and I realized how some patterns of self-sabotage started to emerge. These are behaviors that, consciously or unconsciously, show up in our lives, work, and relationships to derail us from getting what we want.

Here are the seven most common forms of self-sabotage emerging in the Asian clients I've worked with over the years. Take a glance through, and give yourself a score from 1 to 10 for how commonly you might have experienced these behaviors in your daily lives. (1 being "I never do this" and 10 being "I often do this")

1. **Self-Diminishment:** Minimizing how important your work, contribution, or value is to others or even to yourself. Feeling guilt or embarrassment for receiving praise or recognition for things you've worked hard for.

   ___/10

2. **Self-Sacrifice:** Unnecessarily taking on extra responsibility or work for others when you are already overextended, often leading to burnout or unreasonable demands on yourself. Depriving yourself of fun or enjoyment due to feelings of guilt. Feeling shame for wanting to purchase reasonable luxuries, taking time off, or treating yourself due to internal stories of unworthiness. Setting yourself on fire to keep others warm.

   ___/10

3. **Self-Criticizing:** Shaming yourself internally, feeling you're not good enough unless you're overperforming or nearing perfection. Reflexively over-apologizing for things that are not your fault. Taking on blame outwardly for things not in your control. Fearing or feeling that others may be secretly angry at you or disappointed in you.

   ___/10

4. **Self-Censoring:** Struggling with saying no, setting boundaries, or agreeing to things you don't truly want to do. Not speaking up for yourself, holding back ideas or suggestions out of a sense that it's not good enough, only to hear someone else say it and get credit later.

   ___/10

5. **Self-Rejection:** Preemptively rejecting yourself or disqualifying yourself from opportunities or things you want before attempting. Thinking "They wouldn't like me anyway" or "I wouldn't be as good at it as others, so why try?" Difficulty making and committing to decisions. Placing yourself at the bottom of the list of prioritization or leaving yourself off the list entirely.

   ___/10

6. **Self-Isolating:** Withdrawing, hiding, or distancing yourself from others out of fear of being a burden or inconvenience. Thinking "I'll ask for help once I have most of this figured out." This could also show up as emotional self-isolation, in which we are physically present but unable to show our "true" selves.

   ___/10

7. **Self-Abandonment:** Changing who you are, sacrificing your desires, or even bending or breaking personal values to make room for someone else. This happens often in relationships, where a person disowns their needs or worth to try to "keep" their partner around.

   ___/10

As you reflect on the above, you might notice how some show up more often than others. Or perhaps you've experienced none of them (in which case, congratulations on being awesome)! The first step always starts with *awareness*, and then following it with some compassionate curiosity.

Many of these behavioral patterns are tied to other ongoing problems, such as procrastination or feelings of helplessness, and when the patterns show up, they rarely show up alone. They create devastating impacts in our lives that we might later think: "Why did I do that? Why didn't I just say something when I knew what I should do?" which result in further guilt and self-criticism, worsening the cycle.

Over time, I started realizing many of these symptoms stem from deeper issues, starting from our upbringing all the way to how we are treated by those around us in society. Yet the advice we're given tends to ignore the true causes entirely, either because we're misunderstood or those formative experiences are invalidated before we can even address them. So we repeat them as harmful patterns, worsening the symptoms each time.

If you do notice yourself reflecting on these behaviors, take note that while we usually see it as "I should just do it differently next time," we can't ignore the deeper underlying causes of *why* they show up. The causes are almost always a form of self-protection, like an overactive safety system that takes control.

In the next few chapters, we'll start looking at some of the patterns in greater detail, alongside tools and exercises to break free from the less helpful ones. And we'll start with the one that seems to be most prevalent among Asians: The Achiever.

3

Taming the Achievement Monster

Meeting the "Monsters" at Google

Newton Cheng is Google's global director of Health and Performance. For the past fifteen years, he's been coaching and training Google employees to perform and feel at their best, and I'm interviewing him in a video chat for my podcast. My top question: what he most commonly saw as struggles with his Asian team members versus non-Asians.

"I call it the Monster," Newton says.

I asked what he meant.

He explains: "Like self-doubt, a lack of self-worth. . . Like this deep fear of: if I don't keep achieving, the monster will get me."

I pressed further: "So, what percentage of non-Asians had the Monster?"

He thought about it. "I would say, you know, in the general population of a mixed-race group . . . like three out of ten people. If I go into a high-performing tech company, the average might jump to a six." He paused, then added, "And if I take a close look at an Asian American population, it goes to twelve."

On the camera, I can see my jaw drop.

"Wait, twelve . . . *out of ten*?"

"Yeah!"

I cracked up at this. In my mind I immediately pictured some people in the room with two little, snarling green gremlins sitting on their shoulders.

He continued, "If I'm speaking to a more general group, you know, some people feel it, some people don't. But when I spoke to Asian American groups, it's just universal nods throughout the room. And there are people I meet where it's like, oh wow, I thought I had a monster. But you REALLY have a monster . . . That's a twelve."

We talked a bit more about commonalities, and he mentioned how he often sees the monster in immigrants in general. But it seemed that whenever he was hosting a workshop with Asian Americans and asking who felt this, *every* hand in the room would go up. I nodded to myself. If I was in the room, I'd probably have my hand up as well.

I've become well acquainted with my own "monster"—a looming feeling of always needing to compare myself to the people next to me, of wondering if I'm working hard enough or achieving enough, no matter how much I did. I always thought everyone felt this way in society. But this was my first time hearing how much more prominent it was among Asian employees than others. Even for executives at one of the world's more competitive companies, no less.

If our goal is to rise and break through the ceilings of our own personal potential, we need to start by looking at whether there are any internal ceilings that may be keeping us from taking action. This means looking at whether we have taken on societal messages. What did we absorb when we were finding who we are while balancing our cultural identities? What lessons did we learn about ourselves when we were young?

But to get there, we need to take a look at three of the biggest obstacles that most commonly show up along the way: impostor syndrome, comparisonitis, and perfection paralysis.

Impostor Syndrome

You might have heard of impostor syndrome or "the impostor phenomenon" before. It's the psychological phenomenon in which someone feels like an impostor or a fraud in their achievements and believes that any successes they've experienced are the result of luck, or of others having misjudged them.

If you've ever . . .

- felt like you don't deserve your achievements
- worried that people will find out you're secretly not good enough
- dismissed praise from others as politeness and didn't believe it
- dismissed your accomplishments as good luck or timing
- felt you don't deserve to be where you are—your job, your school, etc.
- believed that other people are overvaluing your actual capabilities or that they were "tricked" into thinking you're capable

You've probably experienced impostor syndrome.

When a group of psychologists at the University of Texas at Austin decided to dig a little further into the impostor syndrome phenomenon by examining how ethnicity and minority status affected their findings, what they found surprised them. When compared to every other racial group, they found that *Asian American students experienced the highest rates of impostor syndrome, despite also having higher academic performance.*

In their paper published by the American Counseling Association, the researchers explained further. The researchers had "assumed that the students who are more highly stigmatized and stereotyped as having lower intelligence (i.e., African Americans and Latino/a Americans) would struggle more with impostor feelings." But the Asian American students in the study had the highest average GPAs compared with African American and Latine students. The researchers were then surprised by their study's results, and wondered, "Given their higher achievement, why would Asian American students have higher impostor feelings?"

Researchers went on to propose reasons behind these significantly higher rates of impostor syndrome. "Despite positive academic stereotypes, Asian American students must deal with the stressors of the model-minority stereotype and high parental expectations . . . Furthermore, the model-minority stereotype may, in fact, produce increased anxiety and distress, particularly for those students who do not possess the intellectual capacity or whose interests differ from those presented by the stereotype. When we consider the cultural pressures of high parental expectations and the unique stressor of being the model minority, it is more understandable why Asian American students might be more prone to higher impostor feelings."

The researchers speculated that the model minority stereotype, alongside high parental expectations, led to significantly higher self-doubt and the belief that their success in life or work is the result of "some kind of luck." Asian Americans felt these pressures and this led to toxic perfectionism, external shame, and family shame, even when things were going well.

This was a common phenomenon. In another study titled "Why Is There a Higher Rate of Impostor Syndrome Among BIPOC," researchers found parenting styles common among Asian families were more likely to focus on achievement and restriction, and this led to higher feelings of "impossibly high self-expectations of success."

What was particularly difficult about our impostor syndrome is that *more success* did not help with raising one's self-esteem or belief in oneself. In fact, it perpetuated an endless downward impostor cycle. Psychologist Dr. Pauline Rose Clance discovered this cycle and described it this way:

An Achiever first takes on a task they deem important, such as writing a report or project, and feels self-doubt and anxiety. They'll either over-prepare or procrastinate until the last possible moment.

If they over-prepare and are successful, they'll then attribute their success to their overwork and think: "I'm not naturally good at this, but I can do it if I burn myself out."

If they procrastinate before succeeding, they'll attribute their success to luck or think others were "tricked" into believing their work is good.

Either way, they'll discount any positive feedback by attributing their success either to overwork or to luck, leading them to feel like frauds, which adds more anxiety, depression, and self-doubt. Meanwhile, they'll hyperfocus on any negative feedback as being "the truth."

And then the next task is thrown at the Achiever, and the exhausting cycle begins again.

This endless impostor cycle creates a sort of mental treadmill for many of us. We run as fast as we can without feeling like we ever get anywhere. What's unfortunate about impostor syndrome is it's completely unrelated to how capable you really are or how successful you are, as people experience it across all levels.

On my podcast *Big Asian Energy*, I interview Asian CEOs, leaders, and other experts of their fields. Despite their successes, however, impostor syndrome was everywhere. Case in point: Christina Qi.

Christina's experience is unquestionably impressive. She started her own hedge fund in her MIT college dorm, which would later trade up to $7 billion *a day*. She shared with me how she had started the fund after being rejected by a Wall Street bank that would later become one of her clients (talk about the ultimate revenge).

Her soaring success would later land her picture on the cover of *Forbes* magazine and in the pages of *The Wall Street Journal*. She was honored in the *Forbes* 30 under 30, and across dozens of major publications for her accomplishments and awards. Despite this, she confesses humbly how "no amount of therapy has quashed my impostor syndrome."

"Oh god," I said, "so there's no hope for the rest of us, then."

She laughed.

As she tells me her story, she describes a phenomenon she calls "kid mindset." Even as the founder of a major company, she talked about how she would write emails to lawyers with an automatic tone of apology.

"I'd always find myself saying things like 'Oh I'm sorry to bother you,' which makes no sense. Like, these were extremely expensive lawyers who were working for us. Technically, I'm their boss."

That isn't the first time I've heard this. Many of my clients have described feeling oddly like being a kid, despite the fact that they were advanced in their careers and often in leadership positions. I remember one client telling me she felt she was inconveniencing her employee by telling them to redo a subpar proposal.

These types of experiences are so common, and Christina's story made me think about all the different reasons we might have felt similarly. For many Asian Americans, it's built into our culture that we should respect elders. And when we grow up with authoritarian parenting styles, we might even distrust our own decisions and wisdom in situations when someone speaks or acts in similar authoritarian tones. So I often hear high-achieving and exceptionally capable people share stories of unconsciously undermining their own leadership and authority out of habit.

Which, I often point out, is not unexpected. If every single day I tell a child whatever they're doing is not enough, how every accomplishment is the basis for the next unmet challenge, and it's rude to question authority or those older than you, how could I ever expect them to know when they're considered an equal to others they speak with?

For many of us, we never had a rite of passage that officially says: "You're now an adult. You now have enough right to question those you were previously told to obey." For many Asian families, that elder hierarchy never goes away. And just because you're now a thirty-five-year-old executive managing 200 employees doesn't mean you're not still seen as the kid by your family.

The truth is *no one* is going to hand us a golden plaque to signify our worthiness; we are the only ones who can give that validation to ourselves. In a collectivist family where we're not fully individuated, the dynamic generally doesn't change until the day our parents are old enough that we take on the role of family leader and start caring for them. (And even now, my mom is still not too old to force-feed me food, or to demand I wear more jackets even when it's too warm outside.) But while that might make sense when we're hanging with our family, it doesn't make sense to let that follow us into our workplace, so it's important to recognize when the two roles might affect each other.

At the end of the day, we can't really recognize our own value until we decide to stop letting other people define our worth. Otherwise, we'll keep seeking someone else to tell us who we are, be it a boss, strangers on the internet, or even a romantic partner.

Self-Rejection and Self-Diminishment from Impostor Syndrome

Finish this sentence in your head or in your journal: "I'll finally be good enough for___ when I am ___."

An example might be "I'll finally be good enough to call myself an expert when I know everything there is to know about the subject."

Or another might be "I'll finally be good enough as a leader when everyone I lead admires me and thinks I'm impressive."

Or even "I'll finally be good enough to apply for a job when I can show I never make mistakes."

You can do this for every "not good enough" you might carry, and your responses might surprise you. Because most of the time when I'm working with Achievers, Fixers, or Chameleons, they have absolutely unreasonable, unachievable hidden beliefs about when they'll *finally* be good enough. These are called *competence rules*, and are a way for us to check how we're doing; and sometimes they can seem utterly irrational. There are even some who will say, ". . . Actually, I don't know when I'll ever be good enough. I don't think it's possible."

Yet, they'll have no problem identifying when they consider *other people* as good enough.

That's because in our head, we usually have two sets of *competence rules* that we apply to ourselves versus others. And left unexamined, they're the killer of our dreams.

• • •

One of the common symptoms of impostor syndrome I've seen is self-rejection. It frequently shows up when someone is up for a promotion or a new job, or even wanting to approach someone to ask them out. They feel reluctant to put up their hand or walk over to say hi, because they think, "There's probably someone more qualified" or "They'll probably reject me anyway."

This type of preemptive self-rejection happens *all the time* among my friends and clients, on so many different topics. They'll look at an opportunity and immediately go, "Oh that's not for me," and rattle off a list of competence rules as to why:

- They need more experience.
- There are better candidates.
- They lack leadership skills. (Or negotiation skills, persuasive skills, interpretative dance skills . . . the list goes on.)

I see people self-reject themselves from positions they're more than qualified for, because they believe they need to be *overqualified* to be considered.

This has, statistically, a higher occurrence in women, who are often expected to prove their qualifications more readily than men. In an oft-quoted internal report by Hewlett Packard, they found that among their candidates, men would apply to positions when they met only 60 percent of the qualifications listed, whereas women would apply only if they felt they met 100 percent of the qualifications. This statistic had been quoted by the *Harvard Business Review*, LinkedIn, and books such as *Lean In* and *The Confidence Code*. Other researchers have conducted similar studies and have explored why these results are recurring. The most common reason reported by survey participants is that they think they'd just get rejected anyway, so why would it be worth taking the time to apply?

When we're looking at our self-rejection or self-diminishment, a simple practice is just identifying those hidden competence rules that we have and asking, "Is this true?" Is it true that a candidate can't be hired for a position unless they have been perfect at everything they do? Is it true that the person we want to ask out really needs us to be at a certain weight, a certain height, a certain personality, rather than just being someone who is loving, caring, and everything we already are?

We carry these competence rules everywhere we go, and left unchecked, they only lead us to live a life of inaction and regret.

Perfection Paralysis

I was leading a workshop on how our productivity gets impacted by our own perfectionism, and how when you really break it down, procrastination is often a manifestation of perfectionism, and perfectionism is just a manifestation of our fears.

I asked the group: "Who here has experienced procrastination in their workplace?"

The room was filled with overachievers, so naturally, every hand went up.

I then asked, "Who here thinks it's because you're lazy?"

Once again, every hand goes up.

Everyone I speak to says they believe their procrastination happens because they're lazy. Or they'll use words like *unmotivated* or *not disciplined enough* or *I just don't have time for it!*—even if they also confessed to spending way too many hours binging Netflix and browsing social media.

When we pressure ourselves to be perfect, this can result in perfection paralysis—a paralyzing lack of motivation if we don't feel we can do a task perfectly on the first try. This causes us to hold back on taking action entirely, whenever we feel we might get judged and criticized.

I once spoke to a client who wanted to start a YouTube channel. When I asked him how much preparation he had done, he embarrassedly admitted, "Oh, about four years." He showed me the thousands of dollars of fancy filming gear he had purchased over the years. He had remodeled a full studio in his home. He took courses. He hired someone to give him a full social media strategy.

He had done everything . . . except film videos.

He said every time he was about to start filming, he would notice something missing. The lighting wasn't perfect. His background wasn't perfect. He needed a better lens. He worked incredibly hard and did so much in order to procrastinate doing the only thing that actually mattered.

We can feel intimidated and vulnerable when we open ourselves up to being seen in our imperfections, especially when everyone else seems to have their life together. The belief is often: "If I do this imperfectly, people will finally see I don't know what I'm doing, and they'll judge me for it."

The anxiety of setting the bar so high that you need to do it perfectly on the first go is overwhelming, because we translate *doing something imperfectly* as *being an imperfect person*.

If you're an artist and painted a messy piece, you can either see it as

"Oh man, what was I thinking, I sure messed that up, better try again" or "Oh man, I sure messed that up, I'm just a terrible artist."

At the core of our fear of failing often isn't the failure itself but the label of being seen as a failure, especially if we grew up being criticized for small imperfections.

The irony is that, of course, imperfections are the way of mastering any skill. When you teach a child to walk for the first time, they will naturally fail again and again. Each failure teaches a lesson about how to balance, how to stand, and how to move forward. We don't go to a toddler and say: "You fell down on your first try? Better just give it up, you're clearly not smart enough to walk."

In fact, it is the *willingness* to fail that creates some of the best work we'll ever do. In famed NASA engineer and YouTuber Mark Rober's MIT commencement speech, Rober shared how his own research with 50,000 subjects has shown that the most effective problem-solving comes when people are working without fear of failing. If people were working without being afraid of punishment for making mistakes, they stuck with the tasks longer, learned more, and were more successful. Engineers routinely find that trial and error, rather than expecting perfection, is the most efficient way to solve problems. Unless you're willing to take a chance, you won't ever be able to beat your last attempt.

When we associate our failures with defining our identity, this makes it hard to take action, especially if we've been shamed for our imperfections. After all, if you never *start* something difficult, you can hold on to the belief that you'd be good at it for as long as you want. If you never test yourself, you still have the potential to be competent, yet ironically, the procrastination also keeps your competence from *actually* coming to fruition.

I think this is why so many people leave their dreams in the cupboard. It's easier to keep rewriting your manuscript than to show it to anyone, because then it still has the *potential* of perfection. It's easier to never show anyone the dance routine you practiced nightly in your bedroom alone, because you won't have to face the possibility of making a mistake in front of an audience.

Perfectionism can be hard to break, because we can take on these identities at such a deep level. This limited view of ourselves can become a comfortable crutch we *don't* want to let go of. Psychologist Carol Dweck wrote about this in her book *Mindset,* when she broke down the difference between growth and fixed mindsets. We can become attached to a familiar fixed mindset, when being open to failure can actually open us into a growth mindset. Our fears have a different dimension when we not only fear making mistakes but feel ashamed that our mistakes will define us as failures. This is a key difference: Guilt happens when we *do* something wrong. Shame happens when we *are* something wrong.

Our perfectionism can become a curse. When we say, "I'm supposed to be good at this," this perfectionist expectation can hold us back. At face value, it's a positive thing, but it also creates a deeper self-narration of "So if I fail, I'd be letting everyone down" or "I'd be proving myself wrong, and then I'm not special anymore."

I've seen dozens of extremely talented people who killed promising projects at the start because of this exact issue. They were told they're talented, so anything that disproves their talent threatens the specialness they feel. And when we tie our self-worth to our jobs, to our projects, and the things we own, it takes away from the self-worth we have simply for being us. After all, if we think, "Man, I'm having a bad day, but the fact that I work at this swanky company means I'm still good enough," then anything that threatens others' view of the company threatens how you view yourself.

By separating our own identity from the things we do, we not only have the freedom to experiment, to innovate, and to make bolder leaps. We also see the truth, which is that we are not what we have, or what we do, or what others expects of us. When we start to realize what we do is not who we are, that's when we can stop living in the potential of impotent perfection and in the reality of our greatness.

We are all perfectly imperfect beings. It's who we were at birth, it's who we will be when we die. Perfect in how we are complete as we are, and imperfect in how we are all a little lost, making it up as we go along, and occasionally coloring outside the lines despite our best efforts.

So if you're having a tough day, a slow day, an unsure day, a just-let-me-lie-here-and-feed-me-ice-cream kind of day, remember that it doesn't have to mean anything about *you*. You're not bad at being a good human, you're just a good human having a bad experience.

Loving Your Messiness

To step away from our perfection paralysis, we need to let ourselves be a little messy, and not just in secret. Accepting ourselves for our imperfections can be daunting. I see this struggle firsthand quite regularly when people are in performance mode.

A few years ago, I was leading a public speaking workshop. Before the first day, the attendees were tasked with preparing a performance piece to bring to the crowd: a speech, a presentation, or whatever.

Many of the overachievers in the group would take this exercise extremely seriously and would come with their presentations impeccably prepared. Their performances were memorized, down to the body language, hand gestures, and perfectly rehearsed *dramatic pauses* . . . which usually meant they also seemed a bit robotic and hard to connect with.

To help with that, we added a surprise element to the challenge. When the volunteers stepped onto the stage, they were given additional last-minute instructions that completely messed with their performances, making them deliberately *messy*.

For the actor who brought a Shakespearean monologue, he'd be told he must do the soliloquy in the voice of an ogre.

For the performer who brought a prepared TEDx talk, she'd be told she had to try to sing the script as a song.

Sometimes the attendees are given impromptu instructions from the audience such as "Now do it while you're dancing!" or "Wriggle around on your back like a bug!" or "Do a primal roar!" or "Perform it in slow motion!"

The tasks are all entirely ridiculous, chaotic, and impossible to get right. Which is the point.

Usually about halfway through the exercises, both the audience and brave presenters are doubled over in laughter. But they're also much more comfortable with their messiness. I mean, when you've just spent the last thirty seconds with your eyes closed and tongue out going "blaaaaaaarghhhhhhhh" while pretending to be a squirming beetle flipped over on your back in front of a crowd of your peers, it's hard to take yourself too seriously.

And their performances right after, this time without the ridiculous instructions, are almost always *infinitely* better than their practice speeches from earlier in the workshop. The speakers are more comfortable with their body, they seem more naturally confident, and best of all, they are more connected with the audience.

Whenever we do this exercise, the result is consistently and universally positive, both on the stage and off. People's presence grew—they stood taller, spoke louder. They were more naturally charismatic. And most importantly, they were speaking as themselves rather than as the character of themselves they thought they needed to play.

When we are scared to show the world our inner messiness, we unconsciously also hold back every other part of ourselves, including the parts that make us unique and undeniably interesting. By permitting imperfections, it allows us to discover that who we truly are is actually *better* than our performance selves.

Being seen in our imperfections is naturally uncomfortable because we are inherently scared of being judged and rejected. We all went through a phase in our lives where we may have felt like whoever we were would be picked apart by the dissecting glances of others. These fears are heightened for those of us who grew up in environments that expect perfection, or that tell us that our imperfections will reflect poorly on other people.

One of the more advanced exercises I lead allows volunteers from the group to step up and share a secret self-criticism they hold on to, or an embarrassing or shameful story about their past. Alternatively, they could just stand in front of people and point to an area of their body that they feel is flawed. Sometimes, allowing ourselves to be seen in our imperfections can be deeply freeing.

One by one, volunteers would step forward and share a statement of self-criticism:

"I judge myself for not working out enough."

"I judge myself for not being successful enough to be here."

"I judge myself for not being a better son and not visiting my family enough."

"I judge myself for not being a good enough parent."

"I judge myself for procrastinating."

Sometimes, people would go into greater detail, while at other times, people would just point to a part of themselves, in silence.

After each share, I'd ask anyone else who felt that same self-criticism to raise their hand, so they can see whether they're alone in it. No matter how seemingly specific or nuanced, there was a flurry of hands from others who felt the same exact self-criticism. A soft wave of nodding would drift through the room when people saw that they weren't alone in their deepest fears.

I know how scary it can be to volunteer to stand on stage and reveal your own self-judgments. When I first did this exercise as a participant, I remember stepping forward into the circle and freezing. In my mind, I had prepared to say, "I judge myself for being lazy," and I repeated it in my head as I waited for my turn. But when I stepped forward and saw the dozens of pairs of eyes on me, hearing the weighted silence in the air, I stuttered and said, "I . . . judge myself for being a failure."

The harshness of my words surprised even me, but it needed to come out. I was relieved when about a third of the participants stepped forward, and it felt like a weight lifted. It is as vulnerable as standing on stage without clothes, and perhaps even more so. But that fear is nothing compared to the feeling afterward of lightness and belonging.

In my smaller workshops, I'd invite people to go around the room, find those who they felt most connected with, thank them for their honesty, courage, or vulnerability, and if they feel called, they can say, "I accept you in your messiness."

The wave of emotions that gets released in the room is awe-inspiring.

People break into tears, they embrace one another, and they express relief. When I asked how people felt after, the answers are almost always a variation of: "I've never felt like I could be so accepted for who I am."

Perfectionism can be an intensively difficult thing to overcome because, at the core, it is not about reaching for the best within ourselves but being seen as such. Perfectionism comes with the toxic idea that if we can convince others that we are perfect, then we will be safe from judgment and rejection.

For many of us, perfectionism was often not a choice for us; it was the standard. If you weren't perfect, then by definition you were *imperfect*, which means you were unworthy.

The struggle with perfectionism can consist of cycles of self-punishment. Perfectionists can become addicted to striving for perfection, and when it turns out that we are humans who make mistakes, perfectionists can fall into blame, judgment, and guilt. We can come to believe we deserve to feel shame for falling short.

The only way out of this cycle is knowing our value and accepting our humanity. We need to acknowledge that perfection is not only an illusion, but it actively hampers our success. If we want to be good leaders, not only at work but in our lives and communities, our goal is not to strive for perfection but for excellence and compassion.

Setting a Playdate with Yourself

If you often find yourself gripped by the iron vice of perfectionism in everything you do, you can try setting a weekly "playdate" with yourself.

Playing is inherently, unapologetically messy. But it's also scientifically proven to help us grow. In the book *Play*, Dr. Stuart Brown and Christopher Vaughan dive deep into the neuroscientific research for why "playing," even as adults, is anything but a trivial waste of time. It's one of the seven primary-process emotional systems prewired in our midbrains, and the source of our most basic motivations.

The benefits of play include the essential development of our problem-solving skills, adaptability, intelligence, social skills, and creativity. These benefits specifically come from *free play*, which has no specific outcome goal and puts us into a state of flow. Yet, for many of us, we've been taught since an early age that play is frivolous or unnecessary. As such, many might feel shame for "acting like kids" or guilt for "wasting time." But the truth is, it's an essential practice regardless of whether you're a Nobel Prize winner or someone who just needs a break.

Maybe you've always wanted to play an instrument just for fun. Maybe you actually love Legos, even though you're a grown-ass adult. Maybe you've always wanted to write fun short stories but felt that you had to get all your characters and plots planned out just right before you could get started. Or maybe you tried dancing as a kid and always wanted to come back to it, but like me, you might seem to have been born with two left feet and the rhythmic coordination of a drunk orangutan.

Whatever playful task you attempt, your activity should be untethered from anything of financial consequence, and most important—it should be fun for its own sake. You can still set goals and expectations for yourself, but you should be completely fine without hitting them every single day. At least once a week, schedule a time when you can go and have *playtime*. This is a space without expectations of perfection or excellence or even being good enough, a place where you can have full permission to actually be messy, be creative, and be a kid again.

When I first started doing weekly playdates, I sucked at it. I set a goal of making a cheesecake because I didn't know how to bake, and figured I might as well pick up a new skill for the future. Halfway through, I realized I was still obsessively measuring every ingredient and trying to do it perfectly. I remembered the goal is to focus on the experience, so I decided to get creative. I dove into the pantry and grabbed every ingredient I would rather make the cheesecake with— old walnuts, skittles, those white rabbit candies I loved as a kid, alongside some random green frosting for painting a very crooked smiley face on top.

The outcome was a mess, but I loved it. It was both the least Instagrammable and the most enjoyable cheesecake experience I've had. I realized toward the end, I wasn't even baking anymore, I was an eight-year-old making a mess in my own kitchen, and I hadn't had that much fun in *years*.

During several moments of this practice, my Achiever brain kept nagging at me about how I'm wasting my time because, unlike literally everything else I do, playtime was the one thing that didn't contribute to my professional goals in any way. I felt guilty for having fun, which made me feel restless and pointless. But the pointlessness *is* the point— when you take away the pressures of succeeding, you actually have the space to engage a different part of your brain.

There is no "succeeding" at playtime, aside from having fun. The only way to lose is if you try to win.

Challenging the Myth of Unmet Potential

Tim's parents were concerned that his grades had been slipping and he had recently gotten a B on his report card, a grade that my students often affectionately called an Asian fail.

Tim's dad was not happy about this and emphasized repeatedly to him that this type of atrocity will cause the world to see him as a "loser." Tim's dad couldn't understand why his grades were beginning to slip. They always let him choose his own extracurricular activities and never forced him to do anything he didn't want to do.

But as we talked, it became clear that while Tim's parents allowed him to "pursue his passions," they had no problem yelling at him whenever it didn't match *their* idea of how that path looked. There was a certain irony about being given the freedom to choose his path, as long as his path led to their idea of perfection. Tim could be anything he wanted, as long as it made good money and looked good in front of their friends.

Tim's father insisted they had been so laid back with Tim's upbringing because his own father was very strict, forcing him to take over his family business even when he wanted to take a different career path. It also became clear that Tim's father was trying to relive his own childhood through his son, who had become an extension of his identity. But in doing so, he was unknowingly repeating the very same pattern of behavior that had caused him so much pain growing up, now in an updated wrapping paper. And poor Tim was caught in the middle. I worked with Tim for about a year, and he ended up in a school his parents deemed worthy. He eventually graduated and started working in finance, a career his parents deemed worthy.

Years later, Tim messaged me out of the blue and said he was coming to Vancouver and wondered if we could grab coffee. When we sat down, he immediately admitted he needed help. Tim said he felt stuck, but he didn't know why. He insisted he was fine. He had a fantastic track record with his clients and had exceptional ideas. But he felt he didn't know how to speak up more, which was holding him back. Tim struggled to connect with his peers, especially his white coworkers or superiors, and felt awkwardly out of place.

He was frustrated how his work, which was excellent, was not getting him the recognition he would like, and he asked for help on how to be more assertive and extroverted.

I asked if he felt his standards might be higher than his coworkers.

"Absolutely!" he responded, exasperated. "It feels like everyone else just says whatever they think without a filter. I like to think through what I'm saying and often I just don't feel like there's anything I need to add."

I asked Tim if he wanted to try a ridiculously simple exercise, for fun. I told him to take a breath and close his eyes. For the next sixty seconds, I wanted Tim to imagine what it would look like if there was a little magic genie in everyone's ears that made everything he said sound incredibly impressive, as if he was the world's greatest and most moving speaker.

He laughed, saying, "That would be amazing," and he did it. A huge smile crowded his face.

Then I told him to take a moment and, for the next minute or two, imagine if he was twelve feet tall and everyone saw him as a golden god at the meeting. Again, he cracked up at this visual, albeit a little embarrassed at the arrogance. Like most Asian Americans, Tim has been taught to value humility and not to boast, and imagining himself as a "golden god" felt incredibly disrespectful.

I pointed out this exercise takes place just in his head, he wasn't *saying* he was a golden god or even believing it. I told him he was just doing a fun exercise. Tim finally relaxed and laughed as he imagined himself towering over everyone in the room as a golden god.

Finally, I told Tim to imagine himself in a meeting once again, and this time to see himself as good enough just as he was.

Suddenly, he opened his eyes and narrowed his gaze, hesitating at the suggestion. Tim was deeply uncomfortable with this one. He asked me to explain the logic, his tone defensive. After all, he knew he was good enough. He was crushing it at work and in life. His parents hadn't bothered him in ages. He was totally fine. He repeated this and said he didn't need this, he just wanted advice on how to communicate with his peers better and to speak up at work.

I shrugged and said, "Humor me. We're just having fun anyway, right? What's the harm?"

He sighed and accepted it. He closed his eyes and gave it a try, if only to humor me.

I asked him to picture what it would look like if he was good enough, exactly as he was. To let that idea melt over him for a minute.

Tim took a deep breath, exhaled, and relaxed. His face changed.

And he started to cry.

Exercise: Becoming the Golden God

Growing up in a culture with high expectations, especially for how we are externally perceived, can create some deep self-narratives of inadequacy as we grow older. It's easy to look at what we do or what we say as being the main things to work on. But the internal work of developing unstoppable self-confidence comes first from self-ownership.

We often give ourselves permission to imagine big things because the inherent message is that ambition is socially acceptable, while self-acceptance feels like laziness or complacency. But if we don't start from there, how can we build upon ourselves?

While sitting in a quiet space, take a moment and ask yourself if there are ways in which you feel you're not up to par. Give yourself time to think about if there are areas in your life where you hold high expectations but struggle to meet them.

Then, whenever you're comfortable, visualize yourself as a twelve-foot-tall golden god. Picture yourself walking through whatever it is that you feel not good enough doing. Then imagine it simply being easy because you are a golden god. This might feel a little uncomfortable at first, especially if you've been taught that humility is a top value. But realize that this exercise isn't going to overinflate your head.

Now for the next two to three minutes, ask yourself what it would feel like if you gave yourself permission to accept that you are good enough as you are. Imagine what it would be like if you didn't have to be better, different, or more. Allow the unconditional acceptance that you're worthy and valuable to melt over you. How would that feel?

What would life look like if you felt like that all the time? How much more empowered could you be if you could tackle your challenges from that place of groundedness?

Breaking Free from "Not Good Enough"

The Curious Case of the Missing 8 Percent

When I was in the ninth grade, I once brought home 92 percent on a math test, which was a big deal to me at the time. Contrary to stereotypes, I was born with terrible math skills and it was always a weakness. But this time I had gone through a dozen different practice tests and was genuinely surprised that I managed to luck into a few of the correct answers that I was pretty sure were just blind guesses.

When I paraded my score in front of my mom, she furrowed her brows and asked, "What happened to the other eight percent?"

I deflated like a balloon. And it was my mistake for being dumb enough to show off to her to begin with. It wasn't that she wouldn't be proud of me, but my mom held a general belief that "things could always be better or more perfect." (By the way, *more perfect* is an oxymoron! You can't improve upon perfection.)

Comments like this are similar to the comments from other parents I've heard, though made in different ways:

"Yes, you did well on this presentation. But why didn't you also add the details like I said you should? You would have gotten more points if you'd listened."

"Why did you only get silver? Your cousin got gold last year and said it was easy."

"Yes, this debate championship is good. But it's only regionals. Have you started working on the nationals yet?"

These types of conditional compliments seemed to litter the childhoods of so many people I know.

Some are more comparative and minimizing: "You did well but someone else did better, so your accomplishment isn't really worthy of celebration."

Some are more critical: "You shouldn't be so proud of this achievement as it isn't the best."

And some are more positive, but still conditional: "We're so proud that you reached this goal, but it's not enough."

In extreme cases, I've even seen parents outright compare *themselves* to their children: "When I was your age, I had already won several similar awards and I was working three jobs on the side!"

And the resulting message is always the same: Your wins aren't enough, therefore *you're* not enough, and you don't deserve to be proud or be happy with yourself until you're better.

And at that point, the only solution to determine our self-worth is by constantly comparing ourselves to others.

Comparisonitis

In a study by a group of psychologists from the University of Michigan, the researchers conducted four experiments that compared Americans from East Asian backgrounds with those from white backgrounds, on their views of what they would prefer. They found a surprising disparity.

They asked participants whether, if they had to choose, they'd favor being a "big fish in a small pond" or vice versa—meaning would they rather attend a more renowned university where they perform below average or a less renowned one but perform better. Over half of the Asian adults chose the renowned university, compared to only a third of their white counterparts.

A similar question was then asked about whether they'd rather work for a top global company where they are underperforming, or a smaller company where they're doing better compared to their peers. And a similar result pattern was found.

They found that while white Americans generally valued themselves based only on their individual performances, Asian Americans often felt they had to compare themselves to a much larger group of people, well outside their immediate circle of friends. It didn't matter if you did well on your latest test or performance review, because somewhere out there is someone who's still doing better than you.

Comparisonitis knows no bounds.

In the bestselling book, appropriately titled *Comparisonitis*, author Melissa Ambrosini describes the effect of this type of endless comparison, and the toxic feelings of being not good enough leading to depression, anxiety, overthinking, and regret.

She defines *comparisonitis* as a "contagious, socially transmitted condition that occurs when you compare yourself to others so frequently and fiercely that you're left paralyzed, with your confidence in tatters and your self-worth plummeting." The more we're stuck in comparisonitis, the worse we feel about ourselves, creating an endless loop. We all experience comparisonitis, no matter our background, and most of the time the culprit is identified through social media. A study about the impact of social media on self-esteem revealed that 90 percent of people who use it find themselves comparing themselves with others.

Almost all participants were comparing themselves with those perceived to be doing better than they were.

But while everyone experiences comparisonitis to some degree, collectivist cultures can exacerbate the experience. In closer-knit communities, the comparisons often come not only from ourselves and our parents but from the larger social circles we're a part of. Asian parent groups on WeChat or WhatsApp are filled with other Asian parents spreading news of their children's accomplishments, their recent career changes, college admissions, or competition wins.

When I went to community gatherings, the conversations seemed to often revolve around two things: what's good to eat, and who's achieved what. In these circles, updates about your relationship status, your career prospects, your recent accomplishments, and even your weight can all be under scrutiny.

And then your stats are met with unhelpful reports on other people's experiences: "You're still single? Preeti just got married; you don't want to wait too long!" "Are you still at that nonprofit? I told you there's no future in it; look at Minh, he just got out of school and is working at a big company already." Or even "You gained weight! You should ask Chingyi how she lost all her weight recently; she looks so good!"

The pressures of being on display and being compared to others can start to weigh on our self-esteem without our realizing it. But the real problem with comparisonitis is that we are not dealing with reality. We don't *actually* know the full picture of those we are being compared to. The new job, the fancy trip, or the new toys they just bought are worth celebrating, but we don't know what they sacrificed to get them.

Regardless, we feel like the demand is high because keeping up is as much about pursuing what we want as it is about belonging—if our friends are moving on up in their lives, will they abandon us when they realize we're not "at their level?"

We all know the phrase "Comparison is the thief of joy." And we know that every one of our accomplishments comes with a cost, be it financial, emotional, or otherwise. Even if we think we know the exact costs our friends have paid to get where they're at, we don't know how big the bill will turn out to be a few years from now. These pressures can add up so quietly and yet so quickly.

When we're only measuring our progress by other people's accomplishments, we're always running someone else's race without any idea of their destination or the costs they were willing to pay.

The Path to Feeling Never Good Enough

Yale professor Dr. William Deresiewicz writes in his book *Excellent Sheep* that schools like Harvard, Stanford, Yale, and other prestigious dream schools are pumping out students who, despite being told they can do whatever they want, due to their intelligence and pedigree, seemingly all become robotic, exhausted, and lost. The vast majority of them end up in finance or consulting, not because these were the fulfillment of their potential and capability but because they don't know what else to do, and the degree was the end of the "conveyor belt" of expectations.

Dr. Deresiewicz mentions Asian parents specifically through the example of Amy Chua (author of *Battle Hymn of the Tiger Mother*), and describes her "reign of terror" as "a compound of panicked perfectionism and an infantile sense of entitlement." He says he sees his Asian students returning years later with an exhausted hollowness, feeling lost and purposeless in their lives. And these are the ones who have succeeded—the ones who won the golden trophy and became the Holy Grail story that Asian parents' friends use as an example to shame their own kids.

My perspective differs with Dr. Deresiewicz, however, because I choose to acknowledge the reasons *why* Asian parents like Amy Chua might have felt the need for her so-called reign of terror. In some ways, I can understand the mindset that Chua and other parents like her may have had, and why this parenting style seems to repeat itself through generations. Sure, there's a desire to look good in front of your peers when your child is succeeding in the world, and financial success is a fairly universal desire, but success also carries a different meaning for Asian immigrants because it represents safety and honor.

If you're moving from another country into a new environment, where you no longer have the extended community, family, and social support you once did, failure can feel isolating, terrifying, and disastrous. Social status means acceptance. It means safety from ostracization and from sudden social changes that might put our belonging at risk. If you have money and social status, you have guaranteed security. You don't need to worry as much about discrimination or being outcast when you have money. You're safe, and so are your children. Why wouldn't you want to instill those same values in them to protect them from a life of destitution?

But the question becomes: After a lifetime of chasing gold stars, do they actually end up with what they want? Are they actually safer or more successful? Or are they just burning themselves out to meet their parents' hidden expectations, when they could have established the same security and acceptance in a healthier way?

When I look at leaders I personally respect and admire, they all have a sense of purpose and self-ownership. They're not just hardworking; they're also clear on *why* they're hardworking. They want something other than fame and fortune, which is what leads them to be able to command the attention and admiration of others. They're not deferential, they're not self-judgmental, and they don't do their work for external validation.

Breaking Generational Patterns through Parenting

Perhaps because family is such a big thing in most Asian cultures, I've gotten to hear about a wide range of Asian parent-child experiences from my clients and friends.

The myth and stereotype that *all* Asian parents are the same, or that there's some set rules that all parents follow, is decidedly a myth. While there are existing studies that show Asian parents do show more authoritarian and "tiger" parenting styles than white parents, there's lack of clarity as to how prevalent this style is today. A survey of Chinese American parents of teenagers found that up to nearly 30 percent of Chinese American mothers described themselves as having a tiger parenting style, and an additional 7 percent described their parenting style as harsh. Which suggests that most modern Asian parents, and perhaps more important, most of their kids, view the parents as fairly easygoing.

Our parenting styles can be quite varied. I've met easygoing Asian parents who are endlessly supportive of their children pursuing their passions, as well as strict Asian parents who allowed their kids to study only specific fields, like medicine or engineering.

I've met Asian parents who cared only that their kids marry someone who made them happy, as well as Asian parents who were highly restrictive, refusing to accept their child being with any mate who isn't the race, culture, gender, or even income level that the parents deem acceptable.

I've met Asian parents who are deeply compassionate, caring, and understanding, as well as Asian parents who seem able only to criticize or blame, and are unable to acknowledge any personal responsibility or wrongdoing on their own part.

I've also heard stories of parents who truly break my heart. I still remember as I sat with a client as they shared stories of how they were forced to beg for forgiveness in front of their ancestors' shrines because they missed the mark on an important exam. In another story, a client once shared with me that they were beaten by their parent and made to kneel on uncooked rice for hours in punishment for disobeying their father on a relatively small issue. They showed me scars from when they were hit, and it took everything I had to hold back my own shock. But they shared the story with me so casually and calmly, as if sharing a boring family anecdote. To them, it wasn't abuse, it was love. Even the thought of calling it abuse seemed like a betrayal of their family.

I'm just going to go ahead and say it right now: any kind of corporal punishment in this day and age is not okay. It's abuse, it is proven time and time again that it creates devastating long-term effects, and it needs to stop yesterday. Contrary to idioms that I heard about growing up, like "hitting is caring, scolding is love," neither is true. To a child who is unable to understand that their parents are human and might be venting their own frustrations on an innocent party, the children often take on the story that they are always at fault whenever others are mad and that they deserve whatever they had received.

Fortunately, most Asian parents these days are much more aware of the long-lasting damage of screaming at or hitting their children. But the reason I'm bringing this up is because I think many Asian parents believe that this is what tiger parenting is, when in reality it's actually much less extreme, yet still problematic in subtle ways. When I speak to Asian parents who follow strict or authoritarian parenting styles, they often claim that they're not tiger parents because they're not violent or abusive. They may admit that they will occasionally pressure their kids, but will argue that they do so only as necessary to help their kids succeed. The belief is that while it might be stressful for the kids in the short term, it will ultimately help them in the long term: "They'll understand and do the same once they get older."

And for many children who grow up into parents themselves, they may very well parent in the same ways they were raised. After all, unless we've taken parenting lessons or read new books about parenting, our only knowledge of parenting comes from how we were raised. This is how generational patterns are passed on. If someone was raised with the lessons that "to scold is to love" or that "children are meant to be seen, not heard," and never had a problem with it, they'll likely teach that same lesson to their own children.

But in reality, we *should* break our generational patterns. We should keep the good, and update the bad, because most parents should want to give their children better opportunities and experiences than what they were given. It doesn't require a total abandonment of our culture or who we are—we can decide to pass down traditions like inviting extended family and friends on Lunar New Year but still choose not to pass down any shame, guilt, or patterns of self-neglect. After all, what kind of parents don't want their kids to have a better life?

The struggle is that we often don't know that new ways exist, so the generational patterns are passed down without examination. For example, I often meet parents who seem to think that the only alternative to their "strict Asian parenting style" is a "lazy Western parenting style" that's overly permissive, allowing a group of feral wild children to play and roam as they please. In the eyes of my own parents, the mere prospect of this type of parenting would have led me down a path to where I eventually would have dropped out of school (or worse, attended community art school), gotten a face tattoo, and ended up having to sell blood to survive.

But according to experts, neither of these ways is ideal. There is a third path.

Psychiatrist and education expert Shimi Kang, MD, studied three different types of parenting styles: Tiger parenting, Jellyfish parenting, and Dolphin parenting.

Tiger parents, also known as authoritarian parents, are typically what is pictured when the stereotype of strict Asian parents comes to mind. Tiger parents have high standards and high expectations, and demand obedience to strict rules. These rules are often inflexible, and even unclear, resulting in a lot of "because I said so" reasoning. Often, children feel they are being punished for breaking rules they weren't even aware of. Rewards are also given conditionally, including expressions of approval and love, which are typically given only when the child is doing what their parents say or living up to the parents' expectations, rather than when the child has excelled in their own interests.

Jellyfish parents, also known as permissive parents, are typically parents who try to turn their children into their friends at a young age. They rarely set boundaries or expectations, and if they do, they struggle with following through. They are usually quite comfortable with expressing love but will also steer away from discipline or teaching consequences for actions.

Dolphin parents, also known as authoritative parents, are typically seen as the most effective middle-ground strategy for parenting. They usually have high expectations of their children and set clear boundaries as the final decision-makers in the family. However, they are also much more warm and flexible in listening to their child's opinions and giving them weight in their decision-making. There is a combination of encouraging and loving communication alongside setting rules and expectations. Dolphin parents are often seen as the ideal parenting type by most parenting experts across different cultures, as they typically raise children who are socially confident, responsible, emotionally intelligent, and self-motivated.

Dr. Kang created a helpful chart to identify each category as well as their respective traits. (I've made some adjustments for ease of understanding.)

Parenting Style	Jellyfish (Permissive)	Tiger (Authoritarian)	Dolphin (Authoritative)
Drive in childhood	Drive dominated by the child's demands.	Parent pushing or hovering.	Parent-guided drive of nurturing.
Autonomy	Too much autonomy too early.	Too little autonomy, focus on parent making all decisions.	Gradual increase of autonomy with age.
Instruction	Not enough or absent instruction.	Too much adult instruction, low opportunity for children to learn independent problem-solving.	Instruction when needed, but focus on learning from the child's own experiences.
Discipline	Avoidance of discipline, rules, consequences, or confrontation.	Overfocus on discipline. Parent-determined rules and consequences. A lack of clear explanation when punishment is given.	Collaborative discussions about rules and consequences. Parents maintain authority, but with clear explanations and achievable expectations.
Goals	No clear goals.	Overfocus on short-term, comparative achievement. "Rolling goals" that can never be fully reached.	Collaborate goal setting. Shared vision for the outcome for both parent and child.

Parenting Style	Jellyfish (Permissive)	Tiger (Authoritarian)	Dolphin (Authoritative)
Expectations	No clear expectations.	Parental expectations are enforced with little consideration of the child's needs. Focuses only on achievement, with the assumption that this will lead to happiness in life.	Collaborative expectation setting. Focuses on emotional intelligence, relational skills, self-worth, as well as achievements set from the child's needs.
Drive in adulthood	Not clear or random.	Diminished sense of self, dependent on external reward or pressure.	Healthy, internal motivation that's sustainable and self-replenishing.

Parenting styles are often generational. If a parent was raised in a strict, tiger parenting style, they will usually parent the same way because *that's the way it's done.* After all, it's not as though we can choose the parenting style we experience or even have a point of comparison. We can see only what's on the outside of other families, so we create stories like: "This is just what it takes to succeed" or "Wait until you have kids and you'll see," but we neglect to see the variety of parenting styles that have raised equally successful kids.

Tiger parenting styles differ from Dolphin parenting styles because praise and love is given conditionally. Whereas a tiger parenting message might be "You didn't do well enough on that test, don't be a lazy person or you'll fall behind your classmates," the Dolphin parenting message might be "I love you and I can see that you're working hard, but let's give that another try because I believe in you and your abilities."

Both can maintain high standards, but one is built around a threat, and the other is built around unconditional support.

The stereotype of strict parenting is often focused on punishments—being chastised or yelled at, physically disciplined, or having certain privileges taken away—but the deeper impact can be made by the conditional praise and love. If you're praised only when you bring home a good mark, you quickly learn it's not *you* who's getting love, it's the *grade* that is getting love. So we start attaching a disproportionate amount of pressure to never stop achieving, so that we'll never stop receiving love and acceptance.

When this lesson is embedded deeply in our unconscious, we learn to distrust "unearned" praise or we consider love to be undeserved. Someone giving us a compliment on something we didn't burn ourselves out doing? It must be because their standards are too low or because the praise is just politeness and is undeserved. As such, the idea of loving yourself seems vain and too easy.

This enormously impacts the way we're able to give ourselves recognition or ask for it, because the embedded message is also that approval can only be externally received: You're not attractive unless *others* find you attractive. You're not successful until you achieve external symbols of success. You think you are worthy of love, praise, acceptance, or recognition? Where's your external evidence of that—is it your romantic partner, your job, your car, or house? You're not strong, fit, smart, tough, capable, or even lovable enough until *someone more important than you* has given you the acknowledgment that, yes, you are all these things.

But who the hell says so? And why are we giving the other person's voice that much more weight than our own?

Ultimately, your value can be determined only by you.

The Achiever Treadmill

A major reason why the tiger parenting style creates a longer-term problem is that it results in a dependence on extrinsic motivation—we take action because we desire a reward or want to avoid punishment (carrots and sticks). This is in contrast to intrinsic motivation, where we are motivated autonomously and with internal desire.

Let's say a child is trying to master an instrument at an early age (an experience I'm sure *no* Asian readers can find relatable).

In one instance, a child is told to practice because her parents promise her a reward, like a higher allowance, or is given a threat of punishment if they don't, such as being yelled at or getting certain privileges taken away if they don't practice enough. That's extrinsic motivation.

In another instance, a child practices because she finds enjoyment in playing music or loves the idea of one day playing for a big audience like her favorite musician. Her parents collaboratively set goals with her to help her reach her dreams, and they keep her accountable to her goals without coercion. That's intrinsic motivation.

In Daniel Pink's book *Drive*, the author lists several fascinating studies about how these two forms of motivation can have similar effects in the short term but drastically different outcomes in the long term. We can look at intrinsic versus extrinsic motivation like an internal operating system driving all our daily activities and behaviors.

In one experiment Pink quoted, two groups of students were given puzzles to complete, and were told they would be timed for how long it takes to finish their task. In secret, however, the scientists deliberately left excess time between the puzzles to observe what the participants would do.

In the first session, both groups completed their puzzles at around the same time, as expected, and did the same things between the puzzles, such as checking out the magazines or spending a few minutes playing with the puzzle on their own, unattended. In the second session, however, the scientist told Group A that they would be *paid* for every puzzle solved. Group B was given the same puzzles, but without the promise of reward. Motivated by the prospect of reward, Group A, as expected, did better than Group B.

However, in the *third* session, the financial rewards were taken away. This time around, Group A, now having associated the puzzles with reward, lost their motivation and did significantly worse than in both previous attempts. Group B was never given any financial reward in any session, and in the third session they seemed to become *more* engaged with the puzzles, spending more time with the puzzles than they did before.

The results of the experiment were groundbreaking as it went against all previous expectations and beliefs: it shows that extrinsic motivation—the carrot and the stick—actually ends up *diminishing* motivation in the long run.

Intrinsically motivated people usually achieve more than their reward-seeking counterparts in the long run, and are less afraid of failure. As Pink says, "the most successful people, the evidence shows, often aren't directly pursuing conventional notions of success. They're working hard and persisting through difficulties because of their internal desire to control their lives, learn about their world, and accomplish something that endures." Intrinsic motivation is a renewable resource, creates less fears of negative feedback, and drives from a deeper sense of meaning and purpose.

Extrinsically motivated people can still see results, but the results tend to come in short sprints, and the people run a much higher chance of burning out over time. Because the focus is on the outcome rather than the process, it grows harder to enjoy the actual process of the work, and rarely leads to *mastery*.

But what's most important about intrinsic motivation comes down to *autonomy*. With extrinsic motivation, once the reward or punishment is removed, the individual usually loses all desire to continue improving, because they were doing it only to appease their parents or for the proverbial carrot. This puts them into a state of dependence as they grow older. They may even feel their work is no longer purposeful in the long run, as if they're merely grinding without knowing why, and start questioning their own purpose in life. They have to keep chasing after the next big goal, the next big win, or someone else to validate their success in order for it to have meaning.

For example, Emily was up for a big promotion when she called me for advice on how to prepare for the interview. She had worked on her prep for weeks and obsessed on every detail. And she turned out to be successful in getting the promotion. Afterward, I congratulated her and asked how she celebrated.

Her answer was: "What's there to celebrate? We need to start working on the next level."

This conversation has happened so many times that I started calling it the Achiever Treadmill, because no accomplishment ever seems to linger. The brief moment of celebration of one accomplishment is immediately followed by a quiet panic of needing to strive for the next goal. They never give themselves the space to ask, "Is there a better path where I can utilize my strengths while still enjoying my life?"

From the outside, the displays of shining awards and stacks of accomplishments should reflect the joy and satisfaction of all those achievements. But instead, achievers view them with deep inner criticism, burnout, and a perpetual sense of unworthiness. That's not what success sounds like to me.

This is because the essence of strict Asian parenting is not about oppression, strictness, about hitting them with flip-flops or keeping them from going to sleepovers. The essence is that you do not get to own yourself, because in Asian collectivist cultures, we are an extension of our families and thus not responsible only for our own lives—meaning we will always carry guilt for not meeting those roles and standards.

In that context, parents not only have high hopes for their children but high hopes for themselves *through* their children. If your whole family is one singular unit, then everything you do is a reflection of them. So how can they give up control? What if you make a mistake and make everyone in the family suffer?

There's always room for improvement, there's always room for growth. But that also means there's no room for the acknowledgment of how hard you've tried and how far you've already come.

Getting Off the Treadmill

The problem with the Achiever Treadmill is that it's based on feelings rather than the reality of what was accomplished. We usually *feel* that what we've previously done wasn't big or worthy enough, and we *feel* that what we still have not yet accomplished is what will actually make it big or worthy.

The first step to getting off the Achiever Treadmill is by looking at *reality*, taking a real inventory of the ways in which we have measurably improved. This means being objective in identifying *measurable progress* as a win.

- Did you close more sales this quarter compared to the last? That's measurable progress.
- Did you get off the couch and go to the gym more times this week than the last? That's measurable progress.
- Did you speak up more at the last meeting or class discussion? That's measurable progress.
- Did you set better boundaries with your family when your aunt brought up your weight again for no explicit reason? That's measurable progress, and a healthy one at that.
- Did your recent relationship end with a mature goodbye and best wishes rather than with plates being thrown at you and eighty-two

missed text messages filled with profanity? That's measurable progress. (And, yes, that was a real example.)

When we focus on ways in which we have measurably improved and then actively acknowledge them, we take control of our growth. We can then use this criterion to decide how to move our life forward, evaluating our strategy along the way. And we'll have real, quantifiable evidence that can help us determine whether we are doing enough and deserve a well-earned celebratory break or we need to pivot our strategy and make different choices.

Journaling: Micro Wins

A simple practice of keeping track of the measurable progress in our lives is by keeping a Micro Wins Journal.

In my phone, I keep an ongoing folder of all the times I've achieved a measurable win. Finished a particularly difficult project? That's a win. Got positive feedback from a presentation? That's a win. A nice message from a social media follower who liked a video? You bet that's getting a screenshot and going into the win box.

Over time, it's become a digital scrapbook of random text messages, photos of celebrations, progress updates from workouts, and conversations with clients who made a breakthrough after a session. It didn't even matter what it was about; as long as it felt celebratory in the moment, it went in the journal.

Initially, I found myself often judging the accomplishments, trying to decide if the win was impactful or significant enough to be worthy of mention. But over time, I realized it wasn't the size of the accomplishment in everyone's eyes, it was the impact it made on me that mattered, and by writing it down, it shifted my focus away from where I was in the gap, and moved my focus to where I wanted to be.

That's when things started to really get powerful. I started testing this out on my friends and clients who were all struggling on the Achiever Treadmill. I'd tell them to celebrate the atomic wins: the tiny, microscopic wins they didn't think were even wins. You were exhausted today and still cleaned up your house. That's a micro win. You had the courage to ask someone on a date. You paid the bills and didn't suck *too badly* at your job today. You're still a mess, but you're in a better place than you were two years ago. You made a new friend at work. You got yourself to the gym, even though you half-assed an elliptical for ten minutes. You didn't give up today, even though you really, really, *really* wanted to.

These are micro wins that snowball into big wins.

At first, they all thought the exercise was ridiculous but did it either to humor me or because I wouldn't shut up about it. Over the course of a few weeks, I started hearing back about changes that went much deeper—their perspective changed, they felt more motivated, and they started taking bigger and bigger challenges and seeing measurable progress.

The secret is not about what you're doing, but about the fact that when your brain focuses on acknowledging the small victories, it creates a positive feedback loop of recognition. You start getting more comfortable with seeing progress, and when you look at the bigger picture, you're taking small steps up big mountains. It puts you into a state of gratitude, and your focus lands more on recognizing both the progress and the entire journey. That's how momentum works. It starts small, and then it snowballs, until it becomes bigger and unstoppable.

No matter how small or seemingly insignificant it is, the accomplishment is worthy because you're worthy. That is all you need to remember.

Giving Yourself Permission to Be Amazing

A few years ago, I was speaking to a client who wanted to make a career change. She had a brilliant idea for a new way of running a marketing business and had been working on it quietly on her own for a while.

When I asked her what she was waiting for, she struggled to come up with an answer. We looked at everything from her plans to distinguish herself from her competitors, to her own mindset around why she felt so *stuck* on making the decision to take action, even though she'd done more than enough preparation.

One day, she came to me and said: "John, I figured out what I was looking for."

"Great! What is it?" I asked.

"Permission."

"What do you mean?"

"I feel like I need someone to give me permission to do this. I don't know why, but I went home and I realized, throughout my life, I've been looking for someone else to point to me and say I should start this thing. It doesn't make sense. I'm fully capable of making my own decisions, but that's what it feels like."

For all the Asian people I've met over the years, many of us have grown up with explicit expectations for how we are allowed to show up. We learned that to be good kids, we had to wait for permission or we would be breaking from the collectivist expectations of what is "normal" or accepted.

Maybe when we were kids, we were scolded if we wanted to do something—go out with friends, take a pottery class—that "other Asian kids didn't do." For many of us, that pattern continued into our teens, where we saw the freedom non-Asian kids had to do what they wanted, yet it wasn't appropriate for us to do the same.

It was also common in adulthood. We may have felt more judgments when asking for what we wanted because it wasn't about us alone but how we represented our community. The expectations for the model minority means that we're often holding ourselves to a higher standard. We come to believe that our belonging is conditional, and a break from expectations would bring harsher criticism and judgment from others.

These silent rejections lead us to be more self-critical and more careful about how we step into the light, because to break from the pack is dangerous.

I told her, "I get how you feel. It can feel risky to step out of what is expected of you and to make these big changes. And I could absolutely give you permission just like this." I jokingly tapped each of her shoulders, the way the queen would dub a knight with a ceremonial sword. "There, I now dub you with the permission to go start your company."

She laughed at this, and so did I.

"But the issue is, it's really not about me giving you permission. My permission means absolutely nothing, because then you're still waiting on external validation. You're still looking outward for the confirmation that what you want is okay and acceptable. You need to be the one to give yourself permission."

She asked, "I don't know how to do that. It's not like I'm the arbiter of who gets to start businesses." She laughed at the idea.

"Is anyone? Aside from getting a business license, which you can easily do. Does anyone have the right to stop you?" She shook her head. I said, "Great. Then give yourself permission to not need anyone else's permission."

She laughed. "I can just do that?"

I said, "Sure, you've followed invisible rules all your life. Why not break a few of them?"

The next week, she launched her new project. Unsurprisingly, it immediately started picking up steam. On our next chat, she came back and celebrated: "It felt so nerve-racking to start! But I just kept remembering what you said about not following the rules. And it felt *so good* to click the publish button on my website!"

"I'm sure! Now imagine what else you can do if you weren't waiting for permission anymore."

Trusting our own permission (or trusting our judgment without waiting for permission) is sometimes a scary thing to do, but it's the first important step to allowing ourselves to shine and be seen.

This often means that we stop looking outward for confirmation that it's our time. We should just go out and claim our time, whenever we choose to do so. And we can take action even before we feel we're ready.

This is where we move from waiting for external confirmation to building the trust in our own internal guidance so we can take the leap into the unknown. This is an understandably scary thing to experience. After all, if we've been holding ourselves to this invisible vision of who we are "supposed to be" all our lives, one that is mirrored by the world around us and echoed by our own inner critics, making our own choices can feel like we might be doing something wrong.

Questions I often hear are: "But what if I mess up?," "What if I try this and it turns out I hate it?," "What if I put it out there and no one likes it?"

That's when I usually do that annoying thing coaches all love to do, which is to answer questions with more questions:

- "Hmm, good question, what if you *do* mess up? Have you ever messed up before and fixed the problem?"
- "If you hate it, can you decide to change your mind again and try something else at that point?"
- "If you put it out and no one likes it, can you keep refining your offerings until people *do* like it?"

Usually, the answer is a resounding yes. Just because we've never been tested in *this* endeavor doesn't mean we won't be able to figure it out.

Really, it always comes down to:

1. If things go wrong, can you trust your ability to fix it?
2. Can you give yourself permission to be seen doing something different than what is expected of you?

Finding our awesomeness is about accepting our uniqueness, the ways in which we are meant to shine that might be different from what people have expected of us. It also means we will get looked at differently or even questioned for our choices, which is understandably uncomfortable, but also *necessary*.

You need to give yourself permission to shine.

Claiming Your Strengths

Many of us make the mistake of comparing our seeds to other people's fully grown trees.

We look at a skill, a passion, or a talent we're considering cultivating, and then we become discouraged while looking at other people who are further ahead. We think, "Why bother trying?" And we let our talents remain buried.

I know this because I've seen it time and time again. People who start their path in total uncertainty, and no matter where they are, they end up finding a skill, a talent, a calling that will later become their competitive edge. I've seen people jump into completely new career paths and rise quickly through the ranks. I've seen people launch small community projects that blossom into thriving nonprofits. And I've seen people grow their after-work side hustles into seven-figure businesses.

And 90 percent of the time, they all start with this self-embarrassed confession: "John, if I'm totally honest, I don't actually know what I'm doing. I think I'm supposed to be good at X, but when I compare myself to those who are actually good, I'm nowhere close."

This is especially common with Achievers, who set the bar so high for what they're supposed to do. They don't even consider looking at how far they've come. And they look at the gap between here and where they're supposed to be as a barometer for how well they're doing.

The truth is, most people are "just trying to figure it out." Even for those whose faces are on magazine covers, bestselling authors, people who are at the top of their game—they still get moments when they don't know what they're doing.

The issue for Achievers is that many will use how they *feel* about their capabilities to *measure* them. Their feelings are not always a reliable indicator, because they might use one area's insufficiency to reduce their estimation of their other areas of strength.

Like Shyla, who had a rather lengthy conversation with herself about this: "I mean, I'm not insecure or anything. I know I'm good at what I do. I've been told I'm great at the technical parts of my job. But I feel like I'm not qualified for the position I want, and I won't be good at leading a team."

I asked her, "How do you know?"

"Well, I see people who are so much better at this than I am. Like, I was on a project with a friend from another department, and she's so charming and charismatic. It's like everyone who talks to her walks away feeling inspired. I can't do that."

"Hmm, but do you need to be charming and charismatic? What would you say you do best?" I asked.

"I'm really good at logistics and analytics. I've never missed a deadline because I can usually predict upcoming changes and prepare for them."

"Great. Can that be used as your competitive edge?"

"Yeah. But that doesn't make me a great leader," she said forlornly.

"Well, do you know leaders who are analytical and organized, who are good at what they do?"

She thought about it for a moment. "Sure, when I was in my previous company, we had a manager who was super analytical."

"And were they effective? Did you like working with them?"

"I loved it. I always knew what needed to be done and there were never any unnecessary meetings. I always got good feedback and knew how to improve."

"So it sounds like you created a story about what leadership is supposed to look like, and in doing so, you also invalidated your own strengths. And then you gave yourself a failing mark unnecessarily."

She agreed to an extent, but still wanted to know: "But isn't the ability to inspire and be charismatic an important skill?"

"Knowing how to communicate warmly absolutely is a skill. And one you can easily learn as an add-on to what you're already doing. It's just a matter of learning some new vocabulary and learning to listen. But your leadership style is never going to look like your coworker's style, nor should it, because then you'd be depriving others of what you're bringing to the table."

Claiming your awesomeness is about self-ownership. It is recognizing that even in our imperfections, our strengths hold tremendous value and power in the world if used in the right context. And, yes, that might mean things will be a bit messy.

Stepping Into Your Ideal Self

To demonstrate how quickly and effortlessly someone can immediately feel confident and unstoppable as their ideal self, I often teach an exercise called the Magic Carpet. It can be done anywhere and takes about a minute, and to anyone watching, it'll look like you're just pacing.

I was teaching a workshop and asked if anyone found themselves struggling with impostor syndrome or feeling insecure before an interview, public speaking, or social events. A woman in her thirties raised her hand and shared that she often struggled with feeling not good enough when she's expected to perform or speak, which has hampered her career in a number of ways. She admitted that she would often go home with endless thoughts of "*That's* what I should have said!"

I asked if she'd like to try a quick exercise and invited her up to the stage. Once she was standing in the center of the stage, I asked, "So right now, on a scale of one to ten, ten being unstoppably confident and one being basically feeling like a dumpster fire, where are you?"

She laughed, thought about it, and said, "About five to six."

"Great. That's perfectly fine, so what I'd like you to do is to picture about five steps in front of you and about five steps behind you. All I'm going to do is to ask you to take a few steps forward and backward, and then tell me how you feel. Is that okay?"

She nodded.

"Okay, so about five steps in front of you, I want you to picture your ideal self, using the values we talked about. Imagine seeing a ten-foot-tall version of the most amazing, powerful version of yourself. Someone who's in alignment with your core values."

She closed her eyes, took a deep breath, and then gave me a list of descriptions of her ideal self: "She's strong. She's confident, decisive, and happy."

"Great!" I said. "Can you see her facial expressions? Body language?"

"Yep," she continued, "she's got a huge smile and a look of determination in her eyes." She paused, then added, "She doesn't take anyone's shit." That brought out a laugh from the audience.

"Got it. Confident, decisive, happy, determined, doesn't take anyone's shit. Okay!" With this, I continued, "Now turn around, and at about five steps behind you, see if you can picture the *opposite* of your ideal self. Let me know once you do. Then describe her."

Her body language immediately changed. Even the thought of it seemed to have deflated her, and a look of contempt floated over her face. "She's weak. Does what everyone else wants. She's lazy, unmotivated, and selfish. She's sitting on the floor crying to herself," she said, with a look of disgust, then added, "She looks pathetic."

Wow. "Okay," I said as she resettled back into her body, facing forward. "Now this might feel temporarily uncomfortable, but I'm going to ask you to take a step back and notice how you feel in your body. Better or worse? More or less confident?"

She takes a deep breath, then steps back. "It's worse. I feel a bit weaker. Definitely less confident," she replied. Her body language shifted ever so slightly. Her chest sank. Her voice lowered. Her head dropped a bit.

"I can imagine," I said. "And I'm gonna have to ask you to take another step backward." She paused at first, only for a moment, before taking yet another step back. "How do you feel? Better or worse than before?"

"Much worse. I feel low. Small. I didn't want to do it."

"Is there a place in your body where you're feeling the change the most?"

She nodded, then pointed at her abdomen. "In my stomach."

I continued. "Okay, so let's take a step forward again, just for comparison."

She happily took a big step forward in relief, and her body language shifted back to where it started. I again asked her how she felt.

"Much better. Not fully confident, but definitely an improvement from when I was back there." She gestured behind her.

"Great, now once again, visualize your ideal self in as much detail and clarity as possible. Then take a step forward." There was a hesitance in her ability to cross a threshold. She steeled herself and walked forward. "How do you feel? Better or worse?"

She looked amazed: "Way better. I feel stronger, more confident. Not quite where I want to be, but I also feel lighter." I noted her internal feelings were echoed by her now more upright body.

"Okay, let's take one more big step forward. You should be just in front of your ideal self."

She gladly took a *huge* step forward. Her head is up, her shoulders are back, and an excited energy has formed an aura of strength around her.

"In a second, I'm going to ask you to take your final step forward, right through the visualization where you placed your ideal self. To be fully ready for this, I'm going to count down from five, and when it's time, I want you to take the most powerful, assertive step forward and really *feel* the difference. You ready?"

She closed her eyes and recentered herself, shaking out her hands and shoulders in preparation. Then she opened her eyes, a look of determination gleaming in her gaze.

"All right, let's do this," I said. "For dramatic effect, I'm gonna get the audience to count down with us, okay?" She smiled and gave me a thumbs-up. The audience was loving it, sending their love and support through their voices and energy as we all counted down together:

"Five . . . four . . . three . . . two . . . one, GO!"

Without hesitation, she takes a leaping step forward and lands on her final step.

There's a moment of intensity as she stands, chest raised and heart forward. She centers herself, feet shoulder width apart, closing her eyes to ground herself in the experience. After slightly shaking out the remaining tremors she had been carrying, she takes yet another deep breath, as if to soak in every last bit of the essence of her ideal self. We wait in silent anticipation for her to fully own this moment. There is no reason to rush for anyone else's sake. She owns the room now. Finally, she opens her eyes with a massive smile on her face. She looks lighter, happier, self-assured, as she turns to me and the audience behind me.

"How do you feel?" I ask.

She responds, beaming: *"Like a ten."*

Exercise: The Magic Carpet

This is a practice best done with a little bit of space, about ten feet in front of and behind you. To get the best effect, give yourself some time to really explore how you feel at each step of the process.

1. Start by visualizing yourself standing in the center of a twenty-foot-long carpet.

2. In front of you at one end of the carpet, picture an image of your ideal self. Make the image ten feet tall, bigger than life, even glowing with light. Imagine it with as much clarity and detail as possible, noticing how you look, your facial expressions, body language, even clothing. Ask yourself what words you might use to describe your ideal self.

3. Once you have a clear image in your mind, turn around and position the opposite of your ideal self at the other end. Again, noticing all the details and noting the language you might use to describe that image. Then return to face forward toward your ideal self.

4. Once you're ready, take a step backward, away from your ideal self, and immediately notice if you feel different. Note if you feel better or worse, stronger or weaker, more confident or less confident.

5. Take a step forward, for comparison. Notice again how you feel.

6. Now take two steps back, pausing on the step between, just to track the shift in your physiology and the change in how you feel.

7. Then, return to your starting position. Pause at each step to notice the change, until you're back at where you started. You might notice that you feel a bit different than when you first started.

8. Now, take a step forward. Notice any shifts in your sensations or feelings.

9. Take a step back again; notice the contrast.

10. Then, take two steps forward, taking a pause at each step to notice any shifts. The more time you give your body to acknowledge a difference, the better.

11. Finally, take one big step forward into the image of your ideal self. Notice if your body language has shifted, if you feel different or more powerful in the process.

The next time you're walking into an interview or on stage for a public speaking gig, or any occasion where you want to reconnect with this feeling again, you can "roll out" the magic carpet, and go through the process as many times as you'd like. Then you can continue your life as your new self.

The Rebel Pattern

Aside from the Achiever pattern, the other pattern that I often find emerges as a result of high-pressured parenting is the Rebel. I find that when pressures for overachievement are at overly high or toxic levels, when we are told by others that *we* are not enough if we don't hit external expectations, we tend to go either into self-blame (*What's wrong with me? Why didn't I work harder?*) or into rejection (*I'll never be good enough for you anyway, so why bother?*). This is where I often see the Rebels emerge.

There are two ways that Rebels show up when dealing with tough or unreachable demands. It might start in their actions, where a Rebel will do the least amount of work possible to still get by and not be blamed. In some cases, they may even unconsciously underperform on a project so that they won't be given the same task again. This often happens when someone comes to me wondering why they can't seem to get started on a relatively easy project, or why they procrastinate endlessly on something that *should* be easy. I'll point out that if they keep trying to get themselves motivated by shaming and berating themselves, it's unlikely that their motivation will go up. It's as if there's a part of them that refuses to cooperate, no matter what they do. That's their inner Rebel dragging their feet—by *not doing* something, they're actually expressing a protest.

The other way I see the Rebel show up is when someone seems consistently and reactively contrarian, and they have to disagree with what everyone else says or does. These are people who, no matter what you say, seem to automatically try to go against others. If you say it's hot today, they'll tell you that it's actually cold compared to where they've been. If you say you love sweet foods, they'll talk about how terrible sweets are for you. This is different from someone who genuinely believes in their convictions and is highly vocal about it, as the Rebel will flip-flop in their own statements *solely* to take an opposing stance. It's like a reactive defensiveness, like they're prepared to fight battles where none exist.

The Achiever (or the OVER Achiever) pattern as well as the Rebel pattern usually comes from the same place—it comes out when we feel the need to pick up the shield and sword because we're anticipating some kind of external blame to come. Both will cause us to go into action (or inaction), even when it's misaligned with what we really want, because it's reactive. And neither is coming from our true selves and our true vision of what we want.

Finding Your Vision of Success

It may seem weird for a self-improvement book to say this . . . but self-improvement is kind of a losing proposition. If there's always room for improvement, it also means we're never quite good enough compared to someone else.

Going back to the conversation I had with Newton (the Google guy) in chapter 3, he shared a story about how hard he was on himself one time after a tough day. He was talking to his therapist, who called him out: "You're still trying to get an A on your report card, aren't you?"

He chuckled and admitted indeed that was the case.

His therapist then said, "It's okay if you still want to get an A, but what's important to remember is that *you're* the one writing the test now."

In a world with billions of people, there's always someone who has done more and achieved more than us in one area or another, and we're only ever competing against our *impressions* of other people, not who they *really* are. We don't actually know if that high school friend who just posted pictures of her perfect wedding is actually any happier in her relationship than we are. We don't know if our friend who just bought a flashy Mercedes is actually up to his neck in debt. All we see is what's on the surface of a perpetual competition we never *really* signed up for.

This is where we often go, "Okay, but I still *want* that fancy car, and it's undeniable that Becky's bridal look *is* annoyingly stunning with the Napa Valley backdrop."

Which is a fair point, so long as we know *why* we want those things. Because most of the time when we're in the toxic overachievement mindset, the achievements we want in life are really to impress others or to meet an expectation set by some invisible metric.

The first questions I always ask someone who comes to me for help are what their goal is, how they will measure when they've achieved it, and finally, what they think will happen once they do.

Surprisingly, while everyone has an answer for the first question, many don't have a clear idea of the second, and almost no one can pinpoint the answer for the third. They might come in because they have a career block and want to make more money or because they're struggling in a relationship. They have a vague idea of how they'll be happier once it happens.

So I'll often ask, "When you look back at having accomplished your last big milestones, were you happier after?" The answer is usually a pause, and a recognition that they were happier for a while, but then they went back to being stressed again.

I blame the fairy tales we were told as kids for this, most of which ended on "and they lived happily ever after." But that's not how reality works. Happiness is a state of mind, not a state of life. Even if you win the lottery, you'll eventually get used to the fancy new surroundings and encounter a new, different set of problems.

As an example, I had a client who told me he wanted to make more money because he wanted to buy a fancy sports car. So I said, "Great, let's say a genie appears and gives you this car tomorrow. What do you do?"

He said, "Well, I'll go drive it, of course!"

I said, "Okay, where are you driving? Who would you show it to? Your family and friends? Then what would you do? Where would you go? And what happens after you've done all the things like sharing it on Instagram? What happens the next day? And the next?"

He was stumped. He was so sure this car would make him happy, but now that he was sitting in it (in his imagination), he realized what he really wanted wasn't the car, it was what the car *meant* by association. It meant his parents' approval and recognition of his success. It meant his friends' admiration. It meant social acceptance.

So I asked him, "What would happen if you drove to your parents' house and they criticized you for being wasteful, as you said they often did? Or if you drove it to your friends' place and they didn't seem excited because they liked another brand, or just didn't care about cars?" He admitted he would probably lose a lot of the excitement, and might even question his choice in the first place.

Because at the end of the day, you can buy a fancy car and you'll feel really happy about it for a while, maybe even for months, but after a while, it just becomes a transportation device that takes you to work. Unless you give it meaning, like car aficionados do, in which the car *is* the pursuit. But for most of us, we're looking for something more.

The promise of "the pursuit of happiness" can be really tricky. Because it's not the happiness we're really focused on, it's the pursuit. Happiness is fleeting after it stabilizes, and we usually return to our basepoint. And if we keep dangling that imaginary carrot in front of ourselves without actually asking what we can do to *make* happiness, we can never really stop pursuing it.

The better pursuit is for what *feels meaningful* to us. If you took a tour of your life, you might notice how everything you own was once an idea you had, that the object would do something for you.

I told my client, "Look around at everything you currently own. All of those things used to be money, and all that money used to be time."

I then continued, "Now look at the list of things you want, because all of those things will also cost time. Time is your most important and valuable resource, and because it's finite, as in, we all have only so much of it, it goes up in value the older we get. I don't ever want you to feel that you are settling or giving up any of your dreams, but I want to make sure the dreams for which you're choosing to give up your most valuable resource are actually worth the price you're paying for it."

We looked at his core values—his family, his relationships, and spending quality time with them—and what those values meant. He actually valued time in nature, and the opportunity to spend time every month going on more hikes and spending more time in the mountains.

This is the difference between an "Aligned Vision" and an "Unaligned Vision." When our vision of success is *aligned* with our core values—the things that genuinely matter to us—we get off the treadmill and actually get on a path to *going where we want to go*. When our vision is *unaligned* with our values, our desires are just about external validation, and that vision is aligned with other people's values, not our own.

I had him create a table that looked a bit like the one below, and asked him to fill it out. While both visions might look similar, it's also fully okay if these visions are not the same.

My parents' (or other people's) vision of a successful life is . . .	My vision of a successful life is . . .

When he was done, he realized he had mapped out a life that was completely different from the one he thought his parents wanted for him. It was as though his parents had always been secretly peeping over his shoulders, evaluating his decisions.

But then I asked him to bring the list to his parents and ask them, "Is this really what you wanted for me?" It took him a couple of tries before he had the courage to approach them, perhaps out of concern that telling them what he actually wanted would disappoint them or appear selfish.

He told me later that when he asked, they were surprised because they never expected these things from him. They said, "Sure, some of this was what we thought would help you, but now that you're an adult, we kind of accept you'll find your own path. We don't want you to live our lives, we want you to be happy with yours."

Then he presented them with his aligned vision. While they had a few concerns, they were ultimately glad he *had* a plan for himself, and they mainly focused on how they could help. This was a massive relief for him, and for the first time, he felt that he could be more fully transparent in updating them on his life.

We spend so much of our time trying to go after what we think we *should* want, or what we think others expect us to have, that we often end up sacrificing what we actually want.

Of course, not every parent will be so willing to accept this switch in visions. But I usually find that with enough time, most of these differences end up as "We don't fully understand it, but we get you're a different generation, you think differently, you want different things. And so we'll just have to accept it and wish you the best." Either way, he now has the room to be more honest with them and actually begin to really communicate.

Breaking free from the confinements of our familial roles is a process that takes time and patience, and more important, compassion for ourselves. The symptoms of these roles—the Achiever Treadmill, impostor syndrome, comparisonitis, perfection paralysis—all stem first from our own judgment of ourselves.

Can you, in this moment, allow yourself to take a brief concession of acceptance that you don't need to be different, better, or more?

You are enough, exactly as you are.

Setting Yourself on Fire to Keep Others Warm

Esther the Fixer

Esther runs the social media team for a software company, and she is one of the *nicest* people you'll ever meet. Her voice is always pleasant and nonthreatening, she's humble to a fault, and she is always rushing to the aid of the people around her. She often feels the need to sacrifice her time, her energy, and herself to help others. But she also struggles with saying no because she believes she's letting people down. She feels that her peers accept her but don't really respect or value her time, and she secretly hopes that the harder she works to help them, they'll eventually respect and appreciate her.

Esther carries a strong sense of duty. Her parents always needed her help. Her younger adult brother relies on her and she quietly admits to being "the dumpster" at work ("you know, the one who people dump all the projects on that they don't want to do"). But she continues out of a sense of obligation, jumping from her seat to tend to anyone around who has a problem, even when she's already overwhelmed and on the verge of burnout.

When I asked her why she doesn't just say No, she said, "I'd feel so guilty. Plus, if I don't do it, who will?" That seems to be her answer for all things, along with: "Can you imagine if I stopped?"

"What *would* happen if you stopped?"

Esther thought about it. "I don't know. I guess they'd have to find someone else? My brother would have to find a job?" Then she shook her head "But he doesn't have any experience. I'd have to write his résumé and look for positions that will accept him, and I'd have to drive him to the interviews and probably his jobs. I don't have time to do all that."

I said, "But why would *you* have to be the one to do all these things? He's a twenty-four-year-old college grad with access to the internet. He's perfectly able to figure out how to write his own résumé."

"I guess. But . . . I worry about him. When I was younger, my dad always told me it was my job to take care of him. That as the oldest, I had to make sure he would be okay. Even though as the oldest son, they always expected him to take care of our parents in their old age."

Finally, I pointed out the only way Fixers can let go and finally let adults be grown-ass adults: "Think of it this way. By doing everything for him, you're actually harming him and removing his ability to learn and explore for himself. He'll never get a chance to make mistakes and learn from them. By mothering him, you're smothering him."

That one hit a nerve.

Esther fits the Fixer archetype, through and through. But there is a dark side to her exceptional value of duty and the desire to heal and help everyone around her. It's what's colloquially called nice guy/nice girl syndrome. After Achievers, this is the second most common pattern I see in my Asian clients.

Fixers often play a role in the family as a caretaker. I don't mean just the physical act of helping their parents with chores, but emotional caretaking, like being the family therapist, peacekeeper, or perpetual shoulder-to-cry-on. Fixers are "nice," so they hide their own needs out of fear of burdening or inconveniencing others, and they struggle with any direct confrontation or anything that might *invite* confrontation. They avoid directly communicating any unhappiness, resentment, or anger, in order to remain likable. At the same time, they hope others will someday become aware of their sacrifices and be grateful. Fixers often feel a deep need to fix people, but they rarely allow others to support them because to receive support is to fail at their role of giving.

I point out to Esther that wanting to help others is a great thing, but there's a difference between giving from a place of genuine kindness and giving from the reflexive obligation of trying to be "nice." Fixers can agree to something out of fear of confrontation or fear of being disliked. Fixers often believe that their identity keeps them safe, believing that if they do enough, give enough, and give up enough, they'll eventually *be* enough.

I find many Fixers I talk to secretly wonder if people are mad at them, disappointed in them, or feel let down by them. In her book *Adult Children of Emotionally Immature Parents*, psychologist Lindsay C. Gibson describes how strict family roles often extend into adulthood. This makes sense: a kid who learns they get more attention when they make a joke will likely continue to use that same strategy when they grow up, by cracking jokes around their coworkers. And for kids who believed that being an emotional sponge was a good strategy for receiving love, that becomes a really hard pattern to break.

And that's the problem with filial piety and family duty gone wrong. Yes, being respectful and caring about your parents is great, but it shouldn't come at the sacrifice of a child's basic needs, like unconditional love. The concept of unconditional love is important, because whether or not you were successful in fulfilling your role in the family as a child, you still deserved love.

When you feel it's your duty to fix other people's problems all the time, not only are you robbing them of their right to learn how to handle their own problems, but you're creating problems for your relationships. Fixers worry that if others reject their offer to fix things for them, they're also rejecting the fixer and their worth. And all that leads to is emptiness and burnout.

Because the unfortunate truth is that no matter how hard Fixers work, these patterns are rarely genuinely appreciated or lead to being respected. Behind closed doors, I've heard of nice guys/nice girls being seen as doormats or as trying too hard. They are seen as allowing others to push them around or walk all over them. Or they are seen as telling people what they want to hear because they don't want to rock the boat.

So Fixers are not seen as truly harmonious or as giving from a genuine place. Their giving is seen as people-pleasing and approval-seeking behavior to avoid any criticisms or attacks. Fixers lack the self-confidence of people who give from abundance. Whereas kind and generous people can give, receive, and say no, all from a place of gladness, nice guys/nice girls struggle with setting boundaries and often resort to passive-aggressiveness or emotional manipulation to get their needs met. And because Fixers can't say no, others can't trust that their yes is coming from true desire and availability.

Esther also feels that this is tied to her social conditioning. Growing up as one of the only people of color in school, she felt the best solution to making friends was by being *useful*. She always felt a little bit on the outside with her friend group, where others invited her only because she was the one who was always bringing people food when they were sick or being the shoulder to cry on when they were going through breakups. She questioned whether they would have ever accepted her into their groups if she stopped being the person who only gives and never takes.

I reminded her that without prioritizing her own needs first and setting boundaries to protect them, she won't ever be truly appreciated or recognized for her sacrifices.

She paused for a moment. "But isn't it selfish to only think of what I need?"

"Not at all. By reclaiming your time and energy to focus on growing what you're *really* good at, you can make a much bigger impact in the lives around you. By not honoring your own boundaries, you're depriving people of building *real* relationships with the real you."

Again, this hits home for her. There's always an opportunity cost to what we do. We are our greatest resource, and by investing our time and energy in our zones of genius (where your talent, skills, and strengths all combine), we can actually contribute so much more to the world.

I continued: "The question is, how much do you currently value your time or energy?"

She thought about it. "I guess I don't know. I don't really have a value for it, which is why I'm always giving it away."

"Right, if you don't truly value yourself first, what do you think you're teaching other people your worth is? We teach others how to value us and treat us based on what we put up with."

The realization settles into her, and she asks, "So what should I do?"

"You can start with one of the first words you've learned to say as a child, that you've then spent most of your adult life trying to suppress— you can start with saying no."

Why It's So Hard to Say No

To people who don't understand this, it's hard to explain why *no* can be one of the easiest words to learn, yet one of the hardest to say. Often, I hear of people asking Fixers, "Why didn't you just say no to them?" or "Why not tell them you don't want to?" And the Fixer's answer is often "Because I feel guilty, or because I feel like I'm doing something wrong."

In some Asian cultures where familial hierarchy is particularly emphasized, a direct no to a request or question from an elder or someone in a higher position of authority can be considered rude. So rude, in fact, that some will try every other way to turn someone down than to refuse outright.

Growing up, my mom made sure I learned about the concept of "filial piety," which was basically "respecting and obeying your parents." Similar concepts of the importance of deferring to authority and elders, to be agreeable and nonconfrontational around family, are a common collectivist cultural value across many Asian countries, including in South Asia, East Asia, and Southeast Asia. The idea of familial duty and obedience, in particular, is important, and many of us are taught to not speak up against parents, teachers, or people in positions of authority.

There's nothing wrong with respecting your parents, of course, but when we grow up with the expectation that saying no to parents or authority is a sort of betrayal of our role and identity, it can really screw with our sense of boundaries in adulthood. Instead of doing things for others because we want to, we feel we have to do it because it's our *duty* to say yes.

Imagine receiving a gift and then being told how much the giver didn't want to give it, because they felt obligated to. Even if they never outright say it, you can still *feel* it in the room. When the act of giving is coming from a place of *burden*, it creates all sorts of problems. This is particularly the case with parents who raise their children with messages like: "Look at how much I sacrificed for you" or "Do you know what I had to give up to raise you?"

The subconscious message of sacrificial statements embed the idea that children are a living burden, and even their existence is causing harm to the people they love and need the most—their parents. Love then becomes a conditional transactional act, like a credit card for purchases you never made and you could never pay back. And it can evolve into a toxic sense of obedience.

There is a basic, objective, universal truth: all children *deserve* unconditional love, safety, and belonging from their parents, even if they aren't perfect, even if they make mistakes, and even if they aren't what their parents expected. That is their birthright.

But so much of our feelings of unworthiness, of not being good enough, stems from this one simple need not having been met. Obedient kids who grew up in emotional debt to their parents often become adults who struggle to receive help or support because they can't handle taking on more of that debt from anyone else.

A toxic sense of blind obedience or obligation is, after all, not the same thing as genuine respect or politeness. When parents expect blind obedience, they are asserting that they will provide for the child's needs better than the child can. In authoritarian parenting styles, aka tiger parenting, the answer for everything is usually "because I said so." The parent makes the rules and a *good* child obeys.

If we were shamed for being disobedient, if we were scolded or abandoned when we expressed emotions like anger, we learned that the only way to be safe and accepted was by being passive and giving. When we got shut down for speaking up, we learned how vocalizing our needs or boundaries was *not allowed*. And when we tried to show a different perspective and heard "Why are you being so difficult? Just do as I say!," we learned to feel shame about our instincts and internal guidance.

That's a terrible way to exist. As adults, blind deference and obedience is not a good thing. No matter how many times your supervisor or HR department insists, "We're not a company, we're a *family*," they don't always have your best interests in mind.

It's the same in relationships. Do we really want to raise our children to become *obedient* husbands or wives who can't say no when they're in a relationship or a marriage? Do we want them to remain silent about their needs or to think that their needs don't matter?

I find it particularly disturbing that, even now, these teachings are still being aimed at Asian women. Asian women are taught that defer-ence and obedience is their *value* in relationships or in society. These values are so ingrained in history that even to this day, I still see stereo-types of Asian women who are expected to be submissive or are infan-talized as "cute." The social conditioning seems to say, "If you want to be picked, be good, be deferential, and just sit and look pretty."

When good values, including humility, harmony, and respect are badly enforced, they become toxic. I see this with clients all the time. They get roped into doing things with people they don't like, spend hours having conversations about topics they're not interested in, and fight for a dinner bill they never wanted to pay in the first place. Then they get home questioning, "Ugh, never again" . . . only to repeat the whole thing the week after. Or they start dating someone and say, "I just give and give and give and I don't feel like I'm being appreciated by this guy. I just feel like I'm his mother. Why do I keep attracting guys like this?"

The problem with accepting things out of a sense of obligation is that every time we do so, we're diminishing a part of ourselves that says, "Your needs are as important as the needs of the people around you, and your desires are as important as the desires of others."

Your coworker may want you to listen to their pitch on why Bitcoin is going to save the world, but it shouldn't trump *your* desire to go home after a long day of work, change into your pajamas, and marathon the newest season of *Squid Game*.

What you want *should* be as important, if not more important, than what others want. Not because you're special but because you're the only person who *can* be responsible for your own needs.

For Fixers, the word *no* should be the most important word in your vocabulary, because for every *no* you say to someone is a *yes* you're say-ing to yourself. One of the things I always suggest to Fixers is to practice saying as many *nos* as they can for a week and then compare the differ-ence in how they feel.

Exercise: Taking a "No" Week

In the beginning, Fixers often find saying "no" to be difficult, not because they're lacking a spine but because they don't want to hurt other people's feelings and because they want to appear helpful. After all, if they've felt that their value in the world is to be helpful, then turning someone down also means they're breaking their own rules.

They often end up being overcalibrated for niceness out of fear of overcorrecting to becoming mean. Because when we're overly conscious of our own impact, even a small step toward a healthy, self-empowered balance can feel like they're going to immediately be seen as an arrogant and inconsiderate jerk.

The fastest way to overcome *no*-phobia is to confront it head-on. If we learned at a young age that saying no is unsafe because we'll get rejected, invalidated, or even abandoned, it's important to reprogram that belief so our brains can realize it's actually safe to set boundaries and that we're not going to accidentally hurt anyone by doing so.

A simple way I've learned from many different coaches and my own experiences in doing this is to start with a week of "no."

Every time someone asks you to do something that isn't immediately essential, start by giving a "no" first. (If your boss asks you to do a report that is part of your job, of course that's essential—this exercise applies to nonessential requests.) Then, take a moment and check out how it feels in your body, and see if you actually desire to do something out of a glad heart. If the answer is no, just let the answer stand. If the answer is you actually *do* feel you want to participate, and you have the energy and space to give, then follow your no with ". . . actually, on second thought, sure."

For extra bonus points, don't add an explanation to your "no," at least at first. If they ask why not, you can then share a reason if you have one, or even "I'm not available for that right now" is a perfectly fine response.

This might feel uncomfortable at first, and if it does, it's a green light you're definitely on the right path. We should be as comfortable with our *nos* as we are with our *yeses*, because every *no* we say to someone else is a *yes* we are saying to ourselves.

We are saying *Yes, our time is valuable to us. Yes, our needs are as important and worthy as anyone else's (if not more). And, Yes, I'd much rather sit on my couch watching TV tonight than go out, and there's nothing wrong with wanting that.*

Learning to say no is a practice of self-prioritization, and it breaks the conditioning of undervaluing our own self-worth.

After the initial discomfort, you might notice a change start to emerge. If you practice this enough, you might feel more confident in yourself, because that's the muscle you're building underneath, and you'll likely start seeing people treat you better and with more respect.

But, more important, you'll start to treat yourself with more respect.

Self-Censorship and Self-Abandonment of the Invisible Ones

I often see a pattern of self-abandonment and self-censorship from the Invisible Ones. Whereas the Fixer might try to be overly nice or giving, the Commanders might take over and provide by micromanaging everyone, the Invisible Ones' way of giving is by staying out of the way so they *aren't being an inconvenience or burden.*

Before we continue, I really want to state: preferring to be quiet or not caring to be super social all the time is perfectly fine.

Sometimes we may simply prefer to not be in the spotlight, and I personally don't like it when the common advice is "Stop being so shy and speak up for yourself!" as it only furthers the idea that it's somehow your fault for wanting to be quiet, or there's something wrong with being quiet.

In cultures that celebrate subtlety, choosing to hold our thoughts in quiet contemplation is a communication of respect for the time and space of others. By not hogging the spotlight and, say, choosing to share the thought as an email after the meeting is an act of honoring the needs of others. We can't have a society of people constantly yelling over one another or fighting for the mic. In an ideal world, we'd have workplaces that recognize and fully support both the creative process and feedback from those who wish to be seen and those who don't.

That being said, where we should be watchful is whether we are quiet because we are doing so out of a pattern of self-censorship or self-abandonment, and we withhold ourselves out of shame or fear of judgment. That is quite different from simply not feeling you have a contribution to make.

This is where the Invisible Ones pattern often appears. A common phrase I hear among Invisible Ones is: "I don't want to be a burden." Or when asking for help, "I don't want to cause trouble" or "Only if it's convenient."

As mentioned before, for many of us, especially those from collectivist cultures, asking for help can sometimes feel like we are taking on social debt. If you receive help from someone, it's your obligation to return the favor down the road, and often we might feel pressured to return more than we've received.

The nagging prospect of accidentally inconveniencing or burdening someone carries a lot of social weight. If someone goes out of their way to help you, you might feel guilt or shame for what they have had to sacrifice, including their time and energy. I've even heard of people saying, "There are times at an uncontrolled intersection where I'll avoid making a left turn because I don't want traffic to build up behind me." When I heard it, I couldn't help picturing them taking endless right turns through city streets, driving around in circles until they made it home six hours later.

A friend of mine once shared how she had gotten sick on a national holiday, and instead of asking friends for a ride to the hospital, she instead suffered through a half hour bus ride and a two-hour wait before getting seen. She really didn't want to inconvenience anyone with her tiny "possibly appendicitis" problem.

The struggle with the fear of inconveniencing others negates one of the core tenets of society: we are all far more effective when we support one another. By avoiding asking for help because we're afraid of inconveniencing others, we devalue our own identity.

There's a phrase you've likely heard of—the importance of "taking up space." This isn't just about taking up more physical space (which you are also worthy of doing), but rather, not self-abandoning or self-censoring.

Here's a list of how self-abandoning or self-censoring can look:

1. Not claiming credit for your contributions at work or in relationships.
2. Allowing others to speak over you or cut you off, and immediately thinking, "Oh what they have to say is probably more important anyway."
3. Always being the first one to apologize, especially to those who do not also acknowledge their own roles in conflicts.
4. Avoiding conflict, either by "letting things go" that could have been easily resolved or by outright accepting when someone disrespects you.
5. Holding back ideas or thoughts you want to share, especially about a topic you have expertise in or could be contributory.
6. Turning down or not receiving praise. (Often this is not only out of politeness but outright rejecting it internally as well.)
7. Offering to change who you are when a romantic partner is threatening to leave (out of a desire to "keep" them, rather than a true desire to change for yourself).

The core of self-abandonment is ultimately about feeling that our needs, values, and desires are *less important or worthy* than those of other people. Invisible Ones minimize our own voice, our own desires, and the essence of who we are in order to maximize room for others, no matter whether it makes sense or not.

In this pattern of self-abandonment, we often feel we're the only ones we can rely on in everything we do. After all, you can figure it out alone eventually, right? So why worry your friends? And why take on that social debt and feel like we might be secretly in the red on the ledger?

The Social Ledger and Invisible Social Debt

In many Asian cultures, social reciprocity is a huge value, meaning there is a strong expectation that when you receive a gift, you must reciprocate by giving back something of equal or more value.

That is also why it's not uncommon to see full-on orchestrated brawls break out in Asian restaurants when the bill is dropped on the table. I remember days when my mom would slip me her credit card so I could excuse myself to go "to the bathroom" but secretly pay the bill. I felt like a ninja or a secret agent on a mission. Afterward, a symphony of "You shouldn't have!" and "How did you even do this?" would ring out from the uncles and aunties, signifying I had completed my mission perfectly.

Many Asian people I meet *love* to help others but also find it hard to ask for support, because it feels as if we're demanding so much in the interaction. To give willingly, without expectations of reciprocity, is easy, but to ask someone for help feels like a bigger social weight than the favor is worth.

And most of all, we don't want to trouble others with worry.

Remember how collectivist cultures are all about members taking care of one another? Well, the deeper part of that is that since we're all taking care of others, asking for more than you need is also seen as selfish. So we learn to handle things alone. It's not that we're *better off* alone, but it's less socially demanding than to ask for help. Plus, we don't want to be seen as incapable, right? Tough outer shell and all that?

For many Fixers, asking for help is to be vulnerable. Asking for help exposes that we're not self-sufficient, and, more terrifying, it might be used against us in the future.

These cultural conditions can sometimes lead to our not receiving the support we need. This can directly impact how we are viewed and impact our recognition for leadership, because what's a leader without the ability to delegate to those they lead?

For Fixers, knowing the difference between asking for help and taking too much is important. I find for women especially, there is the added pressure of needing to prove your strengths in the workplace so you aren't underestimated. Adding on to the tropes that often follow Asians, who are already often fighting existing stereotypes of meekness, the stakes for asking for help seems higher. You don't want to seem incapable, nor do you want to appear demanding.

Being clear in your communication can help with this. It's not simply about what you say, but understanding why you might feel social pressure around what you say. The reason many of us find it difficult telling people what we need, or actually seeking help, is the fear that we will be judged or rejected. We're so conditioned to be the helper, not the recipient.

Internally, our work is first to understand that asking for help (or delegating tasks to others) is not about us. Rather, it's about the mission you share with those around you. When you are allowing yourself to receive support, it isn't about selfishness or incapability but a reflection of how no one is an island and we're all in it together.

Overcoming our Fixer patterns is not just about seeing how we're self-abandoning. It's about transitioning away from the feelings of obligation that create toxic debt.

You'll Bring Honor to Us All: How Toxic Obligation Leads Us to Self-Abandonment

When we started looking at the ways Esther might be holding herself back, she'd talk about how this had always been her role since she was a child.

Esther was born to two immigrant parents who left their home to give their children better opportunities. As her parents lacked the new language skills and were busy focusing on running their small convenience store, she was tasked to take care of the household when they were gone. In the family, Esther was praised for how "she's such a little grown-up" or how her parents "never had to worry about her," and she would be praised for being a good daughter because of how responsible she was.

Duty and sacrifice play an important role in this. It's not uncommon for Asians to have grown up with the duty of not only looking after themselves but also making sure the family was taken care of. Esther made sure her brother was doing well in school, that he didn't feel lonely or bullied, and his physical and emotional needs were met. Even further, if her brother wasn't doing well or had run into problems, Esther got blamed for it. Over time, she learned that it's her job to step into her parents' roles at home. (The phenomenon of the type-A older sister feeling pressured to oversee their more relaxed younger brother, almost like a second mom, has come up so commonly that it's been nicknamed "Elder Daughter Syndrome.")

This situation was made harder because, as foreigners in a town with few people who looked like them, her parents had lost their entire community from back home.

"My mom would talk about how when she was growing up, her community and family were always there for each other. If you needed help, there was always someone who would come by later in the afternoon. But now they had no one except us, which meant I needed to step up."

She seemed emotional at this realization, and continued, "It wasn't my parents' fault. They didn't have a social safety net or protection, they were trying their best with nothing. So it was on me to do everything. If I didn't do it, our family would suffer. So I became their safety net." Her voice trembled as she asked, tearing up: "But what about me? *Where was my safety net?*"

This sense of unending duty that Esther feels plays a huge role in Asian culture, especially in the family. For many of us who grew up in a collectivist environment, our job is not only to study hard, make friends, and achieve our own long-term academic or career goals; we also often feel the duty to support our family: emotionally, physically, and financially.

This holds even more weight when our family doesn't have the same cultural support in a foreign environment. For many immigrant families, they left behind the tight-knit community of aunts, uncles, cousins, and friends who could have been called upon and trusted to support them during hard times. This might have been something even as simple as knowing who to call when there's an emergency illness, or if there's someone you can trust to come fix a leak at your house without being overbilled.

In a collectivist culture, families rely on a network of people they know. And suddenly in a new environment, all they have is themselves. This means the load of the extended community is put onto the kids' shoulders. Your duty now is not just to finish your schoolwork but also to check your little brothers' and, perhaps, to go over your parents' business loan agreements to make sure they aren't being taken advantage of.

Self-sacrifice and duty run deep in Asian cultures. Growing up, I was inundated with stories about Asian kids who made incredible sacrifices to fulfill their familial duties: in the classic story of *Mulan*, for example. Mulan begins her journey confronted with the feminine duty of marrying well—not for herself alone but so she can "bring honor to us all," meaning her family and community.

Instead of obeying her family, however, she escapes to fulfill yet another duty—to fill her father's position in military conscription, which is usually reserved for the son. The brave act of self-sacrifice was never for Mulan's own benefit. She didn't step onto the battlefield to win praise or admiration for her capability or intelligence. She did it because she couldn't bear to see her father suffer. Everything she did was for others, and that's what made her a hero. Fulfilling her father's duties. Fulfilling her nation's duties. Fulfilling her familial duties are all celebrated.

She's a hero as long as her heroism wasn't for *her* benefit.

This story, both so touching and powerful, left a strong impression in my own mind as a kid because the story of *Mulan*, and thousands of other stories like it, had taught me how honor and integrity come from self-sacrifice and duty to *others*. When we do something for ourselves, it's selfish. When we do something for others, it's honorable.

This dichotomy made me feel guilty any time I wanted to do something for myself, be it to pursue a career I really wanted or simply to take a vacation. I'd run through mental gymnastics trying to justify why I deserved time off, or how the new career path, which might be different from the one my parents had envisioned for me more than twenty years before, is actually still in line with what they want because it can generate more money. The idea of duty to my parents was allowed to be released momentarily only if I could take on the duty of supporting someone else.

But the truth is when I brought this up with my parents, they looked at me with confused incredulity—they never expected me to work

24/7/365 or to stay in a job *they* wanted for me. They frankly couldn't understand how this was helping them. That last point in particular stood out. I often see Fixers shouldering responsibilities that never truly benefit the people they feel they're helping, because the sacrifice wasn't truly for them; it was for Fixers to feel better.

This led me to start looking at duty with a little more curiosity. At what point is self-sacrifice and duty an honorable, admirable thing, and at what point does it start becoming a little toxic?

The Over-Responsibility of the Commanders

While Esther's main pattern was the Fixer, I've met many like her who end up becoming Commanders.

Commanders are micromanagers. They take control, charge ahead, and are driven to make sure everyone around them is playing their parts. Commanders and Fixers are somewhat similar in that both are in service of others, but where Fixers are happy to tend to others' emotional needs by giving up their own power and control, Commanders will often take leadership, giving out commands or taking on the tasks themselves. (Using the characters of *Everything Everywhere All at Once*, the Commander would be the Asian mom, Evelyn, who tries to control everything in her family's life, whereas the Fixer would be her husband, Waymond, who tries to appease everybody and give them cookies.)

But the difference is that they are far from the "nice guy/nice girl" tropes, nor do they bend themselves to fit other people's expectations. Instead, they go into hyperfunctioning and try to regain a sense of control by directing others. In school, the Fixer was the one in the group project who did everyone else's work. The Commander, on the other hand, was busy sending out angry emails to the team asking why their work wasn't done yet. At least, not done up to their standards. And when everyone eventually fails to live up to those standards—and it's almost a guarantee that everyone shall, since Commanders often expect perfection—they'll often sigh dramatically and say, "Fine! I'll just do it myself!"

It's not that Commanders have unreasonably high expectations for others but that they have unreasonably high expectations for themselves, and they see others' contributions as simply being part of that. If the group fails, then that means the Commander failed, and failure is rarely an option in the eyes of Commanders.

Fixers and Commanders often have the same root sources for their problems and often end up in the same place when they finally take on too much and crash:

Burnout.

Burnout

It was 2016, and I was giving a speech about high performance at a local event.

I was standing in the spotlight, in front of an eager audience of about a hundred people, and all I wondered was whether they could see the sweat slipping down my forehead. It wasn't from nervousness or the heat of the stage lamps, but a searing pain tearing through my abdomen every time I took a breath.

Keep talking, John. Keep smiling. You got this, I kept repeating to myself in my head. I just needed to get through this.

I cracked a well-rehearsed joke and tried not to laugh with the audience, but finally the pain won the battle. "You know what, guys? I'm gonna try something here," I said nonchalantly as I stepped offstage and grabbed a chair. "I'm going to sit down for the rest of this talk, because we should be on the same level. I shouldn't be talking down to you."

The crowd nodded and I was somewhat proud of my improvised solution. The truth had nothing to do with the theatrics. I just knew if I kept standing, I would probably pass out from the pain. But the audience had no idea and appreciated my apparent humbleness as I continued my speech.

It was not the first time I experienced something like this. I had been going through waves of pain for about three years at this point. Countless doctor's visits and prescription medication did nothing to cure it, mere band-aid solutions to let me keep working through the pain. A specialist told me it was stomach ulcers, and when I asked what might be the cause and whether it was hereditary, the doctor said, "No, ulcers could happen to anyone. Could even be stress related."

After the talk, I went home and looked up possible causes for ulcers, and discovered a checklist for burnout. Back then, it was still a relatively new term in my world. The questionnaire asked about whether I was feeling constantly tired or fatigued (*yes*). It asked if I felt I had less time for people, even family or friends (*of course*). It asked if I felt difficulty making decisions (*oh my god*). If I was experiencing forgetfulness (*duh*). If I felt unappreciated or struggled with saying no. (*GET OUT OF MY HEAD, YOU DEMON CHECKLIST.*)

I ended up scoring a near-perfect score on the questionnaire. I momentarily felt proud of my score, until I realized I wasn't *supposed* to be acing this quiz.

We usually associate burnout with overwork, but I've noticed that people who spend a lot of time taking care of other people's needs tend to reach that same point of physical and emotional exhaustion. The emotional toll of supporting those around us is sometimes much more than we can bear—after all, we can fail ourselves, but to fail others and disappoint them can be so much more devastating to a Fixer.

The pressures I was experiencing didn't occur solely when I was actively taking care of others but from my feelings of expectation. I was stressed about not doing enough for others, or stressed that people would be, somehow, angry at me. But the truth is, most of those expectations were not only self-perpetuated, they were created by me.

Once I started realizing the anxieties were mostly created by me in my head, my stomach pains went away on their own, like magic. I didn't realize it, but I had been holding all my tension in my abdomen, and I had concentrated so hard, it was causing physical pain.

Okay . . . Maybe I Might Need Some Help (Perhaps, Possibly)

The two biggest struggles I see with Fixers are:

1. They don't give themselves permission to ask for what they might need.
2. They don't give themselves permission to receive when others offer.

I get it. For most of my life, I sucked at receiving help.

A few years ago, I was going through some rough days. Work was stressful, I was struggling, and I was having a particularly hard time because, on top of it all, the weather sucked. (I often tell people I'm solar powered. I need the sun to function.)

Ji, a close friend I had supported through lots of rough days of her own, had called me up to go for a walk and a bubble tea run. We headed over to a nearby Chatime a couple of blocks up and I grabbed a pair of Taro Milk teas (half sweet, low ice, brown sugar bubbles). We started walking down the streets of Robson and I asked about her day.

Some random updates involving a guy she was dating or something about making kimchi later (yes, she's Korean and, yes, she makes her own kimchi and I was legitimately impressed), she turns to me and asks how things have been.

"Yeah, things are fine. I've been having some blah days with work and all that. But I'll figure it out."

Ji paused and asked me a few more questions. "What do you mean by blah days? What do you *feel* and where?" (She's also a therapist. Can you tell?)

I chuckled and told her, "I dunno, a bit frustrated? I'm fine, though; it's not a big deal. Tell me more about this kimchi thing."

She turned and stopped, knowing my deflective patterns. Then she reached around and gave me a hug.

I laughed, "Oh my gosh, seriously, I'm okay!" Inside, I felt embarrassed that she was making such a big deal out of nothing. I pulled away from the hug.

Suddenly, Ji yelled, "OH MY GOD JUST SHUT UP AND RECEIVE MY LOVE, JOHN!"

I was taken aback for a moment, then after a moment of recognizing how I was avoiding the whole thing, I leaned in. And sank into the hug.

Suddenly, I felt open, connected, and relieved. I held the hug longer and we just breathed into each other. (We have a saying: "Hug till it's awkward, and then keep holding until it's amazing.") Eventually, we both pulled away and continued walking down Robson Street, drinking our bubble tea. After that, the conversation felt more real, and I realized I could share without feeling burdensome anymore, because I recognized the vulnerability and openness released some of the stress, and in that light, I realized my problems weren't insurmountable.

Receiving love and support can be a deeply uncomfortable, even outright *scary*, experience for perpetual Fixers. It goes against our conditioned sense that receiving isn't safe, that sharing how we are struggling means being seen as weak or vulnerable, and at any moment, instead of actually being acknowledged for our needs, we might be invalidated or laughed at by those we open up to.

Asking for help is not just about others *doing* something for us. Sometimes it's a start to share what we're going through, and having that space to be seen and heard.

Most of the time, we know what to do. Have you ever gone to someone for advice for something, and the more you talk about it, the more you suddenly see *Ahas* in a series of epiphany moments that clarify exactly what you need to do, even when the other person didn't make any suggestions or impart any advice?

As social creatures, we often need to be seen, heard, and validated in our experience in the moment, rather than needing to be told what to do. This is why having a community, even one or two friends we can turn to for support, is so immensely important.

I find it's particularly essential this person (or persons) *cannot be our primary romantic partner.* This is not only because relying on our boyfriend/girlfriend/husband/wife/life partner can add additional stress to the relationship. It can create an imbalance in the relationship.

This isn't to say we shouldn't be vulnerable with our partners or share our inner world with them, but there are appropriate limits. After all, a parent probably shouldn't be sobbing to their child about losing their job and how terrified they are about possibly going into debt— that's not something for a child to carry; a child isn't supposed to be your *friend* first. Especially for children who are under ten, who cannot see the world outside of their own immediate circle, they'll always go into self-blame and take on the belief that it's somehow their fault.

In the same way, while you're welcome to share with your partner when you're feeling some added stress at work, it's inappropriate to treat them as a therapist who you dump *all* your problems onto, especially when the problems might involve your partner. If they feel that's their main role in the relationship, to carry your baggage and to caretake you, then they're no longer able to feel fully present with who *they* are in the relationship.

In relationship dynamics, I like to use the "3 Cups" analogy. In an imbalanced relationship, you can picture two cups, each half full. When one cup is getting low, there's an expectation for the other cup to empty itself into the first cup, so the two cups are always taking turns being empty. This is similar to being in a relationship where one person is always tending to the other's needs while depleting their own energy, having to take care of themselves plus the other person continuously. This can work in the short term, especially if one person is a Fixer who feels their need is to be needed, but it often leads to resentment and struggles in the relationship in the long term once the giver feels perpetually depleted and burned out.

In a healthy relationship dynamic, there is your cup, my cup, and the relationship cup. Each of us has a responsibility to find ways to fill our own cup, independently—with our affirmations and self-care, our sense of meaning from our goals and pursuits, our sense of identity from our own creations, and our sense of community from our friends. When we're feeling full, we put energy into the relationship—not just "what do you need" but "what do we need"—such as going on dates, spending quality time together, or even simply having dinner together. Then the relationship itself becomes a replenishing resource that pours back into both cups when it's needed. And from that, if our partner is having a particularly rough time, we can also replenish their cup without depleting ourselves.

This way, we're not *codependent* on each other, filling our cups while emptying theirs, we're *interdependent* on ourselves and the relationship as a source of our wellness and happiness.

How to Ask for Help When It's Hard to Receive

The one question I often have to ask Fixers who feel they need help is: "Did you actually ask for help? Or were you hoping for them to read your mind?" So many Fixers, as duty fulfillers, are so used to *guessing when other people need help and then offering*, they assume everyone else does the same thing.

And I've had to sit through the teary-eyed complaints of Fixers who tell me how they're always the ones running around anticipating other people's needs, but when they tell their friends they're having a hard time, they are disappointed when no one shows up at their door. In these instances, I usually try to ask them, as gently as possible, whether they *actually asked for their needs*.

"What do you mean? I told them what I was struggling with and said how much I wished this could be taken care of, and they had more than enough time and energy to help! They just don't *appreciate me!*"

"Right . . . but did you actually *ask them for what you need*? Did you actually say the words 'Hey, could you come by later this week, I could really use some emotional support?'"

This is often met by a hesitant no or a long diatribe on how they *shouldn't have to ask*—after all, *the Fixer* didn't need to be asked to show up and help, they just did. But that's not how everyone works. We all have different styles of relating to others, and for some, respecting your space while you're going through a challenge *is* the service they think you need.

I understand. Asking for help when we're already struggling can be an incredibly difficult thing, and we certainly *wish* everyone would read our minds, but unless we're living with a bunch of X-Men, that's not going to happen. Thankfully, that's why humans invented language.

Again, for some this might be obvious, but in case it's not, here are some things you can ask for from those around you:

1. **Asking to be heard.** This can be a simple: "Hey, I'm going through some stuff and I could use someone to just listen for a while as I talk through my issues with my life/relationship/work/whatever. Can we go for a walk or grab a coffee?"

   In my household, we call this a "bitch-and-moan session," where if one of us is having a tough day, we'll say, "Hey, do you have a few minutes to listen to me bitch and moan for a while?" And the other person's job is to nod, say empathetic reflections like "That sounds so hard" or "Yeah, I'd be pissed at your boss, too." During the bitch-and-moan, there's no judgment of the content, you can be as petty as possible, and there is *absolutely no problem-solving or advice-giving allowed,* unless you specifically ask.

This is an incredibly helpful tool for many people's relationships. By having a dedicated space where we can vent our frustrations, we have a less likely chance of exploding inappropriately on our other relationships, and thus reduce the chances of conflict.

2. **Asking for advice or feedback.** Most people are more than happy to accommodate this request, and again, it can be as simple as "Hey, I could use some advice (or your opinion) on something. I'm going through X and I've always seen you as someone who really has this part of their lives together."

   Asking for advice needs to be strategic and specific, and remember when you're in an advice-seeking session, you should feel comfortable asking as many follow-up questions as you want, and you should let the advice giver know when you've found what you're looking for so they don't sit there and rattle on for another hour when you already know what you need. Also remember: just because you received advice doesn't mean you are obligated to follow it. Just thank them for their time and honest feedback.

3. **Asking for help.** Be clear and direct in your asks. Try to avoid indirect language like "It'd be nice if someone did this." Instead, get straight to the point: "Hey, can I ask for your help with a project? If you're available, this is what I'd need . . ."

   The key here is to give them information on what you need and what your expectations are *before* they can agree. This way, you know for a fact that they can offer what you need without obligation. I sometimes will add the caveat "And if you're not available for it, that's totally fine, I can find someone else" to make sure they don't feel socially pressured. I often let them know I would be happy to reciprocate the favor if they ever needed it.

4. **Asking for acknowledgment.** This can be a foreign experience for many people, simply because it's not as socially acceptable. But you absolutely can say, "Hey, I'm celebrating that I recently accomplished X. Wanna come celebrate with me?"

   I find it to be life-changing to have people around you who are happy to celebrate things with you. My partner and I hold a dedicated "couple's meeting" every weekend, which starts with a round of our giving each other something we want to acknowledge the other for, like going for the extra mile on a project. We also give each other full permission to say when we want to be recognized for something, and often I'll be working in my office when my partner will burst through my doors with a huge smile and say, "*I want acknowledgment!*" and tell me what she's proud of so we can celebrate the milestones along the way. It's the best.

Exercise: Speaking Your Needs

"You ready for homework?" I asked Sunisa, a thirty-two-year-old entrepreneur at our weekend retreat. She *loves* homework of all types and usually comes back having done more than I asked for, but I had a feeling that this time would be the exception.

At the retreat, everyone gets an envelope with personalized suggested assignments, usually designed to fit their particular archetype. As a Fixer and Commander, Sunisa excitedly stands in front of the crowd, opening the envelope with the eager fanfare of a child opening presents on Christmas morning, and reads it like a sports announcer calling out the winning touchdown:

"This weekend, your homework is to do *nothing*. You can receive and not give. If you want to write notes or a message, you must ask a helper to do it for you. If you would like to eat or to drink water, you must ask someone to feed you. And most important, you need to simply surrender and not micromanage them, but trust them to figure it out."

She gives me a look of surprise, which quickly turns to dread as she realizes I am serious.

After the weekend, at the start of the next day of the retreat, I checked in with her and asked how things were going with her assignment. True to herself, she took the challenge seriously the entire weekend. She said she had her husband do everything for her that morning, including cooking breakfast, getting the kids ready for their activities, and *even putting on her makeup*. I was impressed with both her determination and her husband's surprisingly adept makeup application skills, although she seemed to see the flaws.

She said it was extremely difficult at first, to the point where she almost wanted to cry or at least jump up and yell, "*Stop! I'll do it myself!*" but the more she settled into it, the more she realized why she felt so resistant to the experience.

"My husband joked that it must be nice to have my homework be a vacation and to have everything done for me, but it didn't feel like a vacation. It felt so uncomfortable and vulnerable. I kept wanting to apologize, and I realized I was afraid of letting go. It wasn't just that I wanted to do things myself. I realized I felt embarrassed about needing him, or anyone else. It was a scary feeling."

I told her this was almost always the experience. It can be so difficult for her to let go, not because she needed to always be in control but because the role of being the responsible one was so embedded in her identity.

For many, finding your authentic self is a slow, methodical process, because you need to let your system adjust to something important: instead of being needed by everyone else, remember that you are most needed by *you*.

This doesn't make you selfish or neglectful. In fact, you can be so much more effective if you have a clear eye on where you can receive support, where you can let go and allow people to step into their own self-leadership (especially for those under-functioners who you need to stop enabling), and where you can trust to find balance and still be more than enough.

Giving Yourself Time for Readjustment

When you stop setting yourself on fire to keep others warm, sometimes all you'll hear are complaints that you've turned cold.

Breaking free from Fixer patterns can be a new and sometimes daunting experience. It's not just about learning to give yourself the space and appreciation you need, but when setting better boundaries, people may be confused as to why you've become distant, or complain how you've changed.

The truth is, you *have* changed . . . for the better. When we're giving from a place of "give to get," we're not actually building real relationships, we're building a fantasy. And almost invariably, when I see people discover boundaries for the first time in their relationships, they tend to go a little bit overboard, and often go around telling people: "THIS IS MY BOUNDARY. PLEASE DO NOT CROSS IT."

This is normal. It's an overcorrection, but it's also often necessary. Over time, the boundary will soften and become a bit more flexible, and you'll find yourself being able to firmly say no when you want to, without feeling guilty, and then the yes you do say feels that much more fulfilling because you know you're giving from a glad heart.

It's like jumping from a warm shower into a cold pool. There'll be a little bit of an adjustment period as your body gets used to the change, and then it becomes easier, all at once. After that, there's room for a much more real and intimate relationship to emerge, where both people can feel they have the freedom to be themselves. That's when we can truly be heard, be seen, and *relate* to one another.

Hiding Your Real Self

A Vow of Radical Honesty

For a year of my life, I took a vow of radical honesty.

During this experiment, I was not allowed to say anything that I didn't fully believe was true. Not even a little white lie like "Sure, that eighties-style perm looks *great* on you."

The experiment started when a friend of mine suggested this book to me: *Radical Honesty* by Dr. Brad Blanton. Blanton's basic principle is that most of our deeper internal struggles happen because we avoid having difficult and important conversations. He pointed out that most of the time, even the "white lies" we tell others aren't really stemming from politeness, but fear of confrontation or of upsetting others.

And when I lie or hesitate to tell my best friend that his new perm looks like it was done by a blind monkey, it is not because I want to protect his feelings but because I don't want him to be angry at me. I'm protecting *my* feelings. But in doing so, I'm actually hurting him, as he's capable of handling my opinions.

When I first started the experiment, I gave myself the following rules:

1. I can tell only the truth. This applies to every question that was asked of me, including my true opinions about others and myself.
2. I cannot hold back the truth. If I *didn't* say something that I was thinking or feeling, as a way of concealing information or withholding for fear of confrontation, I needed to go to the person and tell them what I held back.
3. I had to go back and confess to people the lies I remembered telling them.

That third one was the hardest to do, because in the first two weeks of my starting the experiment, I had to sit down with my parents and tell them about *every lie I could think of that I told them growing up.*

I had to come clean about the cigarettes they found in my jacket pocket in tenth grade (no, I was not "just holding them for a friend"), about the time I snuck out in the middle of the night to meet my high school girlfriend, and . . . the fact that I secretly had a high school girlfriend that I had never told them about.

It was terrifying . . . but also liberating at the same time.

I always thought I was a pretty honest person, but I never realized how much of my relationship with my parents was based on a persona I had created, rather than who I actually am.

To my surprise, there was no major blowup. They sat listening with deep intensity and worried looks.

Sometimes there was laughter: "*Of course* I knew those cigarettes were yours! And, yes, I knew you were sneaking out; you really aren't nearly as sneaky as you thought you were."

Sometimes there was genuine shock: "You mean you almost died on your backpacking trip when you were telling us you were fine? Oh my god, I would have demanded you come back immediately!"

Throughout the conversations, which took place over weeks, and sometimes through random phone calls that started with "Oh yeah, one more thing I forgot I lied about . . . ," our relationship deepened. I kept thinking, "Sure they accepted the last thing, but there's no way they'd be okay if I told them *this*!," but they deserved a lot more credit than I first gave them.

In fact, the conversations often went both ways, as they started opening up and sharing their own childhood indiscretions. My mom laughingly shared the time she and my father were on a date that went so late, she almost missed the start of the live radio show she hosted. "We were still racing in your dad's old beat-up car to the station when the intro of the show came on the radio!"

Other times, the conversations led to deeper discussions about our relationship, or why I didn't feel comfortable revealing how alone I had felt during those years I struggled at school.

"I know you and dad cared, but it wasn't about you. I didn't know how to face you finding out that I wasn't as smart as you always said I was. I didn't know how you would react or if you would over-worry. It was just easier to keep it a secret."

Throughout the year, I had countless conversations with friends that were similar to the ones I had with my parents. They usually consisted of my sitting them down, then awkwardly confessing the truth about any past unspoken feelings and half-veiled opinions.

Most of the time, they were things like "I was worried you'd get mad at me" or "I didn't want you to feel worried for me," with a lot of "I didn't want to tell you how I really felt because I was afraid of hurting your feelings at the time, and more important, I didn't want you to hate me for saying it."

At the end of each conversation, the results were almost always the same. We'd laugh about how misguided our best attempts were or how much we wish we had just been honest the first time, as it could have saved us so many headaches all along.

And every time, I'd walk away feeling relieved, more at ease, and stand a little taller.

You don't really know how much hiding our truths cost us until we start undoing it. There were unspoken expectations that have gone un-met, breeding resentment. Long-held, unspoken, or even mistaken be-liefs were formed because we never had the guts to actually say what we needed to say, out loud.

Most of the time, my fears about hurting others by telling them how I really felt was entirely an excuse. Most people are adults who can han-dle the truth, and if anything, I was simply insulting them by thinking they couldn't. But more important, I thought I was so focused on pro-tecting other people's feelings that I never realized the feelings I was most keen on protecting were my own.

Clearing conversations are never easy and often felt to me like I was breaking some unspoken social rule by not shoving down my feelings.

In Dr. Blanton's words, when we stop lying, we start communicat-ing. But at some point, we learned the hidden belief that our honest opinions, experiences, and truths weren't acceptable or welcome. As such, the true version of ourselves isn't acceptable or welcome. So we make up a version that is, and spend tremendous energy hiding and holding back the "unacceptable" parts, to make ourselves more pal-atable.

But at what point did we learn that there was something unaccept-able about us?

And how did we learn to hide?

Whose Rules Are These Anyway?

Throughout these past few chapters, our main focus has been on how social and familial conditioning causes us to create patterns that seem to help us better fit in and succeed. But underneath all those patterns are our authentic selves, the versions most true to our core values and desires.

Finding and allowing that part of us to rise and be seen can feel uncomfortable, especially if we've never been given full permission to express that side of ourselves. This is often when the Chameleon and Charmer patterns emerge.

For me, I learned to hide my true self starting in childhood. The following unspoken rules of my childhood home were complex and confusing, but they were always present:

- There are actions that are helpful to get you better grades and be a better son, and everything else is a waste of time.
- Friends who do not help you earn higher grades are a waste of time.
- Games that do not help you earn higher grades are a waste of time.
- If you have time to relax, you have time to practice your instruments or math questions, or prepare for the next level of courses.
- No matter how well you do, there's always someone who does it better, so stop wasting your time.
- The rules can change at any moment. The bar can be raised at any moment. Be prepared for any moment. You're being watched and graded at any moment.

That last rule is particularly hard to master. For example, I might be yelled at today for sitting in front of the computer and not having gone out to exercise, therefore causing me to become fat or unhealthy. However, if I go for a workout tomorrow, I might discover it was an utter waste of time that could have gone toward my homework.

I could be observed, judged, and punished without notice, which means on bad days, minor infractions like being caught reading a non-educational book could result in being yelled at, yet result in praise the next day.

The rules and expectations were always changing, so I simply braced myself for impact at any given moment. Sometimes, these judgments happened in machine-gun bursts, unannounced and unexpected, like a drive-by of criticisms performed in high-speed staccato:

"What are you reading?"

"Is that for school?"

"Sit up straight."

"Stop shaking your leg; shaking makes you cheap."

"Do people like you?"

"You need more friends."

"People won't respect you."

"Shouldn't you be studying?"

"You need to prepare for your test."

"Your last score was abysmal."

"No, you can't spend time with your friends. If you do, you won't have time to study, and you won't get into a good university. You'll become a failure and won't be able to find a job, become homeless, die alone in a ditch, and everyone will laugh at us."

The best rappers have got nothing on my mom's ability to drop diss tracks.

When I talk to my white friends, they are sometimes surprised to discover it isn't just about academics. Rather, I was feeling that whenever I was in public, it could possibly open me up to an ever-flowing stream of shifting judgments about my appearance, my social performance, and my ability to read between the lines.

This was especially true for my politeness and social performance. For example, here's a pop quiz. If you are at a family friend's house, and it's another Asian family's home, and you are asked if you would like some tea or something else to drink, what do you do?

    a. Accept it graciously and thank the host as politely as you can.

    b. Follow your friend's lead and ask for water because that demonstrates how healthy you are.

    c. Say "Thank you" for the tea but that you don't prefer it. Ask instead for the juice that's sitting on the table.

    d. None of the above.

The room pauses with tense anticipation while they await my response.

The right answer from my parents' view was . . . none of the above. When I correctly turn down this offer, I will then receive the expected polite smile and nod from all adults present. I have successfully passed the basic test of the moment and therefore did not lose "face" for myself, my parents, and all eighteen generations of ancestors before them.

Visiting family friends' homes became an exercise of self-discipline for everyone. The host would then repeatedly insist that you accept the offer of tea, and only after a few polite refusals are you allowed to accept. Additionally, there's often a serving tray of various candies and snacks you don't touch, as if it's purely decorative and contains nothing inside.

Dinners with family friends can also become a stressful orchestration of pop quiz after pop quiz: *Did I remember to pour the tea? Did I pour for the right elder in the right order? If I grabbed the teapot before the other good son did, good job. When he grimaces, he knows he'll pay for that later. Ooh, an auntie just paid me a compliment. Careful. Did I turn down the compliment fast enough? Good, but did I then also reflectively comment on how much I admire her daughter's recent accomplishments? (Something about winning a debate competition?) I don't remember, but I know I'll be told later by my mom. News in the circle travels fast when it can be used against you.*

The way I sat, spoke, looked, spent money (or didn't), and ate too much (or too little) seemed to be all part of the quantum calculus of unspoken rules. This was an ever-changing set of enigma codes to decipher. Then I realized there were ways to hack the system. I became exceptionally capable at pretending to be productive. I learned to summon up the right persona for the right test-grader, seamlessly. I learned how to stay safe by being exactly who they wanted me to be, whether it was parents, teachers, peers, employers, or romantic partners.

The social conditioning around this became even more complicated when I started mixing in non-Asian environments. I learned to be more assertive and direct around white friends, mirroring their language and hobbies, while hiding the more Asian parts of myself so as to gel with them.

Masking to Belong

A 2023 PEW Research study revealed that 32 percent of Asian Americans born in the US say they have hidden a part of their Asian heritage from their non-Asian peers. When asked why, the two top reasons they gave were to avoid ridicule and a *desire to fit in*.

I was surprised to find out how high the percentage was, especially for second-generation Asian Americans (38 percent have hidden their culture) compared to foreign-born Asians (only 15 percent have hidden their culture). After all, being born in the US means English is their first language, they grew up in a Western environment, and they consumed mostly Western culture and media, so they *should* have no questions about their belonging.

Yet so many Asian people I talk to who display Chameleon and Charmer patterns have shared that they act this way because they are subtly treated as an outsider, whether in social circles, at work, or in dating markets. Social media remains flooded with racist videos that say things like "Koreans are all like this" or "This is why I won't date an

Asian," so of course there's a stronger desire to want to distance ourselves from anything that might tie us to our heritage, even if we secretly enjoy our heritage. It's not necessarily internal racism, sometimes
we just feel like we're being pressured to put away part of ourselves in
order to be accepted as "normal."

For many children of immigrants, hiding our cultural identity—the
food we packed for lunch, the music we grew up loving, the language
we spoke at home—is only a part of the expectation to assimilate and
fit in. A friend of mine who grew up in the suburbs of Texas described
this process of "whitewashing yourself" as trying to wash away any last
part of himself that could give away his "foreigner" status, despite having been born and raised in the US. He went as far as wanting to change
his last name to a more Western-sounding one.

I have also had Asian friends who were adopted by white parents
who talked about the struggle between their perceived selves and their
authentic selves. They were raised as white as they come, without any
connection to the culture of their genetic heritage, yet they are *still*
treated as foreigners by people who make assumptions about their skin
color. So they experience an identity crisis trying to merge the two.

Sometimes the Chameleon pattern starts early. In school, we might
lean deeper into a local accent when spending time with friends, or
even research popular musicians to follow, based on what other children like rather than following our own tastes. This is already a normal
part of being a teenager, as we *all* want to fit in and belong, but this is
far more pronounced for Asians because there's something no amount
of makeup or clothes or shoes or Lunchables can hide: our skin color.

For many of us who live in environments where Asians are the minority, we are seen as perpetual foreigners. Because we look Asian, we
are often automatically seen as outsiders, either as recent immigrants
or as visitors. People make assumptions about our language, culture,
and in some scary situations, our loyalty to the nation in which we re-
side. In order to prove our belonging, we become social chameleons,

capable of shaping ourselves to different contexts quickly so as to better fit in.

This might mean we quickly figured out how to be the attentive but not overly outspoken student in class, but when we're with our friends, we suddenly find ourselves channeling our inner socialite. The issue with the Chameleon role, the desire to fit in, can also mean we lose our true voice in the process. Our ability to shape-shift and fit in *everywhere* means we don't always allow ourselves to be who we really are *anywhere*.

At its healthiest, being a Chameleon is a powerful skill that helps us pursue our goals, but only when we know there's an appropriate context, such as at work in a meeting with an important client.

However, when it becomes an adaptive pattern, especially if it's from a deep desire to belong at the cost of our own well-being, it can become a bit toxic. Chameleons may think adjusting themselves can become a form of caretaking—"I can be whoever you want me to be, just tell me and I'll be that for you." They may feel this is a way to earn love and belonging, but it comes at a great cost to their authentic desires and identities.

People don't *respect* someone who doesn't value their true self. If you don't, why should anyone else?

When I see Chameleons at their unhealthiest, they tend to compartmentalize their entire lives based on who they need to be in a range of contexts. They have carefully segregated friend groups, and they generally struggle to bring all their friend groups together with their family groups because they need to maintain an image to continue fitting in with either. They feel fearful showing who they truly are or showing what they really feel. And sometimes, they aren't sure if there *is* such a thing as who they really are anymore. They feel like photocopies of who they're supposed to be.

It never occurred to me that this strange social phenomenon was actually revealing a much deeper wound. I thought code-switching was a social necessity, but at the same time, I worried that being myself all the time would be rude and unacceptable.

This didn't appear to me as a problem until I realized how isolated I *actually* felt. I could fit into everyone else's spaces, but I allowed no one to fit into mine. This led me to codependent relationships and an endless number of acquaintances, yet none felt like "home"—especially among my white friends. If I stood up for who I am and for my values, that meant I would have to accept being disliked by some people. And that, to many people in collectivist cultures growing up in the West, can feel like social death.

The Chameleon and the Charmer patterns are two sides of the same coin. On one side, the Charmer tries to be what they think people *want them* to be: funny, positive, and charismatic at all times, putting on a social performance for acceptance. On the other side, the Chameleon does the same thing but doesn't seek to be in the spotlight, and instead will adapt to any context they're in to be less noticeable.

And after a while, a hidden but subtle lesson started to set in: *In the public sphere, I'm not supposed to be myself but a performance of myself.* So instead of working on myself, I felt like I needed to only work on the appearance—after all, that's what is really being graded, isn't it?

Chameleons and Charmers

For Chameleons and Charmers, who are used to shape-shifting to become whoever others expect them to be, the biggest thing they often sacrifice are the *strengths and advantages of their authentic selves.* They tend to *think* that who they are deep within can't be accepted, so they put on additional roles to fit in.

But in reality, all we need to do is find the alignment between who we truly are and what others need from us, without abandoning our true selves.

For example, Liam found me after he was turned down for a VP promotion at a med-tech company in the Bay Area. We met on Zoom for the first time and, almost immediately, I was charmed by his easy smile. He used to be a therapist and a social worker, which explained why he was so easy to talk to. I could have taken a nap to his soothing tone of voice.

I generally like most people, but with him, I was instantly won over. There was an effortless charm and familiarity to his demeanor that made me feel like I was catching up with an old friend. He laughed at all my jokes, including the bad ones.

"There's no such thing as bad jokes," he said, "only people with mediocre taste."

Damn, I love this guy.

We started diving into his situation. This was the second time he had been up for a major leadership position, but his supervisor said the hiring team felt he lacked a certain "executive gravitas" when he spoke, and how he wasn't confident enough to be a leader.

"I was so confused when I saw that on the report. Why do people keep saying I'm not confident? I think I'm extremely confident. I just don't brag about myself."

He continued to say he didn't *feel* like he was being sidelined due to his ethnicity since it was his supervisor who had suggested he look into coaching. He felt there was something I talked about that resonated with him.

"You mentioned before that I have a tendency to be a bit of a Chameleon and Charmer. I didn't fully grasp it at the time, but the more I thought about it, the more I realized it was true."

"Of course," I said. "What are Chameleons known for?"

He thought about it: "They're good at blending into their surroundings to become invisible."

"Precisely," I said. "You've become so good at blending in with those around you that you're no longer noticeable." I noted this down to discuss later as he continued listing other issues he saw within himself:

- He often tries to make everyone happy, and struggles to take a side as he "can see every side" and wants to avoid hurting people's feelings.
- He feels like he's trying to be what everyone else needs him to be, but he doesn't feel that people really understand who he is.
- He is highly sociable but doesn't really feel he has a tight group of friends who are truly *his*.

He said he's tried everything: He set achievable goals with his teams and keeps them accountable. He reads leadership books, practices active listening. He described how he was liked by all his employees, but the feedback was that though he was deeply caring and attentive, he was not seen as "impactful."

He struggled with the "impactful" part. "I don't understand what this even means. My numbers are great; how can they say that I'm not being inspirational or impactful? My friend says some people are just more 'alpha' than others. Maybe that's just who I am."

"Maybe it's who you are," I said, "but maybe some of these are just learned behaviors. Let's explore who you really are first."

After chatting a few more times, we realized the thing blocking his promotion was that his boss wanted him to be tougher and have more "gravitas," and I wanted to dive deeper into that: "When your boss said that he wanted more gravitas, did you ask for any clarification?"

He said, "No, I didn't. I assumed he wanted me to be more dominating. We just concluded the conversation and said we'd follow up."

"Right," I said. "Ignore the 'executive gravitas' statement from the boss for a moment. The question is not what he wanted to see but what is the request *beneath* the request?"

I used an analogy: "I have a friend, and for a long time she said she only dated tall guys. Then one day, she started dating a guy she was super excited about—they hit it off and got along, they shared interests, he was everything she ever wanted—except he was more than half a foot shorter than her. When she was asked about her 'only tall guys' rule, you know what her response was?"

Liam shook his head.

I said, "She said she realized she didn't actually care about height. She just wanted to feel safe, and she thought the height was what made her feel that. But her new boyfriend made her feel safe because he was attentive and confident, so she realized it was never about the height. Her value was *safety*, and height was the only way she thought she could get that.

"The leadership gravitas your boss is referring to can come from this big 'alpha' energy of dominance, but really what he wants is for you to have a sense of self-assurance and certainty, because what we respect is not someone who is loud or dominating. What we respect is someone who stands their ground."

I suggested, "Next time you chat with him, ask him for more details. Let him know that he can be direct in what he thinks you lack, and ask him questions like: 'What are the most important traits you're looking for in this position,' and if he says 'Someone with executive gravitas,' ask him 'What does that look like in action, and what's the outcome you'd like to see?' Ask for clear examples, and write down the list of things he responds with."

At our next meeting, Liam came back with a list of notes he got from his chat with his boss:

- Make tough decisions.
- Take a hard stance when necessary.
- Be highly independent and keep people on task.
- Handle negotiations with outside providers.
- Handle demands from higher-ups.
- Communicate decisively and directly with the team.

Liam then added, "He also said he needs someone who can hold their own. Not only would I need to handle it without him, but he might also need me to have his back as well."

"Right. So it's not necessarily that he's looking for someone who is domineering at all, which is tough for you because the traits you most hate in people is when they are being aggressive or controlling. But what he's really looking for is someone who is aligned with him to be firmly decisive and to have tough conversations. Are you able to do this, without changing who you are or straying from your values?"

Liam said, "Yes, of course. I'm nice, but when things are down to the wire, I always make necessary decisions and I have no problems drawing firm boundaries with people."

I asked him to list some examples, and after a bit of thinking and looking through notes, he came back with a dozen or so situations. Times when he's had to make tough calls for budget cuts with his teams, times when he negotiated for an incredible deal with a vendor, times when he's more or less led projects to success. It was clear that even though he was soft-spoken, he was still a hardass when push came to shove.

"Great. Let's see what's on the other side of the coin. You've said before, he sees your communication style as being too gentle. But if your gentleness is actually a strength and not a weakness when it comes to having tough conversations, how would you explain that?"

"I'd say it's actually far more effective to have someone who is able to have tough conversations but can do so compassionately. If I have to deliver bad news, I can do so while still making sure people don't feel alienated or hurt."

"That's good. So it's just a matter of communicating this with him. Let's start with a phrase I love, called '*If I could, would you . . .* ?' Basically, it allows us to portray a hypothetical to see if it's a good fit with the person. In this case, it would be to chat with your supervisor, and tell him: 'I notice the things you described that you want in your vision for this role—someone who can handle tough decisions and conversations, handle negotiations from tough providers, and have your back in dealing with the higher-ups—*if I could show you I can do this, would you recommend me for the next promotion?*' Then if he says yes, give him the evidence you've brought."

We prepared a bunch of scenarios of what he would say to his boss's likely questions. Since his boss's biggest concern was whether Liam would have his back, I advised Liam to reassure his boss that Liam wouldn't back down if he needed to stand firm.

A few weeks later, Liam said he got the meeting and shared what we talked about. He said the boss asked him a few questions and gave a few example scenarios, all of which he had felt he could easily answer. His boss said he'll need to chat with a few people and left it there.

Less than four months later, the news came down: Liam would get his promotion. And he was *great* at the new management role. Not only was he able to support his boss, but his team saw the lowest turnover rate in years, because they felt cared for and supported rather than *dominated*.

There are ways to communicate our assertiveness, but the most important thing to know is that there are *multiple* ways to be seen as a leader. Remember, our leadership goals do not require that we "act more white." Instead, we can demonstrate how "acting more like *you*" can get the same outcome.

But there's another layer of this that isn't about the pressures of assimilation. There is a cultural element as well: how we present ourselves to others can be seen as a reflection of our family's social strength, or "face."

Saving Face

In Asian cultures, there is a distinct social pressure and expectation around the "public self" and the "private self," which is much more heavily pronounced in Eastern societies than in Western ones.

The Japanese word *honne*, for example, refers to a person's true feelings and desires, whereas *tatemae* refers to a person's behaviors and opinions when on display. Tatemae, or one's outer facade, must be guided by the social expectations of one's status and position. Failure to do so may create shame, not just for the individual but for the entire group, which is to be avoided at all costs.

The concept of a private and public self can be found in most collectivist cultures. The Chinese call it mianzi. Koreans call it chemyeon. In South India, you might hear it as maanathai kaapaatrum in Tamil. Similar language is also found in many other Asian languages.

Yet, there's really not an English word that truly sums up the full extent of this concept. *Prestige, honor,* or *status* seem limited in their scope. There is no directly translated meaning for "saving face" or "giving face" because while *persona, status,* and *dignity* do overlap in some senses in Western cultures, it's not quite the same thing.

"Face" is not simply about our personal reputation or vanity; it's also about how the group will be perceived. The group could be our family, our community, or even our entire ethnicity.

The loss of face not only brings shame to ourselves or our families, it can bring shame to one's ancestors. In some extreme cases in classical stories, heroes will fight others or even take their own lives to save face.

This is pretty commonly seen in Asian storytelling. For example, there is a common trope in Asian dramas of a main character who struggles with carrying out the social obligation of marrying someone who is suitable for their social status versus being with the person they are genuinely in love with. In these shows, it's not uncommon for the character to "confess" their secret desires to a parent, only to be scolded for not doing their duty.

I've also found this to be a common trope in anime, where a character talks about their internal struggles while maintaining a strong, stoic appearance. Then at the very last moment, they turn around to reveal a single tear falling down their cheeks, hiding their true sadness behind a smile.

Don't get me wrong, it makes for good TV, but it's not great for real people to live the experience. For one thing, we're expected to always keep up a polished, unemotional appearance that is appropriate to our social position. Most of the time, this means putting on a polite smile or just a stoic face of acceptance.

People in many Asian cultures are socialized to believe that your "inner world"—your sadness, your struggles, and your anger—is *messy* and *a burden to share*, even with your family or your community. Therefore your feelings should be hidden.

As a result, I often notice when I meet Charmers at networking events, there's an added polish to the way they appear. When they speak, they pause before each sentence to consider each word, gently sending out enunciated responses. Their smiles are practiced, their questions are nuanced, and they seem to present themselves with an elegant, sophisticated grace.

At first glance, no one would suspect the Charmer is hiding who they are. If anything, it seems as if Charmers *thrive* in the spotlight. They are the life of the party, the ultimate performer, and a master at keeping people dazzled with quick wit and easygoing jokes. They're naturally charismatic and can seem to charm just about anyone they come across.

Where the Chameleon's natural place is to try to blend into the crowd, the Charmer will happily grab the center of attention. They're good at being likable. They can "turn on" their charisma at will and are great hosts. They jump to plan events or the next group adventure, and they never seem to have bad days.

Until you get them alone.

Similar to the cultural reasons for being a Chameleon, a Charmer learned from cultural patterns to keep up "face" in order to protect or promote their family. They also follow the cultural expectation to hide their sadness or weaknesses. In collectivist cultures, where you're supposed to be an extension of your community and not simply yourself, the pressure is extra hard to not be too *real*, especially when confronting tough topics.

This social pressure can show up in family patterns as well. Families may enforce the need to appear polished and happy to be "good." Parents can chastise children for bringing others in the family down, when we're "bad" for being disruptive or for being "too much." When parents invalidate a child's feelings of unhappiness or anger and tell them to get over it or stop making a fuss, they can lead children to feel that their true feelings are not welcome. Some children can take these criticisms as a parent's threats of rejection.

Charmers often show up in sibling dynamics, especially if a brother or sister is an Achiever child. Charmers may not have been the golden child, but they learned to develop an identity in the process of being the person to lift up the family's spirits whenever the Achiever has a meltdown. They realized that by putting on a show, everyone seems to want them around.

Now, being charismatic and charming can be powerful skills. These are skills that individuals can be encouraged to cultivate in a healthy and balanced way, to strengthen, and not detract from, our authentic selves. After all, 85 percent of career success has been attributed to interpersonal skills like communication, and only 15 percent to technical ability. Why *wouldn't* you want to be charismatic?

But Charmers can also approach these same skills in an unhealthy, self-denying pattern. These Charmers struggle to be taken seriously. They also struggle with trust, both in trusting others to accept their darker and messier sides, and in struggling to build trust from others, who feel the connection is superficial. Either way, for some, being a Charmer is a form of self-abandonment, and the belief that your real self, in all its imperfections, isn't worthy of being seen or accepted.

There are glimpses of the Charmer's realities we don't see on the surface. Maybe it's the minute they get home, maybe it's when they're alone, or maybe it's when they sneak off to the bathroom at the party to have a moment to themselves. That's when the smile is dropped and the real self appears.

Charmers may have found a lot of appeal in presenting better than their peers during their social performances. Maybe they were praised for how positive or easygoing they were, and over time, the expectations started to form that that's who they *needed* to be to be accepted.

And just like the Chameleons, Charmers may be overlooked for true strengths as well.

Since the core pitfall for both Chameleons and Charmers is self-abandonment, the solution is to clarify who you are, and what you like and don't like. Often, I get questions like "What should I do with my career?" or "What's my purpose in life?" My answer often is: "It depends. Who are you now, and who do you want to be?"

This question can seem as insurmountable as climbing Everest without a sherpa, but it's actually quite simple: we start with our core values, and we are steadfast in pursuing what makes us feel happy and fulfilled. And that means starting with the *shape* of who you are.

Journal: The Shape of You

A couple of years back, I was leading a workshop on how to express ourselves more powerfully and confidently in relationships and in everyday life.

Immediately, a hand shot up with a question: "Okay, but how do I express myself from a position of power? Like, I can't just say 'Hey, my name is Kevin and I'm freaking awesome.'" The crowd laughed, as did I.

"Yes, you're absolutely right, because your identity of 'Kevin' has no meaning to people other than your parents picked a name from a book years ago. We're still forming the shape of you."

I walked over to the whiteboard and put a big question mark in the center, surrounded by several dotted lines. "Whenever we meet someone, that person is a general, fuzzy idea to us until we get to know their shape. I'm not talking about the physical shape, but rather the shape of this person's identities. So for example, imagine if I told you: 'I love Taylor Swift but can't stand contemporary jazz. I love bubble tea but can't stand overly sweet desserts. I love comedic movies and hate never-ending dramas.' You now have a clearer shape of who I am as a jazz-hating, boba-loving, comedy-watching Swiftie."

As I describe each of these things, I draw multiple small circles to represent each of these identifiers. Then I draw an outline around the whole image, forming a shape on the outside.

"Our preferences help clarify our identity for others, and when we stand by them, we start to form a shape for others to know. This helps them understand where they fit in with you, and what to connect with you on. Maybe we both love scuba diving. Maybe we both hate people who constantly obsess about their cars. Either is fine, but the more we stand firm on these things, rather than flip-flopping on things we love and hate depending on who we're with, the more trust and reliability we build, and the more clear the outline becomes."

The important thing to note is this isn't about agreement. Most of us know someone who doesn't share our passions but who we still deeply respect because they're committed to themselves. We know their shape, and thus we know we can trust it. What we distrust are those who are shapeless, who will take any shape to fit in. Because we don't know who they really are.

Imagine if this wasn't about preferences but values. Instead of hating contemporary jazz, you hate people who mistreat animals. That's a value you hold so strongly to, you'll fight for it every time. Or maybe what you value is precision and accuracy, so when you're at work and your teammate wants you to get something done more sloppily to be finished quicker, you might tell them, "No, this is our project and I won't

sacrifice quality when it comes to our work." This is how we build our shape. As they say, if you don't stand for something, you'll fall for anything.

People who have the Chameleon or Charmer patterns are often too easygoing and remain too reserved about their likes and dislikes. They are worried that their true preferences might accidentally offend someone or push someone away. Or they're so used to being this amorphous blob they genuinely think they like everything. But there's a big difference between actually *liking* something and *putting up* with something. The clearer they can identify what those are, the more *real* relationships they can build.

Here's an exercise to identify your values. Take a piece of paper and divide it into two columns. Then write all the things you value on the left-hand side. These might include honesty, family, creativity, activism, learning, community, etc. Feel free to use the supplied list of values included next for ideas.

Then, write down all the things you stand against in the right column. These might include materialism, strict discipline, disrespect for elders, or selfishness. What's interesting about this exercise is that often, we'll see that one person's value is another's countervalue. Materialism could be seen as greed, or as ambition. Persistence could be seen as stubbornness, or determination.

Then, take thirty seconds to assign a 1–10 value next to each of these, based on how strongly you feel about each.

Things I Value	Things I'm Against
• Resilience (6)	• Selfishness (6)
• Honesty (10)	• Inflexibility (7)
• Growth and personal improvement (8)	• Dishonesty (9)
	• Laziness (6)

Things I Value	Things I'm Against
• Community and family (10)	• Flakiness (9)
• Excellence (8)	• Mediocrity (8)
• Mental wellness (9)	• Injustice (10)
• Spirituality (5)	• Abuse (10)
• Health and fitness (8)	
• Kindness (10)	

Once you're done, take a moment and write down where in your life you are pursuing the things you value. Perhaps you notice your work is important to you because it's where you get to master what you do. But you might also realize you don't make much room in your life for community and family, even though those things are deeply important to you.

You can do the same for the things you're against—where in your life are you seeing these things? Do you notice you have friends who are unreliable and who often cancel on you at the last minute? Do you feel like there is a part of your job that seems unfair or unjust? What can you do to reduce your contact with those people and those aspects of your work?

The more we are living in accordance with our values, the more confident and certain we become. The more we are misaligned, the more fatigued, doubtful, lost, and stuck we'll likely feel. When we envision our ideal selves, we are imagining embodying all of our highest values.

If you're feeling stuck trying to identify your values, here's another way to figure things out:

1. Write down the names of three people who you *most* admire. They can be fictional or real, from the past or the present, alive or dead. For example, Mulan or Batman are totally fine choices.

2. Next to each of these names, write down the one thing you admire most about them. This might be "protecting her family," or "fearlessness."

3. Then, write down the names of three people you *least* admire. Again, they can be fictional, real, past, present, alive, or dead. For example, "Dolores Umbridge from Harry Potter" or "The Evil Stepmother from *Cinderella*."

4. Next to each of the names, write down the one thing you admire the least about them. This might be "judgmental," or "selfish."

5. Take the list of the most important values and qualities you've found through this exercise and put it someplace you can easily spot in your home. Every week, come back to this list and ask yourself, "Did I do something this week where this showed up in my life?" for both your values and countervalues. The goal is to get ourselves in alignment as much as possible, and to reduce situations where we aren't.

What's interesting about this exercise is that it not only helps us see what our core values and countervalues are, but it illuminates elements that we see in ourselves. The things we most admire in others are often the things we most admire about ourselves, and the things we most judge about others are the things we judge about ourselves.

And if you want to use your values to step into your most *confident* self, you can try out the exercise below.

Using Your Value Prioritization to Make Decisions

Fixers, Chameleons, and Charmers find it difficult to make hard decisions if they feel they're letting others down. They feel they need to self-sacrifice and say yes to everything, because they feel obligated by perceived social or familial expectations.

But what if we're not sacrificing ourselves but something else instead?

Every yes we say to someone is a no we're saying to something else. You could be losing time you could have spent with your family, reconnecting with old friends, or spending time on your own, perhaps reading a book. We tend to say yes or make decisions that we don't self-prioritize, because we don't see what we are saying no to.

This is why *value prioritization* is so important.

Recall the values list you made earlier, where you had sorted out how important each one was. This allowed you to form an idea of which values are *more* important to you than others, depending on the situation you're in.

- Family (10)
- Love or partnership (10)
- Education (9)
- Health and fitness (9)
- Career (8)
- Service (8)
- Adventure (7)
- Personal growth (7)
- Spirituality (6)

Once you have this in mind, decisions become a lot clearer. Because when you say no, you're not just rejecting something, you're prioritizing something else that you deeply value, like time with your partner or getting back in shape.

If your boss sends an email asking if you can take on your coworker's project this weekend, your first reaction might be "Hmm, sure, I guess it's only a couple of hours." But if you check your values list, you might suddenly realize, "Wait, if I agree to this, I'd be saying no to spending that time with my family, or I'd have to push back that muay thai class I had been looking forward to taking, and they're both my priorities."

This should give you more clarity around what to do. You can still weigh the urgency or necessity of your decisions (not being on your boss's good side may hurt your family, after all), but if you become aware of what you are actually rejecting on a regular basis, that might help you realize it's time to do some realignment.

Setting Personal Policies with Your Value Prioritization List

When I had a waiting list of clients who wanted to work with me, I often heard: "My situation is really unique, can I just squeeze in for just a bit? How about on the weekends?" I'd have to explain each time a tailored reason why I wasn't available then.

But after a while, I realized, "I don't have to explain in such detail each time. It's just the policy." So after that, I told people, "I'm sorry, I can't make extra room right now; it's the policy." We all understand things like an airline's baggage policies or a store's return policies.

Policies are amazing. Policies allow you to set clear expectations for friends who are flaky, e.g., "I'll be the initiator for inviting friends to hang out, but if they cancel three times in a row, I'll stop trying for a while and let them initiate." They're not as strict as laws or rules, but they give us ways to set expectations.

I found that once I set a policy, people were almost always willing to respect it. Because my decision wasn't personal; my policy was universal.

I realized that I not only had an easier time with my work once those policies were in place; I also saw that the policies made room for me to rekindle my passion in my work.

See, when we talk about "self-trust," we're really talking about "self-confidence." Confidence is your trust in your ability to handle whatever comes your way. What we often don't realize is that our confidence is built on our ability to fulfill our commitments to ourselves.

If we set an ongoing commitment to ourselves, and we always live up to it, we gain confidence. If we have a habit of breaking our own word, we'll lose trust in ourselves and lose confidence. This could be as simple as a promise that we'll wake up early to go for a run, or as in-depth as a promise to reject a high-paying job if the company doesn't live up to our environmental ethics.

Whenever you're in a situation where people are more likely to ask for more than you're prepared to give, start asking: "How can I set up a personal policy here?"

Let's say you want to set some policies around meetings. Meetings can be important, but they often end up cluttering our schedules. Policies might look like:

- I don't take meetings between 9:00 a.m. and 1:00 p.m. because those are my focused hours.
- If you want to set a meeting with me, please email me beforehand so that I know what you want to discuss and the outcomes you want.
- I don't take impromptu meetings unless they're absolutely necessary or urgent.
- If you're late by over fifteen minutes, I'll consider our meeting canceled.

That last point I learned from a friend of mine. Back in the 1990s before smartphones were the norm, she refused to carry a cell phone when she was out. If she made plans with her friends and they were more than fifteen minutes late, she'd simply leave.

When I heard this, I was shocked. "What if they ran into traffic or genuinely had an emergency?"

She responded, "For some reason, after I set the policy, I hardly ever had anyone run into traffic issues or personal emergencies. People just showed up on time, every time." She added, "Punctuality is a measure of respect. If you had a meeting with your favorite celebrity tomorrow, would you risk running into traffic or would you show up early? People respect you more when you respect your own time."

This is a significant point that's worth repeating. We value people who value themselves, and that means anyone who holds the people around them to a higher standard of expectations.

We can also set personal policies with our families.

For example, setting a personal policy with your family might be "We don't make any major purchase decisions without first discussing it with each other." This not only gives you more time to think about your purchases and reduce the chances of impulse decisions you'll regret. This policy also makes it easier to resist pushy salespeople. (This one I learned from my mother, despite her never having had trouble with making the big purchase decisions on her own.)

Or you could set a policy of: "I will always make time for a friendly visit, but I don't provide free work to anyone, friends included." So when friends suddenly call you on the weekend because "Don't you build websites for a living? I just need a few quick things done . . . ," you can quickly reply with "Absolutely, here's my friends and family rate; it's the same regardless of whether you're my parents or my best friend. Just let me know how you'd like to move forward!"

I find that people who are not comfortable setting boundaries can find it easier to set policies. In her book *The Power of Saying No,* Vanessa Patrick, the associate dean of research in the Bauer College of Business at the University of Houston, describes policies as being distinct from boundaries. "Boundaries are like the barbed wire we put up to protect ourselves from outside forces invading our territory. Personal policies are different because what personal policies are, are these pretty red ropes . . . like ones you'd see in a Trader Joe's or a movie theater." She explains that because policies can be set up in advance, they are less reactive. And when policies are designed around our values, we can be truer to our selves.

Setting and communicating personal policies gives our word a sense of gravitas and empowerment, without putting up a big red sign that shouts NO!

Being Seen for Your Authentic Self

There's something ironic about the fact that presenting the best "face" can sometimes result in lowering our internal self-perception, but it's a fairly common phenomenon. After all, if the only times we receive praise or acknowledgment are when we present a more performative version of ourselves, then the *real* version of us underneath doesn't ever get seen or validated.

An exercise we've done in past workshops is the Love Seat. Usually, it happens at the end of a weekend retreat after everyone has gotten to know a lot more about one another, and we'll invite volunteers to step to a chair in the front of the room.

Merely sitting in front of an entire group of people can already be a daunting task (especially for Chameleons who are used to blending in). But we take it a step further and ask them to share whatever is on their mind with the prompt, "Something you don't know about me is . . ." And for the *really* brave, they can try, "Something I don't *want* you to know about me is . . ."

This can be whatever people feel inclined to share in the moment. For some, it can be vulnerable ("Something I don't want you to know about me is that I say I'm on a diet, but I keep a secret box of chocolates at my desk"), and others can be light and easy ("Something you don't know about me is I love hip-hop dancing, which I've never shared with anyone here!") There's no right or wrong when it comes to what to share.

These vulnerable moments are shared, and then the magic happens. After each person's turn, the attention shifts to the audience, who now get to share *how they view the person in the seat* in a three-minute outpouring of love and appreciation. Literally, the audience will call out things they love about the person, from how great they are with people to how capable they are, to even things like loving their style.

Receiving positive feedback, funnily enough, is always harder than receiving negative feedback. We tend to immediately dismiss praise, but we remember criticism. So the task we give to the volunteers in the Love Seat is: you have to *fully receive and accept the love.*

For some people, who have been starved of genuine praise their entire lives, this experience can be so overwhelming that they burst into tears of joy.

If you'd like, you can try this practice with your own close friends or family members. It doesn't have to be something as elaborate as the Love Seat described above. You can simply ask them if they'd want to give this a try. Take turns by first sharing something you may not have previously shared, starting with shallower things and moving into the more vulnerable. Then, the listener would get to share what they appreciate about the first person. Notice if you find yourself wanting to skip past or discount the positive comments, and hold yourself steady as you receive and accept them.

Exercise: The Rock Star Walk

Before we wrap up part 1 of this book, I have one more physical exercise for boosting our sense of confidence and sense of self, specifically for those who have a habit of self-minimizing or self-abandoning.

Sometimes, this minimization can be physical, and we can feel uncomfortable claiming the actual, physical space around us. Some people reflexively apologize when other people bump into them, shrink out of people's way when they walk, and some even feel they're inconveniencing others . . . just for standing where they are!

A simple way to get our system used to claiming space is through a practice called the Rock Star Walk. Picture the way your favorite performer or musician holds themselves when they walk on stage to a sea of adoring fans, and you'll get a sense of what I mean—it's a walk that conveys you own the ground you're treading on.

Don't worry, you won't seem arrogant or weird doing this. In fact, it's most likely that no one else would notice anything strange at all. The idea for this exercise is to convince your mind that you deserve to *claim* the space around you.

Pick a day when you have a couple of free hours. Head to a local area where there's plenty of people but not so busy or narrow that it's impossible for people to navigate around you.

Imagine you're situating yourself on an invisible train track where you can only walk forward, stop, or if necessary, sidestep to the left or right. The goal is to try to stay on the straight track as long as you can.

Then, begin walking through the crowd, holding your head just a bit higher than usual and working to feel comfortable taking up space. You'll probably feel silly at first, but that's okay! The important part is to keep going and get used to the feeling of being unapologetic about taking up space.

As people walk up to you, you might feel the desire to move away. Instead, slow down your pace and allow yourself to claim space. Stay on your straight track for as long as you possibly can. If you encounter someone who is in a wheelchair or who is a senior who may need the space, then obviously get out of their way. Same if you encounter someone who makes you feel unsafe.

As you walk, people may expect you to get out of the way. You can simply slow down and even stop entirely until *they* move. Notice if you feel any discomfort from this. Perhaps this is already how you normally walk, and you are already used to people pivoting out of your way, rather than vice versa. But if not, notice if you feel any anxiety or discomfort. Be curious as to why.

Most people are walking just like you are in this exercise. It wouldn't be any more inconvenient for them to step aside than it would be for you. Reminder: no one really notices anything strange here. Most people walk on autopilot, thinking about a million different things and simply moving to avoid others if they do not first move to avoid them.

After a while, you may notice your walk is becoming more affirming and assertive. You might even notice people will start preemptively giving you space. Some of my past clients have somewhat jokingly called this practice the Moses Walk, because they'll see crowds begin to part six to ten feet ahead of them like Moses parted the Red Sea.

Some of my past clients had truly unexpected experiences and were surprised by people's reactions. One of them recalled that he had stayed perfectly on rails and had seen more and more people parting ways for him, until a stunningly beautiful woman walked up. She seemed so used to people moving out of her way that she nearly collided with him. He literally stopped in the middle of the sidewalk until both of them were about a foot away. He described how she was so taken aback, she stopped and waited for a brief moment, before finally deciding to walk around him.

There might be an occasion when you could walk up to someone who, also like you, refuses to move. Keep slowing down, or even come to a full stop if you need to, until they walk around you. It's not necessarily comfortable, but it affirms your space in the world.

Remember: Your Confidence Can Look Different

Over the past few chapters, we've explored a number of ways in which we can step into our most confident, authentic selves. We've also examined the possible patterns and pitfalls from our familial and social conditioning that could hold us back.

As we talked about earlier, your idea of confidence and leadership can look different from the mainstream ideals of confidence and leadership. It doesn't need to be loud, direct, or domineering, nor does it need to put on a perpetual happy face or become overly adaptable. We contain multitudes, and we should be proud to own all the dimensions of our authentic selves as we work, live, create, innovate, lead, or even pursue relationships.

Perhaps throughout these chapters, you've found bits and pieces of yourselves in these stories. Maybe you've seen how you've been taught to keep your head down and endlessly overachieve and self-sacrifice. Maybe you've been taught that you're not enough, when you are *so much more than you know.* Or maybe you've seen how social pressures to assimilate have made you hide or people-please. Those patterns and conditioning, even self-sabotaging ones like minimizing or rejecting yourself, do not need to feel shameful. They once might have served a purpose in helping you stay safe, but maybe they're not needed anymore. Maybe you're ready to let them go.

The choice is always yours. But remember: your choices can also be an example to others. There are people in your community who look up to you—who need to see your example in choosing to break your patterns, courageously facing the discomfort full on, and accepting the truth of your perfectly imperfect self.

Remember the story of the Golden Buddha. Our authenticity, our values, and our true desires are what makes us great.

PART TWO

. . . . .

BIG ASIAN COMMUNICATION

Now that we've talked about how we can break through our internal ceilings and get to our true, empowered selves, let's move on to the next big part: how to speak, act, and be your most powerful and confident self. This part of the book is all about the practical tools and techniques of leadership communication, so that *other people* can see how amazing you are.

You may recall from the beginning of the book that I mention a study by psychologists that broke down the two metrics we measure everyone by: warmth and competence. When we meet someone who we view as being competent and cold, we might respect their skills but we won't trust their leadership. In the same way, someone who is viewed as warm but not competent might elicit friendliness at best, and pity at worst.

While Asian Americans are often stereotyped in the workplace as being competent and cold, and thus not strong leaders, I started to look at the Asian leaders who have succeeded in spite of those racial stereotypes, and how they overcame them. And when I considered the communication talents of Asian CEOs, entrepreneurs, creators, and *leaders* of their fields, I realized they all successfully managed their teams through two key skills.

First, they're *assertive*. They can confidently speak their minds, advocate for what they want, and unapologetically set clear expectations with their teams and people around them. They don't put up with people trying to step all over them.

Assertiveness is particularly important for Asian Americans, in part because kindness, prioritizing others, and humility are already prone to being misunderstood as easy to boss around. In fact, researchers have found that one key explanation for why the bamboo ceiling affects East Asians more than South Asians had to do with the fact that East Asians scored lower on assertiveness than their South Asian peers.

Second, they're *compassionate*. They demonstrate genuine care and concern for those around them. They're empathetic, and they bring people together in a shared vision for what they want to create, together. They are collaborative, not combative.

Compassionate assertiveness is a deceptively simple practice, but immensely powerful and magnetic. It garners trust and respect without sacrificing any part of who we are. Compassionate assertiveness is a communication tool. We use it whenever we give feedback, ask for our needs, set boundaries, give support to others, or even deal with a microaggression. This way, we are confident and direct without feeling guilt.

And most important, this approach works when we start from the unapologetic ownership of our best selves, including our culture, our layers of identity, and our true values.

In the next couple of chapters, we'll start by taking a closer look at how we might currently be communicating and accidentally *miscommunicating* on these two metrics. Then we'll focus on tangible strategies and techniques that improve our assertiveness and our compassionate communications.

Communicating Assertiveness

The Culture Communication Gap between East and West: High-Context Communication

When people in the West think about leadership communication, they tend to think of a Western ideal of leadership—someone who's extroverted, outspoken, and high on the dominant personality scale. This trope is usually what they think of when they say things like "executive presence" or "leadership potential." But the truth is, the ideal image of leadership can vary depending on what culture you're from.

Leadership is a language. I'm not talking about spoken languages like English or French, but a *cultural language* that covers the social nuances of communication.

An easy example is cultural body language. If you're in Japan, it is customary to see people politely bowing to one another in social settings. It's not uncommon to see two high-powered CEOs bow to each other before starting a business meeting. But if one of those CEOs was in New York doing a high-powered negotiation with a US firm, it would make a very different statement if they bowed to a Western CEO.

Asian cultures communicate differently from Western cultures. In particular, sociologists have categorized their different communication styles as "high-context communication" and "low-context communication."

In the book *The Culture Map* by INSEAD professor Erin Meyer, the author recounts a story with "Silent Bo," a Chinese journalist named Bo Chen who she had brought to a business meeting with one of the top executives at Peugeot Citroen.

Chen was brought on to be a Chinese cultural expert in the meeting, and was highly articulate and extroverted in the preparatory meetings with Meyer. She expected him to similarly overflow with ideas and insights in their joint presentation. However, once they entered into the actual meeting with Peugeot Citroen, Chen fell silent. When the French car executives discussed cultural issues, Meyer would look to Chen to jump in and add his input and examples, but to her dismay, Chen remained quiet and motionless. She continued leading the presentation alone for the three full hours without hearing anything from Chen, until finally near the end of the meeting, when she decided to take the risk of an awkward moment by calling on him directly, asking him if he had anything to share. Suddenly he came to life, smiling confidently and speaking powerfully as he delivered a stellar performance.

Later, when Meyer asked Chen why he didn't speak up earlier, he explained that since she was the more senior person in the room, he was waiting for her to call on him. He had thought, "While I am waiting, I should show I am a good listener by keeping both my voice and my body quiet. In China, we often feel Westerners speak up so much in meetings that they do this to show off, or they are poor listeners."

He went on, "Also, I have noticed that Chinese people leave a few more seconds of silence before jumping in than in the West. You westerners practically speak on top of each other in a meeting. I kept waiting for you to be quiet long enough for me to jump in, but my turn never came."

Chen explained, "We Chinese often feel Americans are not good listeners because they are always jumping in on top of one another to make their points. I would have liked to make one of my points if an appropriate length of pause had arisen. But you were always talking, so I just kept waiting patiently." He recalled, "My mother left it deeply engrained in me: You have two eyes, two ears, but only one mouth. You should use them accordingly."

It wasn't because Chen was shy or introverted; he was being polite. But had Meyer not eventually called on him, this miscommunication could have led Chen to be written off entirely. And there's likely countless others who have lost opportunities that they were more than qualified for, because they hadn't learned how to communicate their strengths in a different *cultural language*. This is not to say that one style is correct and the other needs to be fixed—both westerners and easterners could expand their understanding (and business and leadership opportunities) if both learned how vast the spectrum of effective workplace communication can be.

In the book, Meyer outlines a spectrum of low-context communication to high-context communication, and how it influences body language, verbal messages, nonverbal communication, relationships, and gestures.

Low-context cultures are much more direct in their communication and rely heavily on being explicit in their word choices. Low-context communicators tend to take what is said with the expectation that all important information is clearly stated "at face value."

High-context cultures, on the other hand, usually exhibit more nuanced verbal and nonverbal communication, relying more on reading the tone, facial expressions, environment, and situation to understand the *connotations* of what is said. Taken in context, someone will then "read between the lines."

Individualist countries, such as the US, Canada, Australia, Germany, and Nordic countries, are typically ranked as low-context communication cultures (the US and Canada, specifically, are ranked highest on the scale of low-context cultures), whereas collectivist countries like Japan, China, India, Singapore, and Iran are ranked as high-context communication cultures.

LOW CONTEXT   HIGH CONTEXT

(adapted from *The Culture Map*)

High-context cultures require reading coded social cues. For example, my Taiwanese family knew that when visiting a family friend's house, there were unspoken rules on how to be a good guest. When the host offered food, we were expected to turn down the first offer until the host repeatedly insists, at which point we can accept. You can imagine my confusion, then, when I went to a white friend's house for the first time, and I turned down a generously offered snack. My friend didn't continue to insist, and so I was forced to simply watch him scarf down all the snacks himself. Much disappointment and hunger was felt that day.

Cultural and social language, like any other language, are learned and practiced through observation. These could be things like how to read between the lines of what people say, how to read social cues, to stuff like how to flirt or ask someone out. (Back in high school, I'd imagine my parents would have said, "Stop thinking about dating. Get into a good university and a good career and you won't have to worry!"—oh boy, how wrong that would turn out to be).

The differences between Asian collectivist and Western individualistic social languages are so vast that studies have shown we even talk about *events* differently. For example, when asked to tell a story or explain an event, participants from East Asia were more inclined to explain events with context, spending more time explaining the background and relationships between people, whereas westerners tend to explain events that focus primarily, or entirely, on the individual.

We don't just explain things differently; we literally *see things differently*. In a study by Richard Nisbett at the University of Michigan, the psychologists presented identical images to white American and Asian American participants, then tracked their eye movements when looking at an identical image. What they found was that the Asian participants spent more time looking at the entire picture, including the background details, whereas American participants spent more time focusing on the central subject of the picture. When asked to describe the images, the Asian participants spent 60 percent more time than the white participants on describing the details in the background.

We don't simply have different perspectives; we functionally notice different things.

This also affects how we view ourselves. In yet another study, University of Chicago's Thomas Talhelm worked with scientists in China to test more than a thousand students across different global regions, asking people to draw a diagram demonstrating their relationship to their friends and associates. What they found was that those from individualistic societies tend to draw themselves as larger than their friends, whereas those from collectivist cultures tend to draw everyone the same size. In an added thought, Talhelm noted, "Americans tend to draw themselves very large."

Collectivist cultures also tend to avoid communicating in extremes, preferring to communicate in moderation. Psychologists and sociologists have studied the phenomenon of how different cultures respond to questions based on what's called the Likert scale. If you've ever completed a survey that asked you to answer based on choices like "Disagree, Somewhat Disagree, Neither, Somewhat Agree, Agree," you've used the Likert scale.

The social scientists would give groups of students of different ethnicities and backgrounds sample questions such as: "I am able to do things as well as most other people" or "People who accept their condition in life are happier than those who try to change things," and ask them to respond using the scale. What they were determining, however, was not just the answers to those questions, but *how* the respondents would answer.

What they found was that Black students and white students in the US were more likely to respond in the extremes, either straight "disagree" or "agree." In contrast, both recently immigrated Asian students and US-born Asian American students were more likely to respond with "somewhat disagree" or "somewhat agree." Being in collectivist cultures means that we are less likely to take on an extreme stance, perhaps so as to keep some room for understanding and including the opinions of others.

All of this is to say, every culture expresses themselves differently. A supervisor from a high-context culture might look over a report from an employee and say: "Your methodology was detailed and interesting, but perhaps you might consider a different path next time." For an employee from a low-context culture, this might be taken at face value, and they may walk away thinking, "Oh, she really liked what I did and called it interesting! I must have done a good job." But to an employee from a similar high-context culture, they might take this to mean "This was absolute garbage; go do it again correctly, now!"

In Meyer's book, she listed the differences between how negative feedback is given across different cultures, using this figure:

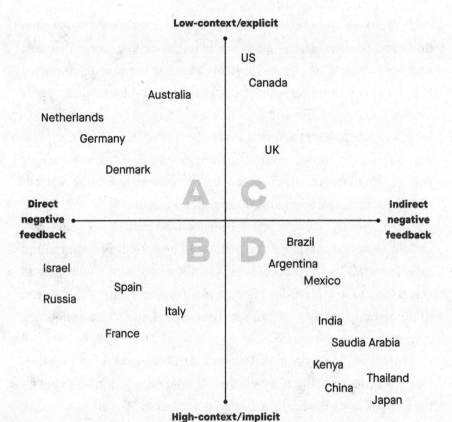

Direct negative feedback:	Negative feedback to a colleague is provided frankly, bluntly, honestly. Negative messages stand alone, not softened by positive ones. Absolute descriptors are often used (totally inappropriate, completely unprofessional) when criticizing. Criticism may be given to an individual in front of a group.
Indirect negative feedback:	Negative feedback to a colleague is provided softly, subtly, diplomatically. Positive messages are used to wrap negative ones. Qualifying descriptors are often used (sort of inappropriate, slightly unprofessional) when criticizing. Criticism is given only in private.

(Adapted from *The Culture Map*)

You can imagine how all this can have an impact on how we communicate, how we observe ourselves in relationship to our colleagues, and how we *lead*. You can also likely imagine how someone from a high-context culture, especially one used to carefully monitoring for tone and nonverbal communications in receiving indirect negative feedback, can feel shocked and brutalized the first time they receive blunt and direct negative feedback. For those of us who work with people from diverse backgrounds, a team leader who understands the nuances of different cultural communication styles is a gem.

For those who are leading or aspiring to be leaders, it's vital to figure out a communication strategy that can be both direct and clear to superiors as well as to subordinates, yet still demonstrates warmth and care. I have to stress: We don't need to change who we are. We just need to use more layered strategies for those who may not have the same cultural language as we do.

This is why I find compassionate assertiveness to be so effective. When we are asserting a position or an opinion, we don't need to be loud, harsh, or domineering to get the point across. We can let the point be powerful on its own merit, even if the message is self-promotional. And if we can do so from a compassionate context, we can be inclusive of the other people around us, demonstrating the warmth and empathy that is our strength.

With that, let's start with understanding *how to be more assertive*.

Aggressive, Assertive, Avoidant

Princeton University lists the four main types of communication styles as Aggressive, Assertive, Passive-Aggressive, and Passive. For convenience, I tend to group passive and passive-aggressive together into an "Avoidant" category, for I find people usually mix the two as they're both coming from a desire to avoid conflict or attack. In most situations,

Assertive communication is what you want. It's kind of like the Goldilocks of communication styles. If Aggressive is too strong, and Avoidant is too weak, then Assertive is just right to be heard, understood, and also respected.

Let's take a look at some features of the three communication styles:

	Aggressive	Assertive	Avoidant
Sounds like	Speaking over others, ignoring others' needs, prioritizing the self over others	Expressing their own experience rationally while still remaining open and understanding of others	Speaking to people-please, or using sarcasm, but not communicating their needs
Emotional tone	Defensive or hostile	Self-assured, calm, and respectful	Deferential, anxious, or resentful
Intention	Dominating, seeks only to be heard and obeyed	Seeks clarity and fair resolution to understand and to be understood	Seeks to avoid conflict or blame
Language	Uses accusatory "You" statements, like "You always do this!"	Speaks factually from observed experience, like "I noticed the last project was incomplete."	Uses mitigating language and hedging language like "I apologize for the interruption" or "I am probably wrong but . . ."

And here are some examples of how each communication type can sound in different scenarios:

Scenario	Aggressive	Assertive	Avoidant
In a group project	"You don't know what you're talking about. Just do what I say."	"I've done a similar project before. I have an idea that I think will work really well, but let me know your thoughts."	Doesn't voice an opinion but complains about the teammates later to others.
Someone cuts you off	"Why are you always interrupting? Be quiet until I'm done."	"Actually, I'm still speaking, and I'd like to finish my thought."	Stops talking and gets quietly angry, or ceases contributing.
Someone claiming credit for your ideas	"I can't believe you stole my ideas. What's wrong with you?"	"I noticed you presented the idea I shared with you as your own. Can we discuss this?"	Feels disgruntled and thinks, "I'll never tell anyone my ideas again!"
Delegating tasks	"Get this done by Monday."	"Could you take care of this by Monday? Let me know if there are any issues."	"If it's not too inconvenient and you have time, would you be interested in taking another look at this?"
Someone makes a racist or sexist joke	"I can't believe you just said that! You're such a racist/sexist!"	"Hey, I know that was a joke, but it felt really hurtful. Can I ask that you don't make jokes like that anymore?"	Laughs along even though feeling uncomfortable, does not want to "cause problems."

Scenario	Aggressive	Assertive	Avoidant
Someone cuts in line	"Hey! Get back! Who do you think you are?"	"Hey, we were next in line. Could you wait your turn?"	Broods quietly.
A friend cancels on your plans at last minute	"You're always so unreliable. You don't value our friendship at all!"	"Hey, I noticed you've canceled a few times recently. Everything okay?"	Doesn't express disappointment, but feels upset and stops initiating plans.
A neighbor's dog keeps damaging your garden	"Control your dog or I'll call the animal control authorities!"	"Your dog has been damaging my garden. Could you find a way to get them to stop?"	Doesn't confront the neighbor, but gets angry and starts to avoid them.

In all the above examples, only the assertive response both gets the point across and seeks to improve the relationship. While the aggressive speaker might seem more powerful or efficient and might get something done in the short term by being domineering and threatening, their style pushes others away and will likely result in lower morale, lower work satisfaction, and higher turnover. Meanwhile, the avoidant speaker isolates themselves because they don't actually communicate what they need, and they end up feeling resentful in the process. Both will end up destroying work environments and even personal relationships.

Being assertive is much more effective long-term, and this approach is really quite simple: speak your mind directly and transparently, and be clear that your words are intended to be constructive.

Aggressive communication can arguably be more closely associated with the Western stereotype of individualistic leadership, while assertive communication can be seen as more closely associated with an Asian collectivist style of leadership that emphasizes harmony, collaboration, and group cohesion.

Beyond that, here are some more tips and techniques to ramp up your assertiveness.

How to Stop Letting Others Talk Over You

One common issue people encounter, and I find this to be a common complaint among Asian women, is getting talked over. I even had a client who told me her coworker (an older white man) would ask her a question, and then cut her off *while she's answering his question*!

We teach people how to treat us based on what we accept and won't accept. And when we let people talk over us, we are teaching them we think it's okay for them to do this, even if we're just demurring out of politeness. I call these offenders power thieves. Those who repeatedly try to talk over you, subtly demean you, or invalidate your thoughts or opinions in public, because that's what they're trying to do—to steal power away from you.

But power can't be taken, it can only be given away by *you*. And if you make it clear you're not going to give it up, the other person will generally back down and look for someone else to take it from.

Let's say someone is trying to talk over you in a meeting. The quickest thing to do in those moments is to call it out. Just say, "Hey [person who is interrupting], I'm not done yet, I'll come back to you in a sec." I find it helps to actually say their name, because people instinctively pause when they hear their names, and it also calls the whole group's attention to their actions. I also add the "I'll come back to you" or "I'll let you know when I'm done" part because it asserts that you're the one to decide when you are done, not them.

In certain situations, if someone has a habit of interrupting, you can just continue talking, as if you don't hear them. If they're particularly egregious, repeatedly say over them "I'm still speaking," "I'm not done," or "if I may continue" in a calm, neutral tone until they get the point. When they finally stop and realize they can't walk over you, say, "As I was saying before the interruption . . ." and finish your thought. If you want to see this done like a pro, look up the video of Kamala Harris's interaction with Mike Pence cutting her off during the vice presidential debate in 2020.

This might be uncomfortable to do at first, but you will get used to it quickly. If you're on a Zoom call or an online meeting, you can even turn down the volume on your speakers, so you're not as bothered by the offender's voice.

And once you're done, turn back to the person who was interrupting you and ask, "Okay, [name], did you have something you wanted to say?" to let them know you are finished, but from an empowered place. You're the one giving them the floor, they are not taking it from you. You do not owe power thieves an apology or justification in these situations. They're the ones creating the problem, not you.

If this happens more than once, I also recommend actually addressing this with them in private. You can say something like "I'm sure you didn't mean to interrupt, but when you did, it made it seem like you didn't want to hear what I was saying. I would appreciate it if you stopped interrupting." If they are really persistent, you can be more direct by saying, "Hey, [name], this is the third time you've interrupted. Please stop," in a calm but *firm* tone. Then hold the silence in the room for a moment, before going back to what you were saying. If they get defensive and try to argue, you can repeat "Just stop," or hold up a finger until the point is clear. Then once they give up, say, "As I was saying before the interruption . . ." and continue.

If you find there are people who do this frequently with others, you can call it out. Let's say you see the interrupter cut off another coworker. Do the same thing as above and say, "Hey, [interrupter name], I believe [person who was interrupted] was still speaking when you jumped in, and I'd really like to hear what he/she/they have to say before we move on."

One thing you'll notice when you start paying attention to this, is the first thing power thieves do is almost always negative. They're never interrupting you because they agree. They interrupt to invalidate what you're saying and to disagree. And the more they do it, the more they just seem to believe *anything* you say should be discounted or refuted.

Power thieves don't only talk over others. One other thing they might do is invalidate or ignore the contributions of others. For example, if you see someone making a suggestion, only to have a power thief make the exact same suggestion a few moments later and claim credit, you should point this out by saying, "That's a great idea. In fact, that's what [name] was trying to suggest before." Or if they claim credit for your idea, you can say, "Yes, thanks, [name], for reiterating my point from earlier."

Stopping power thieves is something we can watch for, not only for ourselves but for everyone else, because they're rarely doing it to only one person. You do not need permission from the person who's being interrupted, because it's not about them. You're stopping behavior that devalues the quality of the entire meeting, which affects everyone, including you.

If someone has a tendency to test your boundaries by showing up a few minutes late each time, say, "Hey, [name], our meeting was supposed to start at 2:00 p.m. For the future, I want to make sure we can start on time as I'm sure we're all quite busy and don't want to waste our time." This statement is particularly effective because they're likely to give an excuse about how busy they are, and your statement reminds them how *everyone's* time is valuable. By not showing up on time, they're wasting other people's time.

Finally, there are people who might test your physical boundaries by hovering over you, standing too close, or even touching you. In each of these cases, speak up in the moment to teach them where those boundaries are: "Hey, [name], can you not hover over me while I'm working?" or "Could you give me a little space?" If you'd like, you can add, "It's making me feel a bit uncomfortable." Once again, find the right tone for you in that scenario.

Boundaries are like curtains. You can close them, but people will sometimes come and try to pull them open. It's as if they're testing you to see if you really care about those boundaries. So each time they do so, make sure to pull the curtain closed again by asserting yourself, more and more directly each time, as in the above examples.

Of course, not everyone who interrupts others is intentionally trying to take their power. Sometimes, people interrupt because they're just too excited or eager to share, and so they can't help themselves. You can choose to be more compassionate in seeing their innocence and soften your tone, but you still can assert your needs and expectations clearly. Remember, you're not speaking up only for yourself, you're speaking up for the integrity of the group.

How to Increase Assertiveness: 6 Degrees of Mitigating Communication

One way of increasing our assertive communication is by noticing when we are using *mitigating language*.

Mitigating language refers to deferential communication that shows up when we speak to someone who has more authority or power than us. People from high-context cultures, as mentioned in the introduction of this chapter, tend to see direct statements as being rude or unnecessarily direct, but this impacts how assertive we are seen by others.

In a study, sociologists Ute Fisher and Judith Orasanu identified 6 Degrees of Mitigating Language, going from the most assertive to the least:

1. **Command:** "You need to complete this project by May."
2. **Team Obligation:** "We should complete this project by May."
3. **Team Suggestion:** "Why don't we try to complete this project by May?"
4. **Query:** "Do you think that completing this project by May could work?"
5. **Preference:** "I'd love to see this project be completed by May."
6. **Hint:** "I wonder if our current deadlines may create a challenge?"

For those from a high-context communication culture, chances are pretty good they've tried to downgrade their communication styles to a question or a hint. Even if what they mean to say is "WHAT IS WRONG WITH YOU? THE OBVIOUS CHOICE IS TO FINISH THIS PROJECT BY MAY OR IT'S NEVER GOING TO WORK," they may end up holding their tongue out of politeness.

Having the ability to use mitigating language is important, especially if you are working with a supervisor who can't handle much direct feedback. But how often are you *defaulting* authority to the person you are talking to?

In Asian cultures, authority and hierarchy are imbued with great importance. Your teachers, your elders, and those who have seniority in your company all hold some sense of hierarchy in your unconscious mind. But the truth is, chances are often good you know better than they do, or you might have information they don't have.

For example, Jackie is the founder and CEO of a successful manufacturing company. She had put together a great team of experienced operators, with one problem—she kept getting interrupted in meetings by one of her employees, an older white man in his fifties who would often interject by critiquing her ideas.

When we chatted, she expressed frustration that she had several conversations with him about the issue, and his response was usually that he was simply trying to help the company avoid mistakes, which "was what she hired him for."

I asked her to pull up her emails and messages from their team conversations, and had her go through them looking for common mitigation phrases:

I suppose

I think

I guess

Perhaps (i.e., "Perhaps we should consider . . .")

Maybe (i.e., "Maybe we could take a look at this option . . .")

What do you feel

What do you think

It might be better

Kind of

I asked her if, in these situations, she was genuinely looking for their feedback, or if she was telling them what they should do. She said she wanted them to receive the information, but she didn't want to be rude.

"The problem with mitigating language is we're actually *miscommunicating*," I explained. "Politeness is important, but you've hired a highly skilled team who are capable of handling direct feedback, and chances are, they are looking for direct feedback from you as a boss. By softening your communication, you're confusing them about what they need to do, and you're robbing them of an easy win."

I gave her a few suggestions:

1. To deal with the person interrupting, you don't have to give way just because they want you to. You can either directly, in that moment, say, "Hold on, I'm not finished yet," or even continue talking without pausing to let him in.

2. When you're dealing with someone who is direct, be direct back. That's their communication style and *you can meet them where they're at.* You're allowed to hold up your hand and say, "Hey, this is the third time you've tried to speak over me and it's disruptive. If you have thoughts, please send them to me in an email after the meeting." You can still value their input, but also be clear how you would like to receive it.

3. When she's writing an email in the future, she should ask herself first: "Can I still be polite while remaining direct and without using many mitigating phrases?" Try to see if you can simply communicate what you want without sugarcoating it. After all, it's a professional environment, not a nursery; you don't need to coddle their egos.

A couple of weeks later, I caught up with Jackie and she excitedly shared how she not only wasn't getting interrupted anymore, but the employee had actually apologized and thanked her for her feedback.

If you're finding it really hard to break habits of using mitigating language, it's okay. There is such a thing as "soft assertiveness," when we can use mitigation strategies while still being assertive. It just requires us to add clarity at the end of our message. In other words, if you're using mitigating language early on, just make sure you conclude your message, email, or meeting with a quick check-in: "Okay, to sum up, this is what I need from you by this date. Is that something I can expect?" or if you started with "Perhaps another strategy might be worth considering," you can then end with "Could you send me a new report by this time next week?"

Adding an assertion of what you're looking for at the end of conversations allows us to get our point across without sacrificing our comfort levels, and is an effective way to establish our authority without feeling like we're being a jerk.

Mitigation Audit

Pull up your emails, messages, texts, or DMs with the people you work with or your peers. Specifically, look at communications where you make *requests or suggestions*.

For each of the messages, give it a grade from 1 to 6 in terms of assertive directness, using the 6 degrees of mitigation listed above. Then at the end, ask yourself the following questions:

- What level of mitigating language do I default to?
- With whom do I use more mitigating language versus direct language? Why?
- Am I being transparent and clear in what I'm asking for here?
- Am I leaving myself wiggle room, and if so, why?
- Would this message have been more effective if I rephrased it to be more direct? What could I have said instead?

The next time you write an email or message to this person, go through it using the 6 degrees list and see if you can be a bit more assertive in your communication before you send it. It might feel somewhat uncomfortable at first, but the practice is well worth it.

How to Stop Apologizing

Winnie, a thirty-year-old accountant who works from home, reminded me of one of those plastic Drinking Bird toys I had as a kid. You know, the ones that repeatedly bow their head into a bowl of water. She spoke

Mandarin at home with her family, and her favorite phrase was "Bu Hao Yi Si" ("I'm too embarrassed"), which roughly translates to something between "I'm sorry" and "Please excuse me." It's a common polite expression of shame or embarrassment for having caused someone an inconvenience, something you say when you bump into someone on the bus or when you're interrupting someone to ask a question.

Winnie's head seemed to be on a perpetual hinge, lightly bowing after every few statements, matched with a mindless apology for things that were mere inconveniences ("I'm so so sorry for being late"—when she was about thirty seconds late).

It got to a point where I pointed out she was expressing apologies for things that were just frankly nonsensical, such as apologizing for lending me a pen that wasn't writing smoothly enough or for how the sun was shining too brightly through her window during a Zoom call. When I noted that she was apologizing unnecessarily, she apologized. ("Have you ever noticed how often you apologize unnecessarily?"— "Yes, I'm so sorry about that.")

I told her a real apology should happen when we've caused an actual harmful inconvenience, and only for something we are responsible for. If you've harmed someone, intentionally or unintentionally, then yes, you should take responsibility, but if something happens that is out of your control, the apology doesn't make much sense.

I told her to modify her apologies into observations about inconveniences she can't control. For example, instead of "Sorry it's so dark in here," she could say, "Wow, the weather is so gloomy today."

Micro apologies aren't authentic, and the more we use them when they're not genuinely meant, the less meaningful they become. A *real* apology should have three elements:

1. Acknowledgment of how your behavior *actually harmed* someone else

2. Apologizing for the damage and for your role in causing it
3. Suggesting a course of action to repair that harm or to ensure it won't happen again

But if she can't actually see any harm, her use of the phrase was diminishing her social positioning without actually *improving* the other person's experience.

We started going through examples of micro apologies, which are habitual, often unconscious acts, such as:

Context	Micro Apology
Actions that are perfectly normal, like small requests	"Sorry, but can I ask you a question?"
Everyday interactions or experiences	"I'm sorry for the mess" (when the space is reasonably clean).
Social contexts	"I'm sorry you're stuck with me as a partner."
Asking for help	"I'm sorry to bother you, but could you help me with this . . ." "I'm sorry, I didn't understand what you meant . . ."
Unrealistic standards	"I'm sorry this wasn't perfect." "I'm sorry I'm a slow learner."
Things that you cannot control	"I'm sorry it's so cold out today!"
Having feelings	"I'm sorry I seem a bit quiet today." "Sorry for being sad, I didn't mean to bring everyone down."
Having opinions	"I'm sorry for disagreeing." "I apologize for this, but I think . . ."

Context	Micro Apology
Being successful	"I'm sorry I got the award; you deserved it more than I did."
Existing, being human	"Sorry I am eating so slowly." "Sorry for being in your way."

Unlike normal politeness, which might include apologizing for things that create inconvenience or harm, micro apologies are generally handed out as a mitigation device. It doesn't always have to be deeply felt, and it can be given out of instinctive politeness. But it still affects how we are viewed and our sense of self-diminishment.

What we may not realize is that even if we're just "being polite," we're still constantly communicating our views of self-worth in relationship to others. We usually apologize more "upward" toward those we view as having higher social status or authority, and less "horizontally," to people we view as being close to us, like close friends or family members, or even our own kids.

For the Invisible Ones who have a less certain sense of self-worth, however, they might see most people around them (including their friends and family) as being higher on the scale than they are. In some cultures from East, Southeast, and South Asia, women in particular are taught how their role is to be more deferential and to give more. In these situations, feelings of worth around taking up space, of receiving or asking for their needs, can bring up deeper discomfort, so apologies are instinctively given to mitigate pushback or blame.

I had Winnie record herself for her future client meetings and had her run the recording through transcription software. After that, I asked her to look up the number of times she said "sorry." In a single meeting, she had apologized nearly 100 times (!!!) unconsciously—or roughly once every two sentences she spoke, including for things she had nothing to do with, such as her client's own calculation errors. When she realized how often she was apologizing, she started to say sorry, but stopped herself and laughed.

Winnie is an extreme case, but she uses a common behavior among the Invisible Ones. It would have been far too much to get her to cut out the word *sorry* from her vocabulary, but I helped her work on rephrasing this habit.

A few weeks later, Winnie and I checked in and she was elated. She talked about how she felt much more comfortable saying thanks to people instead of apologizing, and she noticed how she felt less awkward in her interactions. She was able to recognize that when she was *about* to apologize, it usually wasn't about something she could have been responsible for. Instead, she could bring up the issue without taking responsibility. The result? She not only felt more comfortable around others, but more important, people started treating her better and with more respect.

This is an important point—being humble or being polite is not the same thing as being self-diminishing. You never have to apologize for *who you are*, unless your behavior is creating an actual negative impact in the lives of others.

If you noticed you have a habit of delivering micro apologies, here's an exercise you can try:

Step 1: Micro Apology Audit. Pay attention to how you speak to others and how often you might be using micro apologies in your speech. Notice each time you feel the desire, and ask if this is a genuine apology and if it's needed.

Step 2: Replacing Apology with Appreciation. Every time you want to apologize, see if you can turn it into a statement of appreciation instead. For example:

- Instead of saying "Sorry for being late" try "Thank you for your patience."

- Instead of saying "Sorry for changing plans" try "Thank you for accommodating."
- Instead of saying "Sorry for the question" try "Thank you for explaining."

Step 3: Turn preemptive apologies into direct questions or requests. For cases in which we're making a reasonable request, simply state what your needs are without adding an apology, or acknowledge the other person for their efforts. For example:

- Instead of saying "Sorry if I've misunderstood" try "I want to make sure I understood; could you kindly explain it in a bit more detail?"
- Instead of saying "Sorry, but I disagree" try "I hear what you're saying, but I'd still prefer if you could do this instead."
- Instead of saying "Sorry to call you at this time" try "Is this a good time to chat?"
- Instead of saying "Sorry, but this isn't what I ordered" try "This isn't what I ordered; could you let the kitchen know?"

If you feel uncomfortable during these instances, remind yourself that focusing on the positive, including acknowledging what others are doing right, is more helpful than making it about you doing something wrong. Be patient with yourself in this process and acknowledge your improvement along the way.

Don't lower yourself down, raise others up instead.

How to Promote Yourself

At this point, we've identified how being humble is not the same thing as being self-diminishing, and you can recognize your own worth and value without feeling guilty. So the question becomes: How do we communicate our worth without seeming narcissistic or arrogant?

Many of us are from a background that taught us it's one thing to be aware we're good at something, and another to talk about it in an act of self-promotion. Self-promotion can then feel icky. We might think of negative examples, like someone who is always bragging about the school they went to, or how much money they have.

Bragging happens when someone is claiming attention and praise in a way that is seen as taking more than they deserve. A firefighter reporting how the team saved five lives is not bragging, but your cousin who can't stop talking about her fancy new designer bag is.

There's nothing wrong with talking about the things we're proud of and want to celebrate. The only issue we ever have is if someone is using it to lord over others with the *intention of trying to be seen as better than others.*

If your intention isn't to shame others, sharing what you're good at isn't arrogant, boastful, or "too much"—it's exactly what you're supposed to be doing. Otherwise, how will people know how to come to you for help?

If we are to understand our *purpose* here is to do our best work, then keeping our talents a secret isn't helping anyone. Remember: our accomplishments often aren't able to speak for themselves, and they won't help us claim the credit we deserve if no one notices them.

So how do we get seen when we're in an interview, a performance review, or a meeting with our boss?

Don't brag. *Share.*

Often you'll have the ability to solve a problem for someone else, or you'll have a skill that can make an impact in your workplace or your own business. So the meeting is not focused on *you*, but rather the problem that you can solve.

Here's a simple framework you can try called Struggle-Story-Skill.

STEP 1: STRUGGLE

Think about the skills you want to showcase, and pick a couple you are most proud of. This skill might be your leadership, it might be your ability to create systems, it might be your technical skills, etc. But more important, ask yourself, "What struggles or problems do my skills solve?" and you can start by talking about those problems.

For example, let's say you are really good at helping businesses build websites that don't suck. You could say, "Many small businesses spend tens of thousands of dollars building fancy websites that look really good and are flashy, but they're terrible at converting sales."

Or say you're a teacher and you want to showcase your ability to get kids to stay interested in complex ideas. You could say, "You know how most high school students have a really hard time staying focused when you're talking about things like calculus, and almost immediately you see their eyes glaze over?"

STEP 2: STORY

Next, share your experience with solving the problem.

"I was working with a restaurant that had this beautiful website, but it took forever to load. I pointed out that since 90 percent of their visitors were on mobile, we should build a smaller version that loaded much quicker and allowed you to reserve a table. Within a couple of weeks, they saw a huge uptick in online bookings."

"I've been teaching for years, and I created my own gamification system for learning calculus, which broke down each lesson into puzzles the students had to solve for points. The students loved it and they have done better on the exams than other students in the district."

STEP 3: SKILLS

You've now showcased your experience and shared a story that demonstrates your value. So now, whatever you introduce as your key skills or strengths can be understood as part of that story, rather than just you showing off.

"At this point I've built over fifty websites like this, and they always outperform the competitors."

"I've won two teaching awards for this system, and I've worked with several teachers to develop their own for different subjects. Many of them have told me this is the best system they've ever tried in their classes."

. . .

This is, of course, just one method that would be right for a few different contexts. You might adjust the strategy based on where you are, but the principles are the same—share your skills, and share your stories, and that will help you give context for your accomplishments.

Helpful self-promotion can exist everywhere. Many people never talk about their work with their bosses until it's time for performance reviews. And I often ask them if they'll ever post their celebrations on their work-related social media such as LinkedIn. Take the Struggle-Story-Skill outline above and make it a goal to regularly post your learnings along the way. For example, you could post, "We recently overcame a huge obstacle in our delivery process; here's what we learned."

For those who already often use social media for promoting their own businesses, they might think, "Hmm, this sounds a lot like marketing." And that's because it is, but without the icky *sales* part at the end and without hiding the imperfections along the way. Unlike marketing, the goal here isn't to *only* share our perfect side, but to share the vulnerable lessons, mistakes, and doubts—sharing the scars of our journey and the celebrations of all the things we care about. Remember, it's important to share your knowledge because keeping it to yourself means the world is missing out on the unique essence *you* bring to the table.

How to Improve Body Language

There have been a lot of studies on how much nonverbal communication matters, with things like body language, eye contact, and facial expressions. Without going into the specific debates on exactly *how much* it matters (some studies claim that over 55 percent of our communication is nonverbal) the simple fact is *it matters a lot*. At the same time, I also find most people get a little too bogged down by it.

I've gone through countless popular books that advise people to "take up as much space as possible" (aka "man-spreading"), or to "steeple" their hands (think Mr. Burns from *The Simpsons*, touching all of his fingertips together to form a church-steeple shape with his hands), or to shake someone's hand like you're trying to rip their limbs from their joints to assert dominance, or whatever the new gurus are teaching these days.

In the short term, these techniques might help them feel a bit more confident, but I've never really seen any measurable, long-term results from most of this advice, because they're still *performative*. And when people are being performative, they are focused only on themselves. They can puff their chest up in hopes that people won't notice their insecurities. But their weaknesses are often painfully obvious in the process. This masking behavior is the very opposite of being truly confident. Confident people are directly honest about who we are and what we want.

I recall an attendee in one of my workshops who was clearly being performative. Perhaps he had watched too many YouTube videos on how to be more "alpha" or whatever, but there was always something that seemed *off* about him. His back was perpetually stiff as a board, and he held himself with a puffed chest, raised chin, and fingertips glued together in the aforementioned steeple position. When he moved his hands, he'd break out the same few robotic hand gestures, then snap back to steepling as though he was posing for a photo shoot for *Alpha Bros Magazine*.

The thing was . . . no one thought he seemed confident or powerful. We thought maybe he was in need of some physiotherapy. He later admitted that even though he was doing everything the "experts" told him to do, he couldn't understand why people always felt a little uncomfortable or creeped out around him.

I get a couple of people like this in every group, who are trying to learn all the "right" body language techniques. They end up looking like they're doing some kind of feverish interpretative dance when they're speaking on stage.

When we're trying to focus on the "right" body language techniques, our bodies and our communication become incongruent with who we are. People are intuitively very good at reading all the tiny, microscopic shifts that don't line up. The truth is: You can pretend all you want. You can even fake it "correctly" 99 percent of the time. But eventually, your true intentions will always eventually shine through. It's how we get a gut feeling about a sketchy salesperson or that guy at the bar whose smile feels just a bit *too* happy.

The "right" body language is about *alignment*. Our words, body language, and tonality will naturally align with our core intentions. But when someone has an ulterior motive, their focus is on themselves and how they're presenting, and we can sense it. Not only that, but the more focused they are on trying to maintain control of their body, the more they'll seem self-conscious.

In my workshops, I teach body language for things like public speaking, but never from a "Here's the right way to speak confidently." Instead, I see the body as an *extension* of our communication.

For example, in the workshops, I keep an eye out for "hiding" body language, such as using our hands to cover our face, our necks, or crossing our arms in an unconscious attempt to find safety or comfort. Instead of making someone feel bad, I ask, "What are you unconsciously trying to hide?" And we work on that.

How to Ask for More Money

We can feel comfortable 99 percent of the time, but I find that the one instance where we most often fall back into discomfort is when we are asking for something—for a raise, for someone to buy something from us, or for someone to come up to our proposed fee. If we already feel impostor syndrome or that we will never be enough, we can feel shame about asking for someone to value our work.

I've seen people confidently deliver the perfect speech on how good their work is and how it'll absolutely benefit the person they're talking to, but as soon as they get to the price, they'll unconsciously display small gestures of hiding. They might cover their necks or they might falter in their tonality, or their voice might get a tiny bit quieter. It's almost like their body wants to hide the information they're delivering.

Again, this is because we have a tendency to attach our self-worth to our workplace value. Instead of telling them how much the product is worth, we feel like we're telling them how much *we're* worth. And if we're supposed to be modest and humble, and definitely don't want to seem greedy, asking someone to value our work can feel cringey, as if we're opening ourselves to judgment.

One tip I like to suggest in these cases is to *deliver it like a phone number.*

The price of your services, no matter whether it's in a salary negotiation or you're a freelancer, is not actually about you. It's just part of the exchange of value, and should be listed alongside all the other information you're providing, like your phone number and website information. You just happen to be the delivery person.

When we stop thinking "my salary is a reflection of my self-worth," we can also let go of obsessing over how people respond to us.

Instead of trying to "fix" your body language, fix your focus. Instead of worrying about how you appear, focus on your connection with the other person. What if in every conversation, your focus is on understanding rather than being seen in a certain way?

For those of us who grew up being taught to keep our head down and not claim attention, any time we're speaking up, it can feel a little bit like we're on display and being judged. We'll hyperfocus on whether we're being liked in the moment rather than on whether we're communicating clearly. In high-context cultures we're supposed to be constantly reading between the lines. But the more we realize our salary isn't a measure of our worth, just an exchange of value, we can focus on how to be more effective, assertive, and true in our delivery.

EYE CONTACT

Maintaining eye contact during social interactions is very different between Asian cultures and Western cultures. In numerous cultural studies, sociologists have found that while maintaining direct eye contact has positive value in Western cultures such as in the US or Europe, it often does not for those from Asian cultural backgrounds. For example, in Japanese or Korean culture, children might be taught not to maintain eye contact with elders and those in authority as it can be considered disrespectful. In a cross-cultural study between Finnish participants and Japanese participants, they often found that Japanese participants see a face with a direct gaze to be "angrier, less approachable, and less pleasant" in comparison to their European counterparts.

Comparatively, British social psychologist Dr. Michael Argyle found westerners and Europeans tend to appreciate direct eye contact, and tend to hold direct eye contact an average of 61 percent of the time—41 percent while they're speaking, and 75 percent while they're listening. In the West, making eye contact is a way of demonstrating trust and building rapport. In Drs. Allan and Barbara Pease's book *The Definitive Book of Body Language*, they recommend holding eye contact for about 60–70 percent of the time in conversation.

As adults, most of us don't struggle deeply with eye contact. Chances are good you have no issues with naturally meeting and making eye contact, regardless of your background, but there are two instances where I find eye contact as a topic to be relevant, especially if our goal is to be seen for our assertiveness.

The first is the *avoidant or deferential gaze*, which happens when we make eye contact with someone and then instinctively look down or away. This naturally happens between two people of different power positions, such as a boss and employee. Often the person in a higher power position will hold eye contact longer (called the dominance gaze) while the person who's in the lower power position will avert their gaze more instinctively. It's a subtle cue and there's nothing wrong with it, but if we do this out of habit from childhood conditioning, it could miscommunicate how we feel about ourselves and others.

If you're struggling with holding eye contact, it's important to not jump to the "I SHALL STARE INTO THE SOULS OF EVERYONE I MEET" gaze like a maniac.

Here's a simple exercise you can try, suggested by *The Power of Eye Contact* author Michael Ellsberg:

1. First, find an environment where eye contact isn't seen as threatening. For example, if you're walking down the street in an unsafe or unfamiliar neighborhood, it's probably not the best place for it. If you're in a country where direct eye contact can be seen as rude, perhaps find a friend to practice with instead.

2. Soften your gaze by relaxing your eyes and facial muscles, like you're not trying to focus on any particular spot, but instead taking in a wide view of things.

3. While walking down the street, take notice when someone is walking toward you. When they are about four to five steps away, briefly look at their eyes for a quick moment, long enough to notice the color of their eyes.

4. If they make eye contact with you, hold it briefly, resisting the urge to immediately glance away. Instead, soften your gaze further like you're holding the position but looking past them, until they're no longer in the range of your gaze. To them, you're just looking past them at something in the distance.

5. Once you feel more comfortable with this, try it somewhere stationary, such as at work with coworkers or at a café with strangers. This happens naturally when we go about our lives anyway, The goal is never to make anyone uncomfortable, but just letting your eyes get used to holding the same general position without immediately darting away like you've been caught doing something wrong.

Maintaining eye contact in work situations is important. A study on eye contact during job interviews found that interviewers are more likely to consider an interviewee who maintained a high degree of eye contact to be more credible and trustworthy, and are more likely to hire them. When you're in a meeting or giving a presentation with a small group, you can start by making eye contact with every person around the table before you begin, holding each connection briefly, then mixing it up throughout the rest of the presentation.

How to Handle Difficult People: The AIR Model of Communication

Sometimes, we'll encounter difficult people. You know the ones—difficult, demanding, almost a bit narcissistic in how they refuse to listen to others?

For many of us who grew up learning that we aren't supposed to criticize those who are older than us or who have greater authority, it can be a daunting task to approach difficult people. You don't want to hurt their feelings by being overly aggressive, and the professional context doesn't call for the amount of profanity you're emotionally ready to unload.

In these cases, there's a specific communication model you can use called the AIR model, which stands for Action-Impact-Request.

The AIR model starts with calling out the **Actions** a person has taken that affect you:

"Hey, can we have a quick chat about something? During the meeting, you spoke over me several times while I was getting my points across."

Then move on to the **Impact** their actions had on you:

"It made it hard for me to get my point across and it felt like you didn't value what I was saying."

Finally, land the conversation with a **Request** for the future:

"In the future, would you mind waiting until I'm done before speaking?"

VARIATIONS

You could also add more to each of the sections to facilitate better understanding.

Vanessa Patrick, the associate dean of research at the University of Houston, wrote a great book titled *The Power of Saying No*. In it, she talks about the concept of an "empowered no."

We can empower our language by speaking from our own values and identities. We can do this by separating "I don't" from "I can't." Because when we say "I don't" as a personal rule or conviction, our statements are grounded in our personal values or priorities.

Say a coworker keeps calling you about work on the weekends. Instead of saying, "I can't take calls on the weekends," which almost always invites more questions or challenges, try saying, "Please note: I don't take work calls on weekends." This statement is more grounded in empowerment.

You can choose to elaborate, by saying, "Please note: I don't take work calls on weekends as it's the time I reserve for my family." You are being clear that this is a firm rule based on your principles and values.

My client Ria found this exercise particularly helpful. Ria was leading a team project that had just won their first award for excellence. It had taken many sleepless nights and she was proud of their accomplishment. Most of all, she was excited about her award being announced at the next department meeting, which was led by one of her colleagues. But as he was reading the announcement acknowledging everyone's contributions, she heard her colleague mention everyone on the team's names . . . except hers. *Even though she was the team leader!*

It didn't help that she felt her colleague may have done it on purpose, since she was the only woman on the team, and he had sidelined her before. She was furious, but she also felt she shouldn't bring it up in the meeting because she didn't want to seem confrontational.

On our Zoom call, she vented about what had happened and asked if she should do anything about it. She tried first to downplay it: "Maybe it's not a big deal; these awards are just titles anyway and don't actually affect compensation."

"Well, if it's a big enough deal that you feel mad about it, then it's certainly worth bringing up. After all, how are your managers supposed to see your leadership if they don't know about your accomplishments?"

"Sure, but I don't want to be seen as the person who makes so much noise like it's all about me. It was a team effort after all."

"Well, let's say it wasn't you. If he had named everyone except someone else on your team, would you want to say something?"

"Of course! I always speak up for my coworkers."

"Great, and aren't you a member of the team as well? Do you deserve less recognition than others, especially as the team leader?"

"Fine, but I don't want to seem bossy or demanding. I already feel like an outsider, being the only non-white person in the room, and sometimes as one of the only women in the department." This is a common fear—if our social position is already shaky, we think we should hide ourselves and not cause a commotion, and just "go with the flow."

"Well, if you're already feeling like you're on the outs, then you have nothing to lose. But remember, we are more likely to respect and accept those who know their worth and are willing to speak up for it."

She nodded, but still looked uncertain.

I asked, "What would you say are your department values?"

She paused and couldn't think of anything, so I jumped in: "Based on what you told me, I feel that the people in your department probably value hard work, meritocracy, and leadership, right?"

She agreed.

"So wouldn't setting the record straight be in line with those values? It seems this is demonstrating you being aligned with them in this area, no?"

"Sure, but I don't want to be seen as asking for special treatment or attention."

"But you're not. You're not asking for *extra*. In fact, you're asking for what's equally given—the same recognition as everyone else rightfully gets. And by definition, wouldn't that be demonstrating you're in alignment with them?"

She agreed, and the point seemed to land with her this time. "Okay, but how do I bring this up without making a scene?"

"Easy, just state what happened, ask for clarification, and then give him a choice of how he wants to proceed. This puts the onus on him to right the wrong. For example, something you can say to your forgetful colleague might be: 'Hey, during the last meeting, when you were naming all the contributors of the group, I noticed you didn't mention my name. Can I ask why you left me out?'"

Now, I told her, he might get defensive or even attempt to swipe away the question passive-aggressively. Maybe he'd say something like "Oh, I probably just forgot, don't be so sensitive. It's not a big deal. It's not about you, it's about the team."

I continued, "At this point, you can address the impact directly. Remember you don't have to rebut his defensiveness or even mention the sensitive comment; that's just argument bait. Focus on the actions."

I told her she could reply, "Well, it did mean I was the only one left out of the team, and I'd just like to make sure you're not giving incomplete or inaccurate information. Being accurate is important, don't you think?"

I advised that when it comes to people like this, sometimes what they need is to feel in control, so she should give him a choice of how she'd like him to proceed. She could say, "I'd like to see us set the record straight. Would you prefer to send a quick email to everyone to correct the record, or for me to point out what happened at the next meeting instead?" This way, he's choosing between two solutions that *she* set.

Later on, Ria came back to me with a celebration: "I did what you suggested and it worked! He actually was super apologetic about it and didn't get defensive at all, even though I was prepared if he did. He immediately sent out an email and even went to the managers to talk about how well I was doing. I'm so glad I asked!"

I celebrated with her and the two of us did a little on-Zoom dance session. When we were done, I pointed out: "Even if he hadn't, it still would have been worth bringing up, because it's not just about communicating to others that your work matters, it's also about communicating it to yourself too."

How to Deal with Casual Racism or Microaggressions

If you ever encounter someone who makes a casually racist joke, calmly ask: "I don't get it, can you explain the joke?"

Unfortunately, casual racism and microaggressions toward Asians are still relatively common and often aren't addressed due to "silent minority" stereotypes. More to the point, they tend to be common because they aren't called out often.

This is why most racism you might encounter these days hides in microaggressions, where people will still try to cover their actions by saying, "It's just a joke" and "Stop being so sensitive." When we encounter it, the instinct often is just to ignore and brush it off, but in doing so, we're also passively expressing *permission* for it to continue.

For those who express casual racism knowingly, it's an act of trying to hold power over you—and by doing something that might push your buttons, and pressuring you to accept it, they "win." At the same time, if they anticipate your anger, then they can say, "Stop being so sensitive," to put you on the defensive.

Over the years, I've heard all sorts of things being passed off as jokes—side comments or questions that the asker will claim are innocuous. People might feel it's fine to ask, "Why don't you have a name that's easier to pronounce?" or to say, "This is why I love Asians; you guys never make a big deal of things." Or to wonder aloud, "Do you eat fried dog?"—an actual quote, by the way, from a client's coworker.

And I get why you might want to shrug off their ignorance. You probably *do* have the capacity to laugh it off whenever someone makes a questionable statement or a joke, even if you're rolling your eyes internally. Too often we're told, "It's not a big deal" or "I meant it as a compliment!"

But what we need to remember is that whenever we let things slide, we're also implicitly giving permission to the offender to hurt someone else.

If you encounter casual racism, either aimed at you or toward someone else, it's essential that we speak out, immediately, calmly, and directly.

And we can do it without sounding accusatory.

Conflict around accusations are usually around *intention*. When we call out someone's behavior as being problematic, they usually get defensive because in their view, they aren't bad or racist people. So they're now deeply entrenched in defending who they are, rather than their actions. This makes any attempt at getting through to them impossible. It's like talking to a wall.

But even if someone didn't *mean* to be racist, it doesn't change the fact that there was an impact from their actions. Because what I care about is getting to the root of any hidden racist beliefs, not whether they can hide it better or have to walk on eggshells around me. The way to do that isn't always by shaming their actions, but instead, helping them actually change their beliefs toward us.

Here are some techniques that might allow us to stop further problematic behavior, and even change minds, without creating a screaming match:

TECHNIQUE: INQUIRE AND INSTRUCT

Earlier, I suggested that when someone makes a racist joke, ask them "I don't get it, can you explain the joke?" or "What did you mean by that?" This is a technique I call **Inquire and Instruct**.

Let's say someone says to you: "Oh, you speak English so well." This is phrased as a compliment, which makes it hard to call out as bad behavior. But behind the message is an implication that they assumed you shouldn't. Sometimes, these can also be phrased as backhanded compliments like: "For an Asian guy, he's really good at sports!"

To address these situations, I don't recommend going on the offensive, which puts the person in a defensive position of having to justify their intentions. Instead, just compassionately assume their intent wasn't malicious and then inquire as to their beliefs: "Hmm, you mind if I ask why you thought I wouldn't speak English well?" or slightly jokingly: "Oh, is he supposed to be bad at sports?"

Or let's say someone asks, "Hey, you're good at math, right? Can you solve this for me?"

You can say, "Wait, I'm curious; what made you think I'm good at math?" and allowing them to notice whether they have preconceptions. Or alternatively, they just end up telling you all the ways they've noticed how smart you are. It's win-win either way.

Or let's say you hear someone say, "There was a car crash on the freeway today, probably an Asian driver; you know what they say about them."

You can ask, "No, what do they say?" or "Wait, do you think I'm a bad driver?"

With all your responses, you're presuming innocent intentions, not labeling their intentions as racist. Perhaps the real answer is they saw your résumé and know you have strong math skills. Perhaps they're just ignorant. But either way, your response allows you to shift the debate off whether they had racist intentions, which is almost always pointless.

For all the "It's just a joke" people, they'll stutter for a moment and try to play it off, because they immediately will recognize the "joke" is intended to create harm. But they can't try to pin it back on you for making a scene, because you're just calmly asking about *their own words*.

Compassionate inquiry is effective when people try to hide behind all sorts of statements. I've dealt with "It's just locker room talk!" or

"Well, you're different; I'm just talking about *those* Asians." or "I'm just joking with you; you know I wouldn't say it around other people!" I quickly address these defenses by saying, "Sure, but is this what you really believe about me/us/Asians?"

As for the "locker room" arguments, I can simply state, "If that's not how you really feel about me/us/Asians, maybe it doesn't need to be in the locker room either. After all, it's not something you actually believe, right?"

It's quite common that our friends and colleagues, especially ones who aren't as well educated on the impacts of their actions, are simply unaware. They don't know that their off-the-cuff, unconscious comments could have a hurtful impact on those around them.

They genuinely *don't get it*. And by asking for clarification, perhaps they'll change their beliefs as well.

EVEN IF IT'S REALLY JUST A JOKE

In certain corporate cultures, making jokes at other people's expense is seen as a way of showing closeness. The energy is: "We're so close we can make fun of each other and not be offended." This is something that causes people to feel extra pressure to put up with this behavior, because they don't want to be seen as the wet blanket in a tight-knit group.

However, the problem with jokes about race, ethnicity, or culture is they're not casually ribbing only *you,* but an entire group. For someone who might not be part of the "inside joke," this immediately makes them an outsider.

I have close Asian friends, and we joke about each other all the time. Sometimes we'll lovingly tease each other or rag on each other for fun. We do it with other people only when everyone in the group knows and consents to be part of the inside joke.

With my non-Asian friends, however, I make it clear there are things they can make fun of all day—my questionable fashion tastes, my nerdy obsessions with Marvel movies, my terrible karaoke skills—honestly, almost anything, except race or culture, because then the joke is not just about me.

I'll always politely express what I will and won't put up with in those scenarios. And once I've stated or explained what I'll accept as a joke, I tend to stop being polite. When a joke is made about race or culture, I have gone as far as staring deadpan at them until the silence gets uncomfortable. I've even simply walked out of the room.

I can't police other people's behaviors, but I also don't have to put up with it.

How to Call Out Behavior Respectfully (Even with Your Boss)

A client once told me she had a boss who occasionally made jokes about her Vietnamese background, even asking if her parents owned or worked at a nail salon. She said she thought he was a great boss otherwise and was usually caring, so she didn't want to make a big thing out of it. But it still made her uncomfortable.

My suggestion was for her to address the impact, but to leave the intention as innocent: "You can try saying something like 'Hey, I know you didn't mean anything negative by it, but that question made me feel a bit uncomfortable because it's a stereotype and I'd prefer if it doesn't continue.'"

She asked, "What if he gets defensive or mad at me?"

I said, "What could he get mad at you about? You're just voicing your discomfort, which he says he cares about. If you want, you can add how his actions can have further impact than he knows, by saying, 'Since you're the boss and everyone looks up to you, I'm really hoping you can help set a positive example for others.' This frames the issue as not just about an interaction with *you*, but as an issue of leadership and setting an example. You're pointing out the significance of his role and his responsibilities to the group."

Months later, she told me he not only apologized profusely, he actually started being more vigilant in calling out inappropriate behaviors in others.

Most of the time, unless I know their intentions or they are demonstrating a continuous pattern of outright racism, I avoid using the word *racist* when I address casual racism, because the word immediately derails the conversation and puts people on the defensive.

Instead, I focus on the positives about their identity, such as: "I know you're definitely not the kind of person who'd want to make others uncomfortable" or "I know you're not the kind of person who stereotypes others . . ." or "I know you really value kindness and helping people . . ."

Then instruct them on what you'd like them to do: "I just wanted to let you know this is something that can really help me, and others like me, feel more at ease and do our best work."

How to Deal with "I'm Just Stating the Facts!"

Have you encountered someone who says, "It's only a stereotype because it's true!" or "I'm just speaking the facts!"? In those cases, it's your decision whether you care to actually educate them on the stereotypes, or you just want to make a request for them to stop the behavior.

Let's say my client's boss above wasn't so understanding, and shot back, "Well, don't a lot of Vietnamese people work at nail salons?"

If the goal is to instruct, then she could say, "Yes, because that's usually the only opportunity they're offered in a new country as they're often turned down at other careers" or "Sure, there are many who choose that career path, but there's also lots of people, like myself, who work hard doing other things and we don't want to perpetuate that image. We're not a monolith." No matter what, you can always follow it up with a clear request: "Either way, it makes me/us uncomfortable, and my request is for you to please stop."

There have been situations where I don't even care to further educate someone who doesn't demonstrate a genuine interest in learning. Instead, I'll literally repeat the request over and over: "I understand how you feel, but those words still have an impact, and that's what I'd like to see stopped."

Set Your Intentions, Set Your Boundaries, and Speak without Apologies

As we've covered through most of this chapter, assertiveness is the simple act of speaking up, directly and transparently, while holding a positive intention. This includes saying no, setting boundaries, advocating for yourself, presenting your point of view without fear or aggression, and being direct in asking for your needs.

Before I hop into any conversation with anyone, I like to check in with myself: "What's my intention for this conversation? Is it to understand someone better, to make a deeper connection, or to provide valuable information that could benefit them or us?"

This is an incredibly simple thing to do, but has been incredibly transformative in how I shape the conversation as we communicate. Clarifying my intention helps me frame everything I say from a positive place, because I can check in from moment to moment to see: "Is what I'm about to say helpful for me, them, or us? Is this going to get us closer to understanding each other, or further apart?" Being assertive and speaking directly about what I need, even if I'm giving critical feedback with the intention for mutual benefit, automatically helps me shape what I want to say.

It's important that while we're doing this, we're also setting clear boundaries of what we're willing to accept or not accept from others. I don't put up with people who put others down, and if I sense that's the intention they're coming from, I don't mind being direct in asking them to stop.

There is a wide range of assertive communication styles. Maybe you're on the softer side of assertiveness and are used to using more mitigating language, but you can still be clear in the end about what you need and what you expect from the other person. Maybe you're on the harder side of assertiveness, where you have no problems being direct and straight to the point, but your intentions are still about raising up both you and the other person.

When we're communicating directly and assertively, everyone benefits. There's little room for miscommunication and it brings people *closer* to us, not further apart. We remove the need for guesswork or fears of hurting feelings, because we trust that if we're speaking up for ourselves, other people do not need our emotional caretaking and can handle us as we are.

8

Compassionate Assertiveness

Early on in the book, I mentioned how the Stereotype Content Model revealed a surprising number of people who felt that Asians fit into the "high competence, low warmth" category. I felt absolutely confused by how anyone could think Asians are *cold*. Most places I've visited in Asia are filled with some of the most hospitable, friendly people I've met. (If you spend more than fifteen minutes chatting with my mom, you are under serious risk of being kidnapped to the closest Chinese restaurant, where she will try to overfeed you even if she just met you for the first time.)

The secret formula to charisma is deceptively simple: it's just being more warm in our communication, without sacrificing our competence. A charismatic person is simply someone who emanates confidence and self-assuredness, while still being caring and warm.

And when you take into consideration our conditioning, suddenly the miscommunication of why Asians don't seem warm starts to reveal itself. It's not that we are cold, it's that we've taught ourselves to be as professional and polished as possible to succeed as model minorities.

For example, I had a client named Becca. When Becca spoke about her younger years attending school in Singapore, she recalled being the most outgoing, extroverted one in her class. She was always speaking up in class, had an extremely tight-knit group of friends from school, and she was the rambunctious one. "I hung out with my friends all the time," she told me. "I was really into arts and crafts, and making custom stationery for everyone I met. I had a lot of hobbies as a kid, and planned a lot of activities for my friends too."

Then, her family immigrated to Germany for work. By now, she was nearly a senior, and suddenly, she was alone. She learned the language, and tried everything to make friends. When she did try to connect with her classmates, though, she often hit a wall: "It wasn't that they were mean, but I was obviously the odd one out. They didn't understand why I was into anime, they didn't understand my jokes, and I couldn't understand any of theirs. When you're a kid, the worst thing you can be is *weird*. And to them, I was weird."

She didn't think it was racism or discrimination. She felt the disconnection arose because they were from completely different worlds, which was totally understandable. Unfortunately, when those attempts at finding belonging were met with apathy and rejection, she eventually became more closed off. Instead, she followed her parents' advice to focus on her academics. After all, her teachers had no problems with her because she worked hard and presented herself well, so that's all she spent her time focusing on.

She wasn't born as the quiet, studious Asian kid in the corner, she was trained to be.

When she eventually went to university in the US, she found a few other Asian friends who she connected with easily. But around her professors, she maintained her polished, matter-of-fact demeanor. She was sharp, and eventually went into a corporate position, where she prided herself on her professionalism and performance. Because she felt she wasn't previously accepted when she shared her weaknesses or mistakes, she took extra care not to burden others with them by remaining perfectly polished, polite, and professional in all her interactions. She also stayed away from the drama of her coworkers. When they went to happy hours, she'd go, make polite chitchat, and then head home early.

So when it was time for performance reviews, she was surprised to hear her coworkers found her distant, standoffish, and "hard to get to know." She felt stuck between two identities, both of which seemed unideal. By maintaining what she considered to be polite professionalism, she was seen as cold and distant. But at the same time, she felt uncomfortable sharing details about her personal life. In fact, she mentioned how shocked she felt the first time her coworker told her about their ongoing divorce proceedings, something she considered too personal and private to share at work.

In the collectivist cultural lens, communicating from rationality rather than rash emotionality is a form of politeness. To be too honest is to be considered rude, like you're expecting others to deal with your problems, and oversharing seems selfish and distracting. In fact, when you talk too much about your struggles, you might worry that others may become embarrassed on your behalf and try to help you by changing the topic. And for people like Becca, who grew up without a space of unconditional acceptance or belonging, they learned quickly about "inner circles"—friends who understand their culture and personalities, who allow them to be themselves without being seen as strange or foreign, and about "outer circles"—their colleagues, coworkers, or acquaintances who may not fully understand them. Work is work; it's not a place for their emotional messiness. So as professionals, they practice greater emotional self-control so as to not burden others with their inner world.

I told her she doesn't need to reveal every personal detail in her life, if she isn't comfortable with it. She can connect with others simply through compassion and empathy. It's as simple as saying, "Oh I'm so sorry you're going through that; I can't imagine how stressful that must be." Or she could just empathetically listen and sympathize with others. She could share what she felt in the *moment*, such as frustrations with a particularly challenging deadline. However, the key was accepting that whatever she shared in the moment was fine, and she didn't need to maintain a polished appearance *for the sake of others*.

Our politeness and protectiveness can become misunderstood as distance. Our considerations become misunderstood as apathy, and our attempts at giving others space to share become misunderstood as our having nothing to say. We might actually have plenty to say, but we worry that if we say it all, it might hurt their feelings. So we keep our mouths shut out, out of kindness to them. *You're welcome, by the way.*

But in reality, these unspoken truths and unexpressed feelings create all sorts of problems for us. If you are leading a team at work and they feel intimidated by your distance, they may feel they can't come to you with their real opinions, or they don't feel they can fully know you.

In the same way, if you're up for a promotion among your colleagues but you are seen as too cold and distant, your managers might not fully trust you to invite you in. This is why, when it comes to communication and leadership, the secret sauce is *our compassion*.

How to Lead with Compassion

Every person we meet is fighting an invisible battle.

For those of us from collectivist cultures, especially those with patterns of Fixers, Chameleons, and Charmers, we often have a strong ability to see the struggles others are going through. And as we've seen from the various studies prior, the social values of collective harmony often heightens our ability to read and recognize the experiences of others.

To me, this is an often untapped superpower when approaching *leadership*.

Leadership isn't just about our job positions or titles. We can be leaders in every aspect of our lives, regardless of what we do for work. We can take leadership in our relationship, from setting the kinds of dates we want to go on to long-term visions of the kind of relationships we want. We can lead our communities, making a positive and more inclusive environment for those who are part of it. We can lead with our friends and families, setting a model for the ways we communicate with one another and the depth of connection we want to build. Leadership is embedded in every interaction we hold, and defines all of our interpersonal relationships.

When it comes to the workplace, however, I would sometimes hear from Asian clients who have been promoted to leadership positions that they feel the need to "toughen up." They think they should be more dominant and direct, and they feel pressured to change their communication style to match. And while we've already talked about how assertiveness is a powerful and necessary tool in communicating expectations and boundaries, I also remind my clients that their skill for bringing harmony is *also* a superpower to be brought in, not abandoned.

This might seem counterintuitive at first, especially if the only model of leadership they've seen is the Western stereotype of an extroverted, dominating person, barking commands and demanding everyone make sacrifices. But this incomplete view overlooks another important leadership trait: compassion.

In the book *Compassionate Leadership*, the authors Rasmus Hougaard and Jacqueline Carter conducted two long-term research studies on how compassion can play a role in organizations. In collaboration with *Harvard Business Review* and four business schools, they interviewed 350 executives, mainly CEOs and chief human resources officers, and their staffs. They tracked data on the leaders themselves, and they also studied how their teams rated the leaders. What they found was that the leaders who were rated higher on "compassion" as a key trait received much higher ratings from their employees, including

34 percent higher job satisfaction, 36 percent more organizational commitment, 54 percent increase in leadership satisfaction, and 22 percent less risk of burnout.

They also found the leaders who rated themselves higher on compassion experienced 66 percent lower stress, 200 percent lower intention to quit, and 14 percent higher efficacy than their less-compassionate counterparts.

Compassion is holding the intention of understanding, before seeking to be understood. Especially when dealing with teams with a diverse range of backgrounds, having compassion is especially important, because it builds a bridge of connection.

An example of this in practice can be seen in three parts:

The first part is *compassionate reflection*. When approaching any meetings, especially with those who work for us, it's important we start by checking in and seeing how they feel about their work and their performance. This is the practice of compassionate reflection, which acknowledges employees' challenges and feelings.

Then, *we deliver what needs to be communicated, directly.* This might involve giving critical feedback without sugarcoating. We want to be as honest and transparent in this process as possible, and focus on the problem to be addressed.

Finally, *we set an intention of improving the situation together.* Which means focusing on collaboration and providing support. This helps the person you're talking to feel that they're not alone in the process, and they have a clear understanding of how you can win together.

These three parts don't always have to be delivered like some kind of mathematical formula. Sometimes, you just need to get the point across to someone quickly in a message about what needs to be done, or about clarifying if something isn't up to par. You can be as assertive as you need, depending on the situation, but the *intention* behind your leadership needs to remain compassionate. This means you're still seeking to check in and take on a collaborative role—to find the support they need, to listen to their experiences, and to create collaborative solutions, together.

How to Help People Feel Heard

Without changing the way you speak, the easiest thing you can do is listen to what people are saying, and *reflect it back to them*. I often see people asking questions like "I asked them what they wanted and I listened. I don't get why they still don't feel like they're being heard."

My answer is often, "Well, did you tell them what you heard from them?"

There's a difference between listening and *communicating* what we're hearing. You've likely already heard of techniques like using body language to demonstrate listening skills, such as nodding or reacting to what the other person is saying. Often, especially when we're in a leadership position, our focus is on giving instructions, setting expectations, and giving feedback. And while this might be our jobs, it misses something really basic about human beings—it's not always about the information; sometimes we just need to *feel* heard.

Every word we communicate contains multiple layers. There's the surface-level information of what is delivered, then there is the intention behind the statement, the feelings behind the statement, and the expectations that follow the statement.

When we're in our perfectionist mode, or our Commander and Achiever selves, we can't really *listen*, because that part of us wants to protect our image. But then the opportunity for connection is missed. To fully listen is to not make the communication about *us*, but to first hear to understand the other, then hear to confirm, and then respond.

Let's say you're asking someone to do something and they say, "Okay, but I've been feeling overwhelmed, like I'm drowning in deadlines."

An Achiever or Commander impulse might be to give solutions first and say: "So you don't want to do it? We're all dealing with a lot too. Here, use this time management system."

While this can be effective for some, by doing so, we're also opening them up to hear blame and rejection. Maybe what they'll hear is "Stop complaining, you're not the only one feeling this" and "Here, let me fix *your* problem."

A reflective statement might be: "Absolutely, we've got some big goals to hit this quarter. I can see how this can really feel overwhelming to tackle. I'm sure you're not the only one going through this." This reflects their feeling and reality, without taking on the responsibility of solving the problem immediately.

Then if you'd like to invite them to share further, you could ask if they feel like telling you more, such as, "What are you finding to be the biggest roadblocks right now?"

Once the person feels heard and understood, we can then go into setting goals and expectations, as well as sharing tools: "I can see how it's a challenge, but we still have these goals to hit before the deadline, so let's figure out some solutions that might make it less overwhelming. I have some time management techniques I've found to be really helpful in crunch time; would you like to hear them?"

This gives them a chance for clarification. Maybe they'll say, "Actually, I'm okay, I just wanted to let you know I'm doing my best but I can't handle taking on anything additional on my plate right now," or maybe they'll accept your offer and say, "Yes, please, I'd love to hear it."

Compassionate reflection is not necessarily about talking about feelings, but is *meeting people where they are*. For many more rationally focused individuals, they may not talk about how overwhelmed they are, they'll just say, "I've got too much work to do right now."

In those situations, trying to force touchy-feeling language down their throats—like "Oh, do you mean you're feeling a sense of overwhelm and sadness in this experience of overwork?"—is more likely to draw irritation or confusion, and is totally unnecessary. Instead, just ask them to elaborate, and use what they're saying in your own words or questions.

How to Build Rapport without Saying a Word

The next easy way for us to communicate empathy is by mirroring the other person's energy level and nonverbal communication.

If your best friend comes to you and says, "OH MY GOD, YOU WON'T BELIEVE IT BUT I GOT THAT DREAM JOB I'VE ALWAYS WANTED, MY SECRET CRUSH ASKED ME OUT, THEN I GOT HOME AND I FOUND OUT SOMEONE GAVE ME A PUPPY!"

You probably wouldn't hear that and dully respond: "Uh, okay." Even for the most typically quiet and low-key of us, we'd at least be mirroring *some* of the excitement and energy back to them, right? If nothing else, we could just share how happy we are for them, and say that we're definitely not being jealous *even though that dog is so cute.*

This is a basic human experience, and we can meet the energy they carry—excited, relaxed, contented, motivated—and simply mirror it back through our body language, volume, tone, and all the visible in-visibles in between.

In fancy psychology terms, it's called limbic synchrony, and it's an extremely quick way for us to build a sense of social understanding and trust. Next time you go out, notice the body language of the people who are in pairs. Maybe you'll see a table with two buddies sharing gripes about work, both sitting back, legs crossed in the same direction, their hands gesturing at the same degree of movement. Or you'll see a couple on a date, both with their heads at a slight angle, leaning in.

This concept of "social mimicry" has been examined by a number of different scientific studies, including an experiment where two people, one assigned to the role of a person applying for a job and another applying to be a recruiter, found when the recruiter mimicked the applicant's words at the beginning or the end of the interactions, they got more positive results. It's also why *small talk* is so commonly used at the top of any serious meetings, even though it seems all anyone can talk about is the weather or local sports games—it's a way to quickly build rapport and cohesion. The same was found when the two participants were playing out a business negotiation, where the pairs were more likely to get to a successful decision rather than walking away.

Something as simple as matching the body language of the person you're speaking with, repeating back to them the last few words they say, or matching their tone or facial expression created a sense of community and connection almost immediately. This isn't some Jedi mind trick manipulation; it's about stepping into the shoes of the person you're talking to. When we mimic someone else's body language, we can actually better understand how they're feeling.

This is the result of our brains being really good at feeling what others feel, using what scientists refer to as mirror neurons. In the late 1980s, researchers studying the brain activities of macaque monkeys discovered that when they observed another monkey making a particular gesture, like reaching for a peanut, their own brains cells would fire in the same position. In other words, they could *feel* it as if they were experiencing it themselves.

It brings more meaning to the term "monkey see, monkey do," perhaps to become "monkey do, monkey *understands*."

How to Bring Inclusiveness into Our Daily Language

In 2013, a group of researchers tried to figure out if the way we speak—specifically, the way we use pronouns like *I, me, my* versus *we, us, you*—makes a difference in how much of a leader we are perceived to be. The researchers created a number of separate studies in which language was used in different contexts, including teams who were given a set of problems to solve, a series of informal conversations, the examination of emails with twenty other individuals, and conversations between two people in online chat forums.

Through computerized text analysis, they discovered that across all the contexts, people who used more "other-focused" pronouns like *we, us,* and *you* were seen universally to be of higher status and higher rank, whereas those who used more "self-focused" pronouns like *I* or *me* were seen as lower status and rank.

The implications of language in these studies are fascinating, because when we frame our language by including others, there is an association with higher status and leadership. But it's not quite so simple as saying you should use *we* all the time to refer to yourself, as if you're the queen of England. Inclusive pronouns, like all tools, depend on the context.

Use *I* when taking responsibility and ownership. Whenever I'm acknowledging my own role in something, especially when I made a mistake, I'll outright say: "I had forgotten to include this report . . . ."

Use *I* when giving negative feedback: "I noticed a few corrections that need to be made" versus "You've made a number of mistakes."

I use *we/us* whenever I'm talking about a shared challenge or opportunity: "It's easy for us to forget how quickly the holidays are approaching" or "We're all trying to get to the same destination here."

And I use *you* whenever I'm giving a direct invitation or when giving acknowledgment or praise. "I saw how hard you worked on this project and thought you did a great job at this" or "I'd love to see you share your stories and experiences more. I really appreciate it when you do."

How to Give Constructive Feedback

Speaking of which, this is usually when people ask about how they can give critical feedback without hurting feelings.

As with all the other communication-based suggestions here, it's about finding what fits you best, as we're all different. If you're already very direct, working in some warm or inclusive statements can go a long way. If you're too much a Chameleon or a Charmer, however, maybe dialing it back a bit can be more effective for you.

Except when it comes to negative feedback.

The one rule I have that is universal about negative feedback is to never attach the problem to the person—it is never about: "You aren't good at this" but rather "You didn't succeed at this task." The first has a much higher likelihood to be taken as a definitive identity or character flaw, when it's actually something they can workshop or troubleshoot to get better at.

A handy tool I suggest to people who know themselves to come off as too direct or critical in their feedback is the *I like / I would like* method.

Basically, in giving critical feedback to someone, simply state two parts:

1. What you liked about what they did, so they know what they can do more of.
2. What you would like for them to do differently about the parts you didn't like.

When we hear negative feedback, our brain is usually focused on "Okay, I'll stop doing this," which puts us in an avoidant state, but it doesn't actually solve the problem, because we still have to replace it with something.

By being clear on what you'd like to see, you're setting them up for success:

"*I like* the way you were really concise with your points in these areas; it really got the point across clearly. *What I'd like* to see is a bit more focus on the research and studies, which would help the audience understand why we're making these changes."

How to Handle Blame with Compassion

But what if the person we're communicating compassionately with is also pushing blame onto us? Let's say you and your team just finished a presentation, and there were some mixed reactions from the audience. During the debrief, a team member says, "I think you could have done better on the presentation today."

On the surface level, this is a valid statement of assessment. But this is also a critical point of decision-making for the leader who might see their patterns show up. The Commander or Achiever in us might immediately take responsibility for it and reactively hear it as a challenge to our leadership. This is true especially for those of us who already have a tendency to be tougher on ourselves. One might say, "Well, I told everyone they needed to go above and beyond, and there were parts that didn't get done the way I said."—This would be stepping into defensiveness, picking up a sword to fight a battle that wasn't there to begin with.

Or maybe our more self-critical side might show up and want to apologize, and we might go into self-blame immediately, wanting to reflexively say, "You're right, I really messed up our timelines beforehand."

An easier alternative in this moment is to explore with empathy: "Hmm, what were some things you would have liked to see happen differently?" This still shows you're open to reflection.

When we're in a state of nonreactivity, we can start seeing other people for what they're really feeling. Maybe the person who's pointing out our flaws thought we actually did a great job, overall, but they're used to jumping straight into a tiny detail that needs to be changed for next time, and we're overexaggerating the problem in our minds. If we're not sure, we can always ask.

We could also take a look from another perspective. Let's say the message *is* a criticism of our leadership. Perhaps it was: "I feel like you didn't give us enough time to prepare beforehand."

It is perfectly understandable here to feel a little bit defensive again, but I always remind people that just because someone throws a label of criticism at you, doesn't mean you don't have to pin it on your lapel. The response could be: "Right. It sounds like you were feeling rushed and wanted more time to get things in order."

Remember, we can empathize with a feeling or feedback without taking it as fact. We still have the ability to pause and decide if we agree or disagree, after acknowledging their feelings. If we agree, then the response might be: "You know, looking back, I do think we could have scheduled a few more working sessions to make sure we were fully prepared. I'll make sure to schedule more time for our next presentation. Thank you for the feedback."

Or if we disagree, we could say: "I totally understand in the midst of everything we're doing, it can feel like a time crunch. I feel like time wasn't the biggest issue, but we didn't get all the research we needed. I can see how it must have felt like we were more pressured near the end there."

The simple act of validating the feeling without taking on the blame is an important one, *even* when we're feeling there's criticism in the room directed at us.

How to Be a Great Leader through Vulnerability

I was chatting with Eric Wong, the director of Global Leader Development at Adobe, and I asked him what the secret to great leadership was.

Over the years, he's worked with leaders from all sorts of backgrounds, who have encountered challenges and faced them head-on, and he is a pro at helping leaders navigate conflict.

His answer to what makes great leaders was simple: "Vulnerability."

Time and time again, when we are actually asked *who we want* to lead us, the things we want from leaders are: Sense of caring. Willingness to listen. Understanding. Mentoring. Respect for the team. Able to see the talents of others and lets me do my best work.

We don't want a leader who is standing high up on the podium in a pressed suit of perfection. We want someone who is willing to get in the trenches with us and trudge through the mud and dirt with the team. Someone who is willing to see and understand what we're also going through together. And this is something that should be particularly relevant for those of us who have felt what it means to not belong, because we know how important it is.

We don't want to be told what to do, we just want to feel *understood*.

This is why compassion can be so powerful as a starting mindset to reach others. No matter who we are, everyone is going through a struggle of their own, and compassion is the recognition of their humanity, and our willingness to see them and work with them.

Furthermore, compassion comes from a place of self-empowerment. It comes from a position of giving and willingness to help others. It's kind, caring, and empathetic.

To communicate our compassion, we must first speak from vulnerability, especially from a position of leadership. To be compassionate is about our willingness to authentically show up and accept our own imperfections, and to bring our wholeness to the team, every day.

A great leader says: I can see the challenges you might face, and I'm in this with you. I've got your back and we can do this together.

In the business leadership book *The Culture Code,* Daniel Coyle examines the world's most successful teams and organizations, from the

U.S. Navy SEAL Team Six, to the San Antonio Spurs, to Zappos, and discovered the three key lessons to great leadership and building a great team. In his introduction, he asks what he considers to be "the oldest question of all": Why do certain groups add up to be greater than the sum of their parts, while others add up to be less?

Groups succeed when leaders create belonging, share vulnerability, and establish purpose.

He looked to some of the best CEOs, championship-winning coaches, and organizational leaders in the world and realized there is a magical combination of *setting high standards* and having *unwavering commitment* and *inclusive practices*.

Belonging is an incredibly innate and essential building block of any group. It doesn't matter if you're leading a Fortune 500 company or organizing your local church group choir. If there is no sense of safety, inclusion, and belonging, the members will not play at their best.

Leaders need to recognize *each* individual member as being unique and valued, and leaders can't do that if they're focused only on themselves and how polished or competent they seem. They need to take the time to see and recognize the people they're standing beside.

How to Be More Compassionately Assertive with Ourselves

We're all motivated in different ways. Some of us are a bit more encouraging with ourselves, reminding ourselves of our past successes, and that we're capable of handling whatever the world throws at us. Others might use more "tough love" when it comes to self-motivation, telling themselves they better do what they need to do or there will be great consequences!

We all have a little voice in our head that nags us and points out when we make mistakes or when we do something cringey. A little inner critic jumps out with some harsh words to try to get us to do what the critic thinks is needed to feel safe from judgment. And some days, that inner critic can get *really loud*.

The inner critic is like a watchful guardian, surveilling everything we do and telling us when we're not good enough, so that we'll do what we need to succeed. But it doesn't actually help us. Often, it'll try to criticize us to pull us astray, and in those times, I like to get really firm with it.

Practicing compassionate assertiveness with ourselves starts by recognizing where that voice comes from and treating it with compassion. Perhaps it was a voice we learned in childhood (remember the earlier quote where *the voice our parents use when we're kids becomes the voice we'll hear when we become adults*?), or perhaps we created it when we were in school as a way to keep us from doing embarrassing things. It's a fear-driven response, and can exist even when what we're about to do is perfectly safe.

In those times, I like to picture my inner critic as a person, and I even visualize them. After all, they're a part of me, and they'll always be around. The trick is knowing when to get them to quiet down.

One of my inner critics is named Bob, and he looks like a forty-five-year-old accountant with square glasses, a green vest, and elbow pads on his blazer. He holds a clipboard and grades everything I do and tells me when he perceives I'm doing something wrong. Bob tends to speak up a lot when I'm feeling a bit insecure about my work, like when I'm giving a big speech to an auditorium full of people. He might go down his checklist and say, "Well, your jokes aren't really that funny, and you're trying too hard. No one really cares about this, and you should probably just cancel the event before everyone finds out how terrible this is." Bob can be *absolutely savage*.

Whenever I hear Bob, I'll take a moment and go, "Oh hey, Bob. I see you're here, so it must be because I really care about this, and it's really important to me that I do a good job." And I'll shift my thoughts to go into my compassion and gratitude: "Wow, I'm so excited I get to do this. Even if my jokes aren't great, it doesn't matter because maybe one or two people in the audience might appreciate it, and isn't it great that I care so much and that I try so hard?"

After I give Bob a little love, I then ask him to leave: "Hey, Bob, I know you're worried about us not doing a good job here, but I trust myself, and even if I'm not perfect, I can go out there and have fun and rock the stage. So you don't need to be here right now; why don't you go and sit down, and I'll tend to you later?"

At this point, I find the little inner critic voice will usually be gone.

Then, I can focus on being assertive with myself. I start looking at what I still need to get done, and tell myself, "Okay, I still have to rehearse this speech, so I'm gonna set a goal to do three full run-throughs before the end of the week, so I can do an excellent job when I'm on stage and really help some people."

Compassionate assertiveness is a simple practice but massively powerful once we get used to putting it in action. It makes sure we aren't discounting ourselves internally or feeling we're always not enough. But at the same time, it's not just us sitting endlessly in front of the mirror telling ourselves "I'm good enough" over and over without ever taking action.

It's important that we can be compassionate about who we are, give ourselves the love we need, but then also leave the warm cocoon of healing so we can *go get things done.*

Human beings are social animals, and most of the time when we feel stuck, it's because there's something we need to say to others that we struggle to get out, or there's something we need to hear from others that we struggle to ask for. So often, the problems we face really just come down to us not speaking our truths. We're afraid of how it might affect others, we're afraid of how we'll be seen, and as a result, we end up letting things get worse and worse.

Speaking our truth takes tremendous courage, but it's also the most powerful tool we have for solving problems and getting what we want. And if we can hold the compassion that allows us to act from love and care, as well as the courage to speak assertively and directly to the needs that are being underserved, we can join forces to break through just about anything.

Our greatest strength will always lie more in our community, not in trying to take on the world alone.

. . . . .

PART THREE

BIG ASIAN COMMUNITY

Community, for Asians and the Asian diaspora, is a big part of our values and cultural identities. Yet many of us might still feel isolated, even when we're in a crowded space, because our belonging is often conditional. We might feel that we have to act or be a certain way in order to be accepted by our social environment or even by our own families, who might have different ideas of who we are supposed to be than who we truly are.

Social acceptance for the Asian diaspora, especially those living in non-Asian countries, can come with multiple barriers. In the most recent study published by STAATUS Index, *only 22 percent of Asian Americans polled said they feel like they belong and are accepted in the US*, the lowest of any ethnic group. Even worse, nearly *half* of all Asian Americans report feeling *unsafe* in the US, due to their race.

Social acceptance is one thing, but that isn't the whole picture of who we are as people. In order to get the fully nuanced version of ourselves, we also need to look at how we are accepted in our families and whether we can fully accept ourselves.

Acceptance of who we are is a big topic, because we are now starting to realize what a significant role it plays in *everything*. Without self-acceptance, everything from our physical health to our mental health can become negatively impacted. And in order for us to belong and thrive, we need to heal any lingering symptoms that might have made it hard for us to truly be ourselves.

In this part of the book, we'll examine three major areas where our sense of acceptance—in society, in our families, and within ourselves—might encounter roadblocks, and may affect our well-being without our being conscious of it.

The first two chapters will look at the history of Asian acceptance in Western society, as well as the barriers that still plague us to this very day. Then, we'll look at how familial dynamics can make us feel emotionally isolated, even in adulthood, and examine techniques in improving our relationships with our families as adults. Finally, we'll take a look at the topic that is often seen as taboo within Asian societies: mental health, and healing our wounds.

You may feel some hesitation toward some of the topics covered, but it is a necessary process to access the community you are meant to be a part of.

Remember: you deserve to be surrounded by a community that accepts you for who you truly are.

Barriers to Belonging

The problem with belonging is it's usually seen as an on-off switch. The belief is that as long as we're not outright *rejected*, it must mean everything has been done for us to belong. But in reality, that's not actually true. We can be invited into the room without ever being actually known, acknowledged, or accepted for our values and beliefs.

There are different levels of social belonging. In social psychology, researchers show how belonging can be measured in both objective and subjective dimensions. An objective belonging might come when someone is invited to a group event, or when they become a member of a social group. At the starting level, it might be very transactional—you're a part of a group because you paid the annual fees to be part of a club or community group. But just because you got through the door doesn't mean people are actually interested in or curious about you.

The subjective layer is more in-depth, and measures things like how much emotional connection someone feels to those around them. This may mean people know, like, and trust you. People ask you questions about how things are going, they form deeper relationships with you, create inside jokes, and even invite you to connect outside of that club or social event. It's the feeling of having your ride-or-die crew, or a core group of friends who truly *know* you.

Perhaps this is why so many Asian people I talk to share the paradoxical experience of feeling *lonely in a crowd*. They're told to network and build more connections, so they end up at endless networking events or meetup groups where people trade feigned over-enthusiasm while secretly thinking about whether to file the conversation under "Must follow up" or "Forget about immediately once I figure out an excuse to walk away." You know, the events where you sip gallons of lukewarm coffee served with a side of lukewarm conversation as people shuffle about the room, trading names they've already forgotten before you finish introducing yourself. Even the most extroverted of us, at the end of the night, can often feel a sense of shallow emptiness, as we are still on the outside looking in.

But belonging is what we all truly want. At the highest, most connective level of belonging is the feeling of *total* acceptance—meaning we can be ourselves, including all of our little quirks and imperfections. It's where we are fully accepted by the people around us, even when we're not at our best, when we're tired, introverted, socially awkward, or just having a bad day. It means we can belong as we are, when we're not expected to provide something for others or expected to perform a certain way.

For many, including myself, this is a rare sanctuary that is hard to find. In certain cases, it may not have been offered by our families, so we never got a blueprint for what we should expect or accept. We start lowering our expectations, happy with whatever crumbs of connection and acceptance are offered to us, without realizing we could set better standards and teach others to treat us better.

But why is it harder for us to feel that sense of belonging and acceptance, not just in our friend groups, not just in our workplaces, not just in our communities, but even in our own *country*?

The answer might be found in our history.

A Brief History of Asian Ostracization

Before we dive into why belonging is such an important topic for the Asian diaspora, it's important to first understand the history of how Asians were often viewed in Western countries.

The US and Canada have had a problematic history when it comes to the treatment of Asians, from using terms like "Yellow Peril" to arguments on how Asians were unclean and unfit for citizenship.

When one nationality is attacked, like Japanese Americans or Chinese Americans, *all* Asians end up being discriminated against because to non-Asians, it seems we all look alike. And historically, we were welcomed only while we were considered useful (such as if we were willing to work on railroads for below-market value, or were helpful for the space race), but ostracized as soon as we're not.

The modern ostracization began in the 1800s, when some white people spread propaganda that Asians brought diseases to North America, especially in San Francisco, leading to the infamous Chinese Exclusion Act of 1882, the first law in the history of the US barring immigration based on race. Despite its being called the Chinese Exclusion Act, its elaboration into the Immigration Act of 1924 went on to restrict all other Asian immigrant groups regardless of nationality.

Following the Chinese Exclusion Act were some of the most brutal "driving out" eras of this time, where large-scale violence, such as the Rock Springs Massacre and Hells Canyon Massacre took place. Chinese immigrants were stabbed, burned alive, starved to death, or shot. They were accused of taking jobs from white miners.

Similar laws in Canada were established that banned almost all Asians, including South Asians, or added "head tax" rules, making it extremely difficult for family members to immigrate from Asia, but much easier if one was coming from Europe. Laws and rules were put in place to make North America as unwelcoming as possible. Asians weren't welcome to do any well-paying work, resulting in most of them working in the only services they were allowed—cooking and cleaning. Hence the commonality of seeing Asian laundromats and restaurants, and why you could find Asian restaurants across even the tiniest California towns, as historically they were driven out of major cities.

The justification against Asians were initially social denigration—Asians were said to be carrying filthy "tropical diseases" and were considered to be dirty or unhygienic. This perception was historically so extreme that, in the early twentieth century, American officials in the Philippines (at the time an American colony) said the Filipinos had "unclean and uncivilized bodies" and used this to justify continued US colonial rule. It is perhaps unsurprising why anti-Asian racism spiked during the 2003 SARS outbreak and more recently, during COVID-19.

Anti-Asian racism continued well into WWII, in which seventy-five incarceration sites and concentration camps were set up across the United States under Franklin Roosevelt's famous Executive Order 9066, placing all Japanese Americans in concentration camps. California declared anyone with 1/16th or more Japanese lineage had to be incarcerated, and Colonel Karl Bendetsen went on to say that anyone with "one drop of Japanese blood" fit under the rule of incarceration—regardless of whether they were mostly white, or if they were second- or third-generation American citizens without any ties to Japan whatsoever.

By comparison, during WWII, German and Italian Americans were never incarcerated en masse. Those who were investigated or incarcerated needed to actually be suspected of disloyalty or have been proven to be working against the US. But Japanese American US soldiers, who were actively fighting against Germans and the Japanese, watched as their own families were put into concentration camps. Imagine risking your life for your country, fighting its enemies, and then seeing your family jailed.

Incarceration wasn't the only issue; most white citizens didn't want to be around Japanese people. A March 1942 poll conducted by the

American Institute of Public Opinion found that 93 percent of Americans supported forced relocation of Japanese people.

It wouldn't be until 1943, right after the Japanese concentration camps were set up, when the Chinese Exclusion Act was stripped. It wasn't out of a desire to be more accepting of Chinese migrants but because the government wanted to build a transpacific alliance with China, against Japan and the Axis powers. Once Japan was defeated in WWII, that story began to change.

Around the 1960s, the Black civil rights movements began to take shape, and in order for racists to combat that, a new narrative began to form. Magazines and newspapers began printing stories of successful Asian Americans who came from humble beginnings and had achieved prosperity. To enforce institutional racism, many cultural outlets sought to divide racial minorities and started pointing to Asian Americans, who were still largely confined to their own segregated communities, as being examples of "good" minorities, as few were involved in activism or political uprisings.

This "model minority" narrative, among other issues, created a conflict between Asian American communities and African American communities. During the LA riots of 1992, Black and brown neighbors erupted in fury and protests at the injustice of the acquittal of the four police officers who had beaten Rodney King. While the LAPD protected wealthy West LA neighborhoods, they stood by as Black and brown neighbors burned down much of nearby Koreatown.

Given the extensive history of anti-Asian racism in the West, one would think things have changed dramatically since the 1990s. But the reality is, while a lot of the obvious discrimination has faded, there are still pervasive remnants of bias and discrimination that keep us from truly feeling we are accepted or belong, and it creates very tangible, significant problems that have gone unnoticed or unrecognized in our society.

Let's fast-forward to today and see how things have panned out.

Barriers to Belonging: Whitening Résumés and Perpetual Foreigners

One noticeable way our belonging is challenged today is through the invisible discrimination we encounter during our job searches.

A Harvard Business School study in 2017 found only 11.5 percent of job applicants of Asian descent received callbacks when their résumés included references to their ethnicity or race, like their "foreign-looking" names. When their résumés were "whitened" by removing any of their ethnicity markers, including things like changing to more Westernized names, their callback rates nearly *doubled* to 21 percent.

Perhaps what is most ironic is the study found companies that promoted themselves as "pro-diversity" often were just as discriminatory, if not more so. One of the study's co-authors, Katherine A. DeCelles, notes: "This is a major point of our research—that you are at an even greater risk for discrimination when applying with a pro-diversity employer, because you're being more transparent. Those companies have the same rate of discrimination, which makes you more vulnerable when you expose yourself to those companies."

This cold truth is, sadly, not a surprise to many Asians. More than a third (36 percent) of Asian students who were seeking jobs and internships "whitened" their résumés, and two-thirds mentioned they knew friends or family who did so. Whitening résumés includes things like changing their names to be more Western-sounding—like substituting Luke for Lei—and they also "Americanized" their interests, adding activities such as hiking, snowboarding, and kayaking that are more commonly associated with white Western culture.

"One Asian applicant said she put her 'very Chinese-sounding' name on her résumé in her freshman year, but got noticed only after subbing in her American nickname later: 'Before I changed it, I didn't really get any interviews, but after that I got interviews,' she said."

Even after we get the job, however, there are still blocks to belonging.

I've heard so many complaints about how it feels to be identified
and pigeonholed as "the Asian one," but my clients often hadn't known
that this experience comes with a name. It's the result of what's called
the "Perpetual Foreigner Syndrome," which means that because we
look different (as in, not white), we're automatically assigned the identity of being "the Asian," rather than the people we actually are.

This usually comes out in subtle ways that don't seem overly problematic at first glance, such as having our names mispronounced, or
god forbid, when we get the "Sure you're from New York, but where are
you *really* from?"

"Um . . . you mean which hospital in New York was I born in? I don't
know, where are *YOU* really from?"

These casual flubs and questions are sharp reminders of: "Oh, right,
it doesn't matter if I was born here or if I'm a citizen of this country, I'm
still seen as a foreigner."

We are *told* by our workplaces that our culture is celebrated. Sometimes colleagues or even bosses add patronizing comments such as "Oh,
you're Korean? I love K-pop and kimchi!" or the immediate assumption
that we must identify first with our hereditary culture. I mean, what if
someone is Korean but loves heavy metal and dueling banjos rather
than BTS? There's nothing specifically wrong with people wanting to
connect when that's all they know about our culture, but sometimes
that type of celebration makes us feel even more different.

Examples of the Perpetual Foreigner Syndrome usually involve
things like getting randomly grouped with other people of similar ethnicities: "Oh, my friend Darren is also Japanese; I gotta introduce you
guys!" or the assumption of a stereotype based on the way you look:
"Hey, John, you're Asian, can you calculate the tip on dinner for us?"

Sometimes, this might even lead to people mistaking you for

another Asian person, which has happened to me at least four or five times now. It is particularly amusing, because usually when I meet the other Asian guy I'm being confused for, we'll look at each other knowingly, like, "Yeah, you too, eh?"

A hilarious example of this being called out on social media was when Emmy Award–winning Kumail Nanjiani (*Silicon Valley*, *The Big Sick*) posted, "A day may come when I am not mistaken for another brown actor. But it is not this day."

In response, Kunal Nayyar (*Big Bang Theory*) posted, "Every time I get recognized for you I think, 'Man, I wish it were true:)'"

This was followed by Kal Penn (*Harold & Kumar Go to White Castle*, *House*) posting, "I have taken credit for both of your accolades in the last 2 weeks so I guess I owe you each a photo, half a beer, and an awkward extended hug."

This feeling of "Sorry, Wrong Asian" is well documented across multiple industries. Journalist Jeff Yang asked people to share their #SorryWrongAsian experiences on social media, and he reported on the responses in a *Guardian* article:

> "I was mistaken for Margaret Cho in the women's room of a NYC theater . . . while attending a performance by Margaret Cho"
>
> —Korean American podcaster Kristen Meinzer

> "A primetime TV booker asked if I'd do a debate panel with former White House chief of staff Reince Priebus. I said it wasn't my wheelhouse and I couldn't get down to the studio in time. She insisted and arranged a satellite truck to come to my house. She'd meant to book Neera Tanden."
>
> —TV correspondent and radio host Nayyera Haq

> "At my old studio we used to have food catered in for late-night work . . . One night we got a ton of sushi brought in. Being budget-

conscious, I asked the caterer, 'What the hell?' Apparently he'd mistaken one of my other Asian employees as me and asked *him* what the next night's order should be."

—Video game producer Josh Tsui

"For about a year I had a colleague at the White House who confused me with another Asian co-worker so often that the other Asian guy and I would frequently trade notes given to us by the colleague but meant for the other."

—Ronnie Cho, former associate director of
the Office of Public Engagement under Barack Obama

"I was doing an event that had a couple of chefs involved—Momofuku's David Chang and Kogi Taco's Roy Choi. We were all on stage speaking and I was DJing . . . Sitting down to eat, someone—pretty recognizable!—waved me over and started the conversation with 'Thank you, chef!' I wonder who he thought I was . . ."

—Platinum-selling producer Dan "the Automator" Nakamura

I found these examples hilariously relatable. I've been "Sorry Wrong Asian'ed" probably dozens of times through the years, which has given me lots of food for thought. We're all subconsciously influenced by how others view and treat us, so if we're being confused for someone else, or if we're being asked whether we are good at math (or if we can fix their tech issues, or if we can opine on political events in Asia), these micro-aggressions are yet another reminder that we're still *not quite* like everyone else. I mean, I do love sushi and curry, but that's because those dishes are delicious and have nothing to do with my ethnicity.

After experiencing all these little reminders over the years, I started to avoid talking about anything related to my culture or ethnic background. Not because I want to deliberately keep it a secret, but because I didn't like being constantly othered.

As it turns out, I'm not the only one who does this. A PEW Research study found a staggering 39 percent of Asian adults under thirty have deliberately hidden their culture, food, religion, or even clothing from non-Asians out of concern for how they'd be seen or treated.

And it's not just immigrants who are trying to assimilate. As it turns out, those who are born in the US (second-generation onward) are even more likely than recent immigrants to hide their cultural background from their friends, with 32 percent of US-born Asians choosing to actively hide their culture versus only 15 percent of immigrant Asians. For multiracial Asian Americans, many said they hide their heritage "to pass as white." Being Asian has become a liability in our lives and careers.

Perhaps this is why I, like many Asian people I've spoken to, have at some point in their lives felt it was easier to spend time with other Asian people. It's a feeling of belonging that says, "You're not the *other* here."

True societal belonging should never pressure us to hide who we really are. Society should allow us to proudly carry both parts of ourselves, and celebrate our cultural heritage as well as any new identities we choose to take on. But over time, by being told we are better appreciated for being more "white," we have created a guarded version of ourselves. We have gotten so used to being told "it's not a big deal," that we started to believe it ourselves.

But it absolutely is a big deal. At a much bigger scale than we could imagine. The way we are perceived and the ways we are treated hinder us, and become the barriers to our unconditional belonging.

Barriers to Belonging: The Myth of the "Model Minority"

During the pandemic, when anti-Asian hate crimes spiked 339 percent across the US, I was invited to give a speech at a rally in my city. When

I told my mom about the event, her response was "Anti-Asian racism? Are there people who are racist against Asians?" She didn't say this because she doesn't understand that it happens. So many of us are so used to brushing off things like microaggressions that we start to accept them as a normal part of life.

Most of our stereotypes—hardworking, keeping our heads down, not causing problems—create a space of *conditional* acceptance. That is, we are accepted for who we are so long as we can blend in and assimilate well enough.

At the time, presidential candidate Andrew Yang spoke up in an attempt to address the rise of anti-Asian hate by tweeting the following message:

> *We Asian Americans need to embrace and show our American-ness in ways we never have before. We need to step up, help our neighbors, donate gear, vote, wear red white and blue, volunteer, fund aid organizations, and do everything in our power to accelerate the end of this crisis. We should show without a shadow of a doubt that we are Americans who will do our part for our country in this time of need.*

He also wrote a *Washington Post* op-ed restating his advice. I want to say that I absolutely believe in Yang's positive intent here. Rallying around civic duty and community can be a great thing in general. But unfortunately, his statement also implies that we need to *prove* our belonging once again. This sentiment is reminiscent of the days of Japanese internment camps, when even Japanese American soldiers who were fighting for the US overseas were robbed of their property and told they needed to prove their loyalty to America. For years, we had been conditionally accepted, but suddenly, our acceptance became deeply fragile.

The first time I heard the term "model minority," I genuinely thought it was a compliment. I mean, who doesn't want to be seen as the *model* for anything? Doesn't that just mean we're seen as extra smart and successful?

There are even terms like "Asian exceptionalism" to describe the impression of Asian excellence in academia and career success. For a long time, I thought that was a good thing. The thing is, this "praise" isn't about celebrating Asians, but rather putting us into neat little approved boxes, where a dominant white gaze can assert their ability to assess "good" from "bad" minorities. And then we are used as political pawns.

In the words of Viet Thanh Nguyen in his *Time* magazine article on the model minority stereotype: "This is what it means to be a model minority—to be invisible in most circumstances because we are doing what we are supposed to be doing, like my parents, until we become hypervisible because we are doing what we do too well, like the Korean shopkeepers. Then the model minority becomes the Asian invasion, and the Asian-American model minority, which had served to prove the success of capitalism, bears the blame when capitalism fails."

Not only is the model minority stereotype used to shame other races, it's also a way for public systems to ignore real issues all ethnicities face. This stereotype sweeps Asian Americans like Hmong, Laotians, Cambodians, and Vietnamese, who were typically less economically successful, into the same group as East Asian and South Asian nationalities who were more successful.

The model minority myth also seems to fade when it comes time to attack specific *national identities*. For the past few years, questioning the loyalty of Chinese Americans became acceptable. Laws banning Chinese nationals from buying homes mean anyone who *looks* Chinese was being forced to prove their background in order to find habitation. More important, the concept made no sense to me—if foreign investors are the issue, why not just ban all foreign investment entirely? Though anti-Asian hate seems to have died down, it's just shifted to a more specific group to attack.

I've seen the same general stereotypes about many different Asian national heritage. Disgusting tweets or comments stereotyping Indians and Indian diaspora as rapists, posts that generalize all Koreans and Korean diaspora as misogynistic. How did this become okay?

Anti-Asian racism is often hidden in Anti-Asian-National-Heritage racism. It's historically easier to justify attacking a nation you're in competition with than to admit that attacks are actually racist toward a whole people who have nothing to do with governments abroad.

The model minority myth can be dangerous. The message is: "This is what good Asian Americans are supposed to look like, act like, and be like. They don't complain, they do what they're told, and they know their place in society. And if you try to speak up, we will make an example of you."

If Asians speak up about being kept out of leadership roles by the bamboo ceiling, or about racial bias when getting turned down for research funding or turned away from educational opportunities, the answer is always the same: "Other races have real struggles, you don't. The racism you face isn't real racism; the problems you face aren't worth addressing. And most important—don't complain."

And since we aren't *allowed* to complain about our position in the hierarchy of the current system, we use any anger or frustration we experience and turn it toward someone else—our own community.

Barriers to Belonging: Token Olympics

Another way where belonging is broken, especially at work, is through tokenism. I was at a brewery with Eric, a second-generation Asian Canadian friend I had just met.

We were two beers in and I was already getting tipsy because I'm an absolute lightweight who can't handle alcohol even if my life depended on it. My face was tomato red with the "Asian glow," and we were talking about what it's like to be Asian at work in environments where there aren't many of us.

The concept of competitions between Asians comes up, and he confesses something I felt was powerful: "Sometimes, I feel this pressure to compete against other Asians in the room because there are fewer of us. Even when *we* first met, I felt this instinct to size you up and see what you're about. And I don't always feel that way around white guys."

I nodded aggressively and pointed at what he just said, spilling a bit of beer in the process. "I get that! Like I both find familiarity and camaraderie around other Asians, regardless of their ethnicity, but also this pressure to compete!"

He raised his mug and I raised mine to toast in agreement. He chugged the rest of his beer as I covertly took a small sip and put mine back down. If there's a competition here, I'm definitely not winning it. He gestured for another beer, then said, "I don't know why I've always felt that way, even during high school when I was playing football or in my fraternity, and then later on at work."

I really appreciated his honesty, because this is something I've heard from others before. I've heard of it as "the Asian seat at the table," and I've taken to calling it "the Token Olympics."

Even with the recent rise in diversity, equity, and inclusion initiatives in most companies, these changes seem largely to be about surface appearances—adding the occasional "diversity hire" to boardrooms and teams that used to be an entire ocean of white faces. These initiatives rarely extend beyond corporate lip service; just making sure their end-of-year company photos hold some semblance of diversity (and even putting them up front on display). While I can give some kudos for those who make genuine attempts to create inclusive measures, the reality is most organizations, especially those not as high-profile, still largely treat Asian employees as an afterthought—a self-congratulatory checkmark to be added at the bottom of company quarterly reports or HR memos.

As such, most advice given to Asian Americans can largely be boiled down to: "See? We're promoting and making hires, we've done our part. If you want to succeed, you just need to speak up and network more." But studies show that while Asian American employees are *twice as likely* to join and participate in employee-led groups like Asian Employee Led Resource Groups, almost a quarter of Asian American workers still report feeling excluded in discussions about inclusion at their workplace.

Asian employee resources are generally a low priority for most companies, even ones with more robust diversity initiatives. Returning to the issue of model minorities, it usually means we get whatever is left over in the company HR budget, enough to throw a pizza party but not enough to actually address the real problems. Asian employees are left to fend for themselves when it comes to seeking mentorship, support groups, and leadership advice, which can be additionally uncomfortable since the model minority expectation is we're supposed to have everything together *before* we're accepted. So the very *act of seeking* belonging, ironically, puts our belonging at risk.

This further leads to other problems, like gatekeeping or "crabs in a bucket" mindsets—describing the phenomenon of how a bunch of crabs in a bucket will try to pull each other down if one attempts to climb out. Similarly, if our acceptance is conditional, and we're only really offered a couple of token seats at the table, it means we're pitted against one another for those one or two diversity spots. Just imagine a group of employees, all qualified, but fighting it out like the Thunderdome: TUNE IN TONIGHT AS TWENTY ASIANS ENTER, BUT ONLY ONE WILL GET PROMOTED!

Sometimes, this phenomenon starts early in our lives. Many Asian high school and college students have expressed to me they needed to compete more with other Asian students for opportunities, from extra-curricular competitions during high school to university admissions.

As one student shared with me: "There were times I felt my parents didn't care when I was comparing my progress against white friends. They would say things like white people were different, because they didn't face the same expectations or challenges."

The student went on, "When we were applying for universities, all of my friends knew listing your ethnicity as Asian meant you were limiting your chances of acceptance, because we aren't seen as an under-represented minority group. We needed higher SAT scores, higher GPAs, and we needed to do more sports or extracurriculars that other Asians weren't doing. We were all racing to the same destination, but were running on a narrower track against ourselves."

There's this subtle sense that losing a promotion or an opportunity to a white person is more forgivable as they are supposed to have more resources, more opportunities, so we don't always measure ourselves by the same rulers we measure non-Asians.

Back when I was at the bar with my drinking buddy, I shared these observations. Eric laughed and agreed: "Exactly. It's not uncommon for people to climb the ladder and see there are fewer and fewer Asians the further up they go, so it can feel like you're competing against others for the token spot. Because you're not competing against everyone else there."

He thought further, and shared, "We're just . . . interchangeably Asian, competing with other interchangeable Asians."

We laughed a bit about this, but between the laughter, I could sense the discomfort of shining a light on something that both of us had long discarded in the "Sure but what can you do?" box.

Inter-Asian competitiveness, or the phenomenon of Asians feeling the pressure of competing against other Asians for white acceptance, is a sentiment I've witnessed many times. It's the feeling our "true" com-petition is not against everyone else, but first, among other Asians.

Barriers to Belonging: Gatekeeping, Internalized Racism, and Inter-Asian Racism

If we weren't given permission to compare ourselves to white peers, it can result in Asians being more critical against other Asians and create gatekeeping along with inter-Asian racism—that is, Asians demonstrating racism against other Asians. Racism is a problem, no matter who perpetuates it.

In Ali Wong's Netflix special *Baby Cobra*, she calls this out in a joke: "I think my husband and I have a huge unspoken understanding between each other, because he's half-Filipino and half-Japanese and I'm half-Chinese and half-Vietnamese. So, we're both half fancy Asian . . . and half jungle Asian. . . . The fancy Asians are the Chinese, the Japanese. They get to do fancy things like host Olympics. Jungle Asians host diseases."

This is something I've observed more from past generations than newer ones, but they still cause problems of alienation. Colorism, which is judgment of those who have darker skin colors, is also a common problematic phenomenon. It's not only racist but also classist, due to the association of darker skin with those who perform physical labor outdoors, and it needs to be addressed whenever it comes up.

Inter-Asian racism creates destructive results for Asian diaspora who are all fighting for acceptance and belonging as equals around the world. If anything, we have a greater responsibility to educate and stop ignorance when it's perpetuated because it causes far more harm when it's coming from our own communities, places where we are supposed to experience acceptance and belonging.

This also extends to cultural and ethnic gatekeeping. A common discussion, for example, arises when Americans use the term "Asian" only to refer to East Asians, but not to South Asians, even though culturally we are far more alike than different. We may speak different languages and eat different foods, but we share similarities in our collectivist cultures, our core values, and our upbringing. South Asia is clearly part of Asia. I understand if someone who is South Asian does not identify as Asian, but this choice should obviously be made by each individual for themselves, not by anyone else.

Once, while I was attending a conference with Asian speakers, I was sat next to a woman of South Asian descent. After exchanging the usual pleasantries, I asked how she was enjoying the event. She confessed to me how she's always felt a bit out of place at the events as they were usually filled with East Asian participants and speakers, and how South Asians were typically invisible in these groups, or even outright excluded: "Someone came up to me and thanked me after a panel, and for speaking up for Asians, as if I was an ally and outsider speaking up for another group. She was surprised when I said that I *was* Asian. She didn't seem to know that India is part of Asia."

These kinds of conversations can often explode into arguments online. When Bangladeshi American Audrey Barikdar shared a screenshot of a post debating whether South Asians should be on Subtle Asian Traits—a Facebook community with over a million Asian members around the world—she noted the number of comments that outright claim South Asians can't be Asian because they're brown.

The message was clear: if your skin is darker, you're not welcome to identify as Asian or with other members in the Subtle Asian Traits group. That message, however, disregards simple facts and embraces a distorted view of Asian identity.

The kind of submarginalization that happens to South Asians has created a divide in Asian diasporic communities, with many people of South Asian or Desi descent feeling that they're being judged even in designated safe spaces.

Dr. Suraji Wagage, a clinical psychologist and cofounder and director of the Center for Cognitive Behavioral Therapy and Mindfulness, talks about how spaces of inclusion for Asian diaspora are often guilty of the very exclusion they seek to banish. "When you hear the term 'Asian American,' who do you picture? If you talk about eating 'Asian' food, what type of cuisine do you mean?" She says, "I personally always feel uncomfortable checking 'Asian' when required to select my ethnicity on a form . . . Asian Americans and the AAPI community are not monolithic, though we are often described using umbrella terms, comprising individuals of over 50 ethnic groups from over 20 countries."

When these discussions are brought up, often the response is, South Asians themselves do not always identify as being Asian, preferring to self-identify by their heritage such as Indian or Pakistani over having to debate the association to East Asians. The same issue extends to those of Persian descent or those from West or Central Asia, especially those from Muslim backgrounds since they face further roadblocks in the West.

I find the argument behind these subgroups to be more detrimental than they are helpful. If a Japanese diaspora can find enough commonality with Malaysian diaspora as both are Asian, while still maintaining individuated national identities, why would it differ for Cambodian diaspora or Indian diaspora? And more important, why would we choose to divide ourselves further and marginalize each other, when our goal is to fight for greater recognition and understanding?

This same gatekeeping results in a kind of "No true Asian" fallacy, or feelings that someone is "not Asian enough" because they don't prefer Asian food, don't speak the language of their ancestors, or don't take an interest in Asian culture. Statements like: "How do you not know this, you're Asian!" subtly suggests there is a kind of cultural performativity that has to take place for our already-fragile acceptance, *even in our own communities*. That's a problem.

Years of assimilating, and a long and messy history of colonialism, has resulted in some deep wounds around our ethnic identities. If being Asian is seen as a liability in our work, our social acceptance, and our relationships, it isn't a surprise when there are people who not only hide their identities, but who start to join in on the dominant group's judgment of their own ethnicity.

One of the members of an Asian support group I facilitated once confessed that growing up in a small Texan town, he felt ostracized being one of only a handful of Asians in school. Initially, he would sit with other Asian Americans during breaks and become friends, but when he saw how an Asian friend of his was being bullied by a group of white students, he feared the wrath would turn to him. Instead, over the next few years of his time at school, he found himself spending more time with the "popular" white kids, and never spoke up to defend his past friends even when the bullying continued.

"Anytime someone pointed out things about me that were considered Asian, I'd get defensive. I'd say my mom forced me to learn the language. I'd throw away Asian lunches my parents packed and would rather stay hungry than be seen eating weird food. I'd stay quiet or even join in when Asian jokes were being made. All throughout college, I made sure to only make friends with and date non-Asians. I hated everything about being Asian. I hated my hair color, my eyes, my skin color. I just wanted to be white because it was the only way to not get attacked or stand out."

By the end of his confessional, he was shaking and in tears. He felt so much shame and regret over pressures to eradicate a major part of who he was because it was the only way for him to find social acceptance. Even years later, after embracing his heritage and community and finding pride in his Asian identity, shadows of that pain still lingered.

I've heard so many heartbreaking stories like this over the years, secret identity crisis confessions from both men and women. The stories stem from how they rarely saw Asian characters in media who were heroes or respected, or as a way to hide parts of themselves from being seen as "the other." Some learned to join in judgments against "fobby" (fresh off the boat) Asians—meaning those who were new to the country, and were seen as socially awkward or didn't know how to fit in. That judgment extended to all the features of Asian heritage, including language, appearance, or culture.

This phenomenon of "internalized racism," meaning those who may have developed racism even against themselves and peers of their own race, is also an unfortunate result of years of outright or subtle anti-Asian racism. Especially for those who grew up being conditioned to believe that white people—either their practices or culture, or even just who they are—are superior. Some Asians can adopt a white mindset that results in self-hatred or hatred of their own racial groups without realizing it.

In the words of Nadra Kareem Nittle in her article on internalized racism: "Overall, those suffering from internalized racism buy into the notion that white people are superior to people of color. Think of it as Stockholm Syndrome in the racial sphere."

I've seen firsthand the way internalized racism can be devastating to our community. Clients have shared with me videos from Asian social media users who outright say they refuse to date or marry people of their own race, and instead advocate for dating white or non-Asian romantic interests. Often, the person in the videos or the comments say it isn't that they're discriminating against their own race, but they see all their dating prospects as fitting into certain stereotypes—too close to family, expecting to live with parents until marriage, or traditional family values.

While a part of me can understand how internalized racism can stem from a desire to protect oneself, it doesn't change the fact that some people are using racial discrimination against their own race. Some people live with a generalized view about *all Asians of the opposite sex*, while neglecting how they themselves would likely object to being painted by the same overarching brush.

I can empathize with the anger and hurt after seeing those videos, especially because it comes from other Asian diaspora. Not only does it affect our self-perception and self-esteem, it also feels extra hurtful because it gives those who are already racist toward us ammunition to use against us: "See, even they hate themselves. That's why we're better."

As much as I'd love to celebrate how there seems to be more social acceptance of Asians in the media, the amount of harm created by years of marginalization goes deeper than what's often recognized. Which brings me to the shadow of "Asian acceptance"—the fetishization and emasculation of Asians.

Barriers to Belonging: Fetishization

When it comes to dating, Hana noticed she kept running into the same problem.

The vast majority of the non-Asian guys who'd slide into her DMs seemed always to have the same patterns. They'd go on dates, and while things seemed to go well for a bit of time, she'd notice they always have the same few behaviors or requests.

"One of the biggest red flags is how often they include mentions of my race when talking to their friends. I once dated a guy who would introduce me to everyone as 'my Asian girlfriend.' The first couple of times, I didn't think much of it, but then he'd ask me to say sexy things in Korean when things got intimate or to wear 'Asian' outfits when we went on dates."

Over time, she started to keep track of various "fetish flags" her dates would display. In the beginning, they were usually well concealed, such as in small mentions of how much they loved "women like her" who were "cute and innocent" or comments about how Asians make better wives because they're loyal and don't argue.

If asked more about what they meant, the response is usually a shrug, followed by: "I just like what I like." And further defensiveness is often wrapped up in sentiments of: "Take it as a compliment! Isn't it flattering we find Asian women attractive?"

When it comes down to it, fetishization is a form of objectification, not actual appreciation. In other words, it's not that they're attracted to the women themselves, but to the specific features of what they think Asian women represent to them: submissiveness, domestication, and white worship.

In Hana's case: "It feels dehumanizing in a way, like I'm just an Asian wrapper for them to show off and they don't really care about who I am unless I'm going along with what they want me to be or how I should look."

Asian fetishization has a long history in the West, rooted in the violence of colonialism. Asian women historically were seen as either "dragon ladies," who were sexy, dominant, and dangerous, or "China dolls" and "lotus blossoms," who were subservient and geisha-like in their innocence and docility.

These were common in Western books, movies, or plays such as *Madame Butterfly*, *Miss Saigon*, or even *Austin Powers in Goldmember*. The narratives around them usually involved Asian women who were either in need of rescue by strong, heroic white men, or had to be liberated from the meek, cowardly Asian men. This is worsened by sex tourism to countries like Thailand, in which certain foreigners of those places would specifically target underprivileged locals who turn to sex work out of necessity.

Of course, this doesn't suggest all white people in interracial relationships are fetishizing their partners, or that their Asian partners are participating in white worship or experiencing internalized racism. That's a myth that needs to be abolished, and Asians should obviously feel free to date whoever they want without having to fight off the label of self-hate. Most interracial couples I know in those relationships tend to have perfectly healthy dynamics of mutual respect and admiration for the person beneath the surface.

But the trend is still common and problematic enough that it needs to be addressed, because it still creates feelings of unsafety or uncertainty for so many—am I being objectified and fetishized for my race? Or does this person genuinely like me for who I am? The fact that this question still needs to be a filter in this day and age is frankly embarrassing for our entire society.

While Asian characters in modern television shows still often face stereotyping, the "Asian sidekick" perception is shifting. Complex female Asian leads, such as Kamala Khan's depiction of Ms. Marvel, are showcasing far more in-depth and empowering characterizations of Asian women.

The main benefit of these goes far deeper than simple representation, but actual characterization—pulling back the surface of our racial identity to reveal the human experiences underneath. No longer are we confined to generic "exotic" foreigners who are proficient in kung fu or tech, but multifaceted real characters who have strengths, weaknesses, hopes, and dreams.

And that's what we need more of—not just Asian people who are seen as cultural stereotypes, but actual *human beings*.

Barriers to Belonging: Emasculation of Asian Men

On the opposite side of the spectrum of fetishization are Asian men who, historically, often face media stereotypes of being feminine, unattractive, and *emasculated*.

Similar to the fetishization of Asian women in Western media, there is a catalog of films depicting Asian men as comedic punch lines, like Long Duk Dong from *Sixteen Candles* or as "Asian sidekicks" like Sulu in *Star Trek*—Asian stereotypes who do not fit into Western perceptions of masculinity. Not only that, but it was almost impossible to see Asian men in a sexually desirable light in television or movies.

When martial arts actor Jet Li was given the lead role in the 2000 film *Romeo Must Die*, a reimagined *Romeo and Juliet*, the end scene initially had him kissing his co-star Aaliyah. But at the last second, the script was changed to his hugging his romantic counterpart instead. Though a reimagining of *Romeo and Juliet*, friend-zoning Romeo was head-shakingly flabbergasting. When asked why the scene was changed, the director Andrzej Bartkowiak explained: "Mainstream America, for the most part, gets uncomfortable seeing an Asian man portrayed in a sexual light."

Since the 2000s, there's been scarce improvement. Asian romantic leads, either East or South Asian, are almost all Asian women with white male romantic partners. This isn't only in film or television, but in advertising, media depictions, and even among celebrities. Interracial couples featuring Asian women and white male counterparts are a staple in scripts, especially stories involving some kind of white savior, and yet the reverse is shockingly rare.

The scale of this phenomenon stems from a pretty long history of anti-Asian racism. Early depiction of Asian people "as members of inferior races, depraved heathens, opium addicts, and Yellow Peril invaders were common" throughout the 1800s, and early Asian diaspora masculinity was largely constructed to seem threatening. Then, in the 1900s, perceptions of Asian American men went from dangerous to emasculated and weak, as many were forced into jobs like cooking or laundry, traditionally seen as feminine work.

Online dating sites have revealed how Asian men and Black women were the two groups that generally received the lowest number of matches. For years, the stereotypes plagued the dating prospects of Asian men, where the only exposure their prospective dates had of them were essentially caricatures. In a 2018 journal article, more than 90 percent of non-Asian women said they wouldn't date an Asian man, and 40 percent of Asian women said they would not date an Asian man. Another study found Asian men are twice as likely as Asian women to be single

(35 percent to 18 percent), and in online dating, where choices are made quickly, based on an initial picture swiped aside, Asian men received fewest unsolicited messages from women.

This type of online dating racial hierarchy and sexual racism is almost inescapable in today's world, since so many people now turn to apps for dating. To know you've been excluded from the selection process purely because of your race, before you've even had a chance to send a cute message or friendly hello, undoubtedly sucks. This is particularly disheartening for Asian men who are told they've been dematched because they've been doing what's expected of them—working hard and keeping their heads down, fitting into the model-minority box that they've been told they need to fit into—while also being told that's the problem.

Fortunately, positive change seems to be happening, albeit still extremely slowly.

Starting with the media, TV shows like Andrew Koji's Ah Sahm character on Netflix's *Warrior,* or Daniel Henney's Lan Mandragoran character from Amazon Prime's *The Wheel of Time* are displaying more traditional masculine characters. Simu Liu's *Shang-Chi* showed both the strength and the depth of Asian-diaspora heroes. And of course, hottie Henry Golding from *Crazy Rich Asians* raised the heart rates of many fans when he took his shirt off to reveal his six-pack, the perfect image to go with his stunning smile.

This, alongside the newfound popularity of Asian TV dramas or musicians like the global K-pop craze BTS, seemingly heralds a positive change in the way Asian men are perceived. Anecdotally, more and more of my single Asian male friends have reported how dating experiences for them have improved, with a sudden jump in the number of matches on dating apps.

In my interview with Asian dating coach Aisen Li, who refers to himself as "the Asian Hitch," he shared a funny story about a white male client who said: "I wish I was Asian; you guys seem to be so much more popular with women." We both laughed at this because it wasn't so long ago when many people had the opposite sentiment, which shows how things have progressed in a few short years.

As with every generation, progress is being made and things are getting better. But before we break out the champagne and the RACISM IS OVER banners, it's important to note we are still in the early, fragile phases of true acceptance and integration.

The movement for true Asian acceptance is only beginning and may face more challenges before it gets better. We need to vote with our dollars and our choices to support the idea that, yes, Asian men can be pretty damn sexy.

Again, You Belong Here

When we are taught that our belonging is conditional, it leaves us little room for mistakes. We can feel pressure to appear perfect, both culturally and socially, and we can be fearful that any mistakes could mess things up for everyone else. Hiding mistakes, vulnerabilities, and imperfections can seem like the safest move. However, doing so might hurt us more than we know.

All of us are shaped by our societal, cultural, and familial conditioning. It's like an operating system that's been installed in our minds, guiding us on how to act so we fit in, belong, and thrive. Most of the time, we're entirely unaware of it, and we play out the roles we're given without realizing why we're acting the way we do. This conditioning can show up when we feel guilty for something we don't need to feel guilty about, or when we feel the need to put others before us, or when we choose to hide ourselves to avoid accidentally offending others.

We need to break free of this conditioning so we can recognize our real selves and fulfill our true potential. To do so, we need to start with the awareness of when we are in our roles. These roles we take on are not about being false, but a conditioning that has helped keep us alive and safe. The problem is that this conditioning also hides our true, authentic selves. Our real selves are infinitely more powerful—after all, anything our role self can do, our real self can do better. And once you break through barriers to belonging and tap into your authentic self, an incredible change starts to happen.

Owning Our Belonging

Building Belonging: A Rising Tide Raises All Ships

Now that we've addressed some of the barriers to belonging, let's talk about how we can break down the boxes we're in, build more spaces of belonging, and reach out and support others as they break their own barriers.

Jaya was one client who memorably found a way to do this is at work. Jaya was frustrated with her company's total lack of support for training and development. Management kept telling her they were aware they needed employee development programs for their under-represented groups, but *it just wasn't a priority this quarter*. Years went by and it seemed as if nothing was going to get better, so she took matters into her own hands.

She approached a few of her Asian colleagues she was close to and decided to throw her own leadership training program in her living room on the weekend. For the first meeting, she invited a friend with leadership communication training to come and create a workshop for the group. She provided snacks, and six people showed up. The event went well, and everyone shared how much they learned from the experience. They then set a date to do it again a month later.

At the second meeting, they had eleven people, including other colleagues who had heard about the event and expressed interest. Once again, Jaya provided the snacks. This time, they added a hands-on activity and a discussion group after. And this time the group was much more comfortable contributing different ideas and resources. Once again, the day ended with their planning another event in the next month.

By the third event, Jaya's living room was getting overcrowded with more than twenty people in attendance. They decided to break out into groups and watch short video training sessions, which one of the members had created. People dived deep, shared personal stories about feeling excluded, traded name cards and book suggestions. This time around, everyone brought their own snacks to share, potluck style.

By the end of the day, however, they didn't plan another event in the next month. Instead, they gathered everyone's signatures and wrote a collective letter to their company's management showing that this was not only needed, but there was a measurable demand for it. The collective power of the group, which quickly spread to other departments who had heard of Jaya's actions, proved to be too much pressure for management to ignore. An AAPI Employee Resource Group (ERG) was created, with full funding.

Jaya became the de facto organizer for the group and grew it to over two hundred members across different departments in the company. They still hold monthly workshops and training. This time, the company paid for the snacks.

I love Jaya's story because it is so incredibly simple, yet so inspiring. Going in alone to demand that your boss provide resources can feel intimidating and scary. What if our needs are deemed not important enough? What if we feel guilty, as there are other groups who also need support and aren't getting it first? Are we even allowed to ask?

Of course we have the right to ask, and it's important to know it isn't selfish to ask, because we're also looking to empower others around us. A rising tide raises all ships, and by taking the lead in creating change instead of waiting for others to create it for us, we are actually empowering others to do the same.

Sometimes, there's a reluctance to claim support for Asian individuals because it can feel selfish or self-serving. I recall a conversation with a past client who wanted to create an anti-Asian hate event, but felt self-conscious because he didn't want to overshadow the struggles of his Black friends. I said that if he wanted to support his Black friends, he should absolutely do so, for the two issues serve the same outcome, fighting oppression and violence against minorities.

When you're creating spaces of support, you're stepping into the service of others. Even if you seek the same benefit that would be given to others, it isn't only about you. The change is there to help everyone.

If collectivism is one of our top values, why not treat it as a superpower?

For a lot of people in the Asian diaspora, the hesitance to create groups stems from the fact that they don't want to be pigeonholed. But, ironically, being part of a group is what frees them from being seen as "*that* Asian person." Talking about Asian struggles to the general population, who might not understand the issues, can carry the threat of looking like you're participating in the "oppression Olympics," as if you are a rabble-rouser who is self-victimizing. But when you're part of a group collectively seeking change, that perception fades because you're no longer fighting only for yourself.

Collective bargaining gives us more leverage and protection, especially for those who are new to an environment and are still trying to find their footing. As such, creating spaces of belonging is something almost any one of us can do. It's literally an invitation to people who share a common interest and desire, and finding a time and space for belonging.

I love seeing people create networking groups, mastermind groups, resource groups, or even the "Let's all hang out and grab lunch together sometime" groups at work. Everyone has different comfort levels of how social they want to be, but I've never met anyone who didn't appreciate being invited (so long as they're not *pressured* to go). Even if it takes a few attempts to get the ball rolling, the long-term effects are almost always worth it.

Building Belonging: Being a Champion for Yourself and Others

So far, we've talked a lot about stepping into our self-confidence and self-ownership so we can be more assertive and direct at work, but the truth is that even a lot of the powerful leaders and confident communicators can face obstacles to belonging.

For example, what do you do if you're outright told by your boss you "don't count" as being diverse when asking to start a mentorship program for Asian diaspora colleagues? Or what if you witness discriminations or microaggressions happening to you and other Asian colleagues?

Even for the most confident of us, it's not uncommon to feel the issues aren't worth addressing, since we don't want to seem like we're creating problems for others. And more important, there's a fear of real, tangible consequences to speaking up, even in private. What if speaking up interferes with our careers? What if things go badly and our boss then holds a bias against us? What if our boss labels us a bad team player and gives us a bad performance review for "not fitting in"?

There is no easy way to address hidden racism, but there are strategies. Sometimes, the easiest way to handle it is just by asking a trusted colleague, one who wouldn't be affected by a potential racist employer's wrath, to speak up for you. They can send a quick note saying they observed some bias, even without naming you.

Another thing you can do is approach your HR department and, while pointing out how the bamboo ceiling can exist in other companies and industries, ask if they would consider offering leadership development programs that can help Asian employees get on track for management roles.

The main thing is to talk about this with other Asian colleagues, and then approach the workplace leadership as a casual group. It can feel a lot less intimidating when we're not alone in advocating for ourselves. This is why I often remind people how speaking up is not an act of championing ourselves only; it's for others too.

Share articles, research, or studies listed in this book with others in your organization. Educate people on common issues you've seen where people aren't speaking up for themselves, but should be. Speak up for one another, be an advocate for one another. And soon, you'll notice others rallying around for you as well.

As a champion for change, we can choose to be "the troublemakers" for others, because that's the privilege and responsibility we have.

Building Belonging: Mutual Support

It makes me sad whenever I hear someone from an Asian background talking negatively about another race or deriding another Asian culture. While I know racism between Asian countries exists, I feel we're just perpetuating more hatred, which makes us easier to divide. Though this book's main focus is to help our community rise up, it never calls for any community to take a seat or to feel shame.

There is a long history of other communities coming to our aid, and vice versa. Asian-Black solidarity in the US has had its roots since the 1800s, yet so much of this information goes untaught in school. During the waves of anti-Asian immigration policies in 1869, US civil rights leader Frederick Douglass famously said:

I submit that this question of Chinese immigration should be settled upon higher principles than those of a cold and selfish expe-
diency. There are such things in the world as human rights. They
rest upon no conventional foundation, but are external, universal,
and indestructible. Among these, is the right of locomotion; the
right of migration; the right which belongs to no particular race,
but belongs alike to all and to all alike. It is the right you assert by
staying here, and your fathers asserted by coming here. It is this
great right that I assert for the Chinese and Japanese, and for all
other varieties of men equally with yourselves, now and forever. I
know of no rights of race superior to the rights of humanity, and
when there is a supposed conflict between human and national
rights, it is safe to go to the side of humanity.

In the 1950s, representatives from Asia and Africa gathered at the
Bandung conference to discuss what decolonization would look like.
Starting in that same decade, Grace Lee Boggs, a Chinese American
activist, worked to fight against the struggles for racial justice in De-
troit, and did important work in protesting anti-Black racism.

Yuri Kochiyama was an activist, a Japanese survivor of the internment camps, and a friend and supporter of Malcolm X. She fought
alongside him for Black civil rights in the 1960s. She also did notable
work in advocating for Puerto Rican self-determination, joining the
Young Lords Party, a civil rights organization committed to Puerto Rican independence. In 1977, in possibly one of the coolest stories of
cross-racial support, Kochiyama joined thirty demonstrators in occupy-
ing the Statue of Liberty, and hung a Puerto Rican flag from the statue's
crown. One of her famed quotes was: "Build bridges of understanding
and empathy, even in the face of adversity."

After Vincent Chin's murder in 1982, African American leader Rev.
Jesse Jackson and the NAACP played a major role in bringing national
attention to Chin's case as the victim of a brutal hate crime. In his "Rain-

bow Coalition" speech to the Democratic National Convention, he referenced the case and the rise in anti-Asian violence, and spoke about American solidarity across racial backgrounds.

In the shadow of 9/11, hundreds of Japanese Americans in Los Angeles gathered to protest the mass arrests of Muslims. Fred Korematsu, a civil rights leader who contested his incarceration in WWII to the Supreme Court, filed amicus briefs in two Supreme Court cases challenging the detention of Muslims at Guantanamo Bay, Cuba.

Throughout the history of the US, there have been countless cases of cross-cultural collaboration where we have stood shoulder to shoulder in the common fight against injustice, and this work continues today. Creating belonging for ourselves is as much about creating belonging for others, because our humanity is linked, and we're at our best when we're united.

We can support other racial groups in so many ways, from attending rallies to protest against oppression of Black, brown, or Indigenous communities; to showing up to food drives for low-income communities; to forming BIPOC ERGs at our workplace; to donating to causes that affect cultures aside from our own. We collectively benefit whenever we challenge systems of inequality.

When we include other marginalized communities—the LGBTQIA+ community, the disabled community, or any groups we see as struggling against a system they can't overcome—we gain a deeper understanding and compassion for those around us, and it gives us an opportunity to learn and widen our horizons.

This isn't about addressing others' issues just on a surface level. We must extend genuine care and compassion for all people. It's not "you against me" but "you and me against the patterns that keep us down" or "you and me against the systems that keep *anyone* down."

Building Belonging: Asian Community Groups

In 2016, I was going through a breakup and all the heartbreak and "what am I doing with my life" worries that comes with it. My brother-in-law recommended I join a men's community group he was leading, thinking it could help to have a space to talk about my life problems.

The group was held in one of the member's apartments, with all twelve of us (plus two of his cats) crammed into a small living room, shoulder to shoulder in folding chairs around a circle. I was the only Asian person in the room, and for the most part, all we did was talk about what we were going through in our lives.

The first few meetings, I couldn't really figure out what I was doing there, aside from placating my brother-in-law, who insisted that my life would change from being a part of the group. At the time, I just couldn't see it. Why are we talking about our problems, taking time out of our busy lives that could have been spent working?

But the longer I stayed, the more I started to see benefits. By talking about our problems, and feeling safe from judgment, a sense of camaraderie emerged. Life can be hard, no matter who you are. We're all going through our own individual struggles, and having someone to talk to can be a powerful thing.

In our ancestry, we had natural community spaces. We'd go hunting together or farming, or simply sit around and talk about life as we did things like weave baskets or sing songs or do community dances in courtyards. There was a natural sense of camaraderie that formed a social glue based on mutual understanding. We've now replaced get-togethers with apps and social media, and we lost the community that was present.

Later on, I was talking to Colin, an Asian friend of mine, who also led and facilitated groups like the one I was in. We shared how amazing it was to have a space of unconditional belonging, but also how we wished there were more Asians in the group. There were times when the both of us had felt the desire to talk about certain experiences, like our Asian upbringing or feelings of being a minority, but we had held ourselves back from sharing. So we started an Asian community group, calling it the Waking Dragons. We joked about how the name reminded us of *Dragon Ball Z*, a show we both liked as kids.

Initially, we wondered if we could convince other Asians to be a part of it, so it was initially filled with our own Asian friends. But over time, people kept inviting others to join, and our little group started to grow. We had members from across North America, from California to Texas to Calgary and Toronto, and each week, we met on Zoom to chat about our lives, struggles, and goals in our work, lives, and relationships.

Most people who came to join the groups realize they've felt like they'd been fighting alone most of their lives, even if they were married, had plenty of friends, and had families around them. After all, you can't tell your kids at dinner about your marriage problems, or complain to your employees about how you're not sure if you can make payroll. They first tried going to their friends but found most were interested only in shallow conversations about where to eat or what shows they're watching and didn't understand how to hold space without judgment.

The stability of the weekly group meetings ended up becoming one of the most reliable, solid communities in my life. Whereas friends might move away or disappear into relationships, the group remained solid, and members had one another's backs. People would volunteer to help each other move, even flying to different cities to support one another through particularly difficult times. There was a sense of bonding and unity—we celebrated one another's wins like our own, and gave tough love when necessary.

The results of these groups have been absolutely incredible. I've seen people from our groups:

- Find the courage to leave toxic relationships
- Double their incomes after getting the moral and emotional support to chase after new career goals
- Discover their true passions and launch their dream businesses
- Find the courage to come out to their families

And the fact that we all shared a similar cultural connection deepened the experience even further. I never realized how much I was holding back when I was with non-Asians, just because I assumed they wouldn't find my experiences relatable. In the Waking Dragons group, we talked about family, upbringing, struggles, and I was surprised by how many shared experiences and shared passions we had. We watched old movies from Hong Kong and Japan, went to Indian food and culture festivals, and I even learned how to make pad thai from scratch. (I mean, *I* call the dish pad thai, though my friend who taught me the recipe still refuses to acknowledge my efforts as such.)

Ji-Youn Kim calls this experience Diasporic Joy—the joy of reconnecting with our own culture and all of its incredible expansiveness. This joy comes from sharing experiences like going to Asian movie nights, enjoying Asian snacks, and introducing others to music or hobbies that were part of the greater cultural sphere.

These little experiences have deepened my appreciation for Asian culture tremendously, especially learning from other Asian communities. I got to see my Korean friend's family make kimchi from scratch. I learned more about Pakistani and Indian history dating back centuries. I saw my own family dynamics reflected in my Filipino friend's. The more I saw our differences, the more I realized how similar we really are.

And the more I experienced, the more connected I felt to a part of me that I had not previously gotten to see. I realized that while my white friends never excluded me and I'm deeply appreciative of that, there was a kind of warmth I felt from my Asian communities, like a mix of poignant knowing and acceptance that envelops me as soon as I see them.

It feels expansive, exciting, and also deeply connective.

It feels like coming home.

Big Asian Family

can't quit until my parents die."

In my interview with Amy Yip, the author of *Unfinished Business*, she recounted working with a VP at a major bank who was trying to decide whether to leave her current position to pursue a dream career path. When asked why she hadn't already left, she said, "I can't leave yet. My parents were so proud of me being a VP of a major bank that they'd be heartbroken if I left. *I'm waiting for my father to die so I can finally quit.*"

The sentiment felt both stark and extreme, but also goes to show how much respect and obedience can be present in the Asian culture of filial piety.

No two families are the same, no matter who we are. Some are strict and formal, others are relaxed and easygoing. But *all* families have their struggles, because if there's one thing I've learned about family, it's the more closeness and intimacy, the more opportunities for friction.

Asians are big on family closeness. Take living with parents even after you become an adult. Between 40 percent to 60 percent of adults in Asian countries live in multigenerational households (meaning at least two generations of adults living together). The expectation becomes even more apparent with young adults, between ages of twenty-five and twenty-nine, who mostly have their own careers, spouses, or their own children. In India, for example, 65.3 percent of men aged twenty-five to twenty-nine live with at least one parent. In South Korea, 64.9 percent in the same age cohort reported living at home with at least one parent. That number doesn't change dramatically after marriage, as 59.5 percent of married Indian men and 50.3 percent of married South Korean men reported living with a parent.

This trend doesn't change much even when we move to Western countries. PEW Research has found that while only 16 percent of white Americans live in multigenerational households, 29 percent of Asian Americans do—that's almost *twice* as high, and the highest of any other racial and ethnic group. This uptick is shared by immigrant communities in general, but there is the added cultural factor of Asian filial piety—the duty of a child to obey and respect their parents, and to care for and support them in their old age.

Feelings of family duty run particularly deep among many of us from Asian backgrounds. As adults, we often keep close if somewhat multilayered relationships with our parents. They often depend on us as much as we do on them. We need to make sure they're properly cared for, to ensure that they're not lonely, or to make sure their computers are working properly. We're often taught that since they provided for us in our youth, it'll be our turn to provide for them in their twilight years.

And with that closeness come expectations, obligations, and pressure—all ingredients for a powder keg of conflict.

Our family of origin is usually our first and most important space of belonging, and yet one we often have the least amount of control over. After all, we can't choose our parents or the families we were raised in. It's kind of a take-what-you-can-get scenario, and no matter how hard you try, you cannot change who they really are.

But what we *can* choose is how we interact with them. Remember, just as we accept them for who they are, you also must accept yourself for who *you are*. You deserve the same love, respect, and understanding as anyone else in the family. And you can change your relationships with your parents by deciding how you communicate with them.

For example, I've spoken to dozens of people who have secretly revealed to me how they sometimes still feel guilty for making a decision that might go against the expectations of their parents, such as choosing a career path their parents didn't approve of. Or picking a partner who differs from their parents' expectations, such as not having the right job or being from a different race or culture. There's almost a stereotypical gripe we have: "They told me not to date throughout school, but then once I was in my mid- to late twenties, they suddenly were frustrated I still haven't settled down and had kids yet."

Sometimes, the solutions they come up with are just to hide details of their lives when talking to parents or to go along with what their parents want. Their parents might still lecture them on how to manage their jobs, relationships, and lives, even when they're well into their thirties or forties.

Of course, love ties us together, but there are also expectations, obligations, demands, and friction. The closer we are, the more challenging that relationship can become, and the more complex those *expectations* become. Oftentimes, when I hear these topics being brought up by Asian adults among white friends, the response is often: "I don't get it; why don't you just do what you want, or leave?"

The answer is not so simple. Because most of the time, we do *want* our parents to still be an important part of our lives. We don't want to let them down or fail in our duty to care for them. I've found no matter how much physical distance we place between us and our families, the emotional connections can still run deep. Even for those who have chosen to go low contact (or even cut off contact) with their family members, they're still deeply affected by them emotionally. We love them, we don't want to sever ties; we just wish they would understand us and what we need.

Almost always, when there's a conflict in the family, it's because someone feels their needs aren't being met, or they're feeling they don't matter to you, or vice versa.

Our families *should* be our first space of unconditional belonging. After all, we should be able to be fully ourselves around the people who *created* us, shaped us, and taught us to become who we are. But ironically, sometimes the family home is the place where we first learned to hide who we were in order to belong.

Therapist Sam Louie in *Psychology Today* describes how many of his Asian clients share frustrations when talking about their parents continuing to dictate or lecture them on their lives, and the impact this has on their mental health. He lists common topics, such as: "How to succeed in school or professions, how to date, how to improve their marriages, how to be a 'better' person, but also mundane aspects of life such as how to be 'healthier' (e.g. what you should be eating, how you should be sleeping, etc.)." This might come from parents, as well as from any other extended family, such as aunts, uncles, and grandparents, as they force advice upon us on topics we might in fact be more knowledgable about. And in those instances, it's easier and perhaps more respectful for us to politely excuse ourselves to our bedroom to scream into a pillow.

If this sounds a little like the self-censorship and self-abandonment we talked about in the previous chapters, you'd be correct. After all, where else do we play out our familial roles more evidently than with our families?

The pressures of these expectations, which can seem as deceptively joyous as a parent walking around bragging about our work accomplishments, can reset our internal GPS on who we're supposed to be. After all, even our younger teenage selves knew the feeling of disappointing our parents was far worse than pissing them off.

Over time, these little lectures on how we're doing things wrong, or praise for how we're doing things right by *their* standards, start to calcify into our internal guidelines of personal and familial duty. And if we don't step back to see if who *they* want us to be is truly in alignment with who *we* want ourselves to be, that sense of duty can start to transform into toxic obligation.

The difference between duty and obligation comes down to the intention and source. Being of service to our community and our families is a noble, admirable trait. The acts of giving up our own leisure time to drive our elderly parents around or to care for them in their twilight years can feel incredibly fulfilling. The love and bond of family can be powerful in lifting us up and helping us feel supported. When things are going well, "Family comes first" can be a perfectly wonderful value that is not only something to be admired but something that can give us a sense of greater purpose.

When we feel like we're fulfilling our duty, we're being selfless and good. It's an expression of our love and care for someone who loves and cares for us. But if that incredible gift of duty comes from a place of self-abandonment, where we feel we're not doing it out of love but out of shame, guilt, and resentment, our duty becomes a toxic obligation.

That's when all the joy, the good, and the beauty that comes from deeper connection fades. Instead, we become ashes of ourselves as we burn ourselves out.

Rebuilding the Bridge as Adults

In many cultures in the world, there are ceremonies for transitioning from childhood to adulthood. Adulthood is important because as we grow up, we go through a period in our adolescence when we figure out who we are, separate from our family identity. In Jungian psychology, this is called individuation. From adolescence to adulthood, we learn to stand on our own and develop our full sense of self and *become our own person.*

At an early age, this might be figuring out your own identity, personality, and true self. It might mean breaking from familial roles, prescriptive gender identities, familial values, and just about anything. That self-discovery can be bumpy and occasionally awkward, especially when we look at old photos of our blunder years and go "Oh my god I can't believe I went through a goth phase."

If we have a family that supports us in this exploration and accepts our journeys of self-discovery, we'll eventually figure out who we want to be. But if our families are more strict about who they expect us to be, this can create some long-term struggles. When we experience constant micromanaging, we might start questioning our own decisions, feeling anxiety around who we are, and deep doubts about our sense of purpose or sense of self. And if we get used to abandoning our true selves in this stage, we often get used to abandoning ourselves in our future relationships as well.

In Western, individualist societies, the transition to adulthood is usually marked by a child moving out or starting their own life. In close-knit, collectivist families that live together with strong familial hierarchies, the transition can look a bit different but ultimately still have the same result. That is, if you lived with your parents but they were totally fine with you being whoever you choose to be, then your path is no different from those who moved out. Becoming fully individuated doesn't have to mean leaving your family. It's entirely possible to have a healthy self-identity as an equal adult in a multigenerational home.

Problems arise if you reached adulthood but weren't given the full permission to figure out who you were, because your parents required you to become whomever they expected you to become. Sometimes, this can create longer periods of feeling stuck, lost, or even like you're a perpetual child.

Being able to reconnect with our parents *as equal adults* is, however, an absolutely essential stage of our lives. We're not being selfish to want our parents to treat us with more respect. If we were equal adults, that would also give our parents permission to be themselves around us.

By the way, when I say "equal," I don't mean that you can't still respect your parents as your elders, or respect the family hierarchy that you choose to value, or look up to them as your parents. Ideally, you would take full responsibility for your self-ownership, just as your parents do. You're equal human beings in that regard.

The parent-child roles we had in our childhoods aren't meant to be kept for our entire lives. After all, how can we go back and take responsibility and care of our parents in their old age (if that's what you choose to do), without shouldering the responsibility and care of ourselves first?

We're *supposed* to go through a growth period, and then we're supposed to come back and reengage. In adulthood we take responsibility for ourselves, and we can also rebuild a new and deeper relationship with our parents. With this shift, *they* also can break free from the roles they were in.

The change to a more *equal* relationship, however, can be challenging for some parents, because they might feel cemented into their roles and are comfortable in them. But the change is necessary if we want to have a closer, more authentic relationship.

And for those who still feel they're a kid around their parents, this can take a little mental restructuring.

Kennie's Story

For example, I was talking with Kennie, a twenty-eight-year-old, second-generation Korean American. She's been struggling to tell her parents about a relationship she's kept secret because her partner is a woman of a different race and culture, and she fears her parents would not be able to accept her.

"I've tried to sit down and talk to them about it so many times, but each time, I struggle to get the words out. My partner is really understanding and patient, but it's not fair to keep her a secret anymore. I feel like I'm stuck between her and my parents. I'm at a point where I'm considering not telling them until after we get married, so they can't interfere, but my family is important to me and I don't want to cut them out."

When I asked why she doesn't tell her parents calmly and deliver it as a fact, she said, "I can't, they just treat me like I'm still a child."

I asked, "You said previously you have a strong personality and don't take crap from people. So what would happen if a friend of yours ever tries to talk to you like a child or talk down to you?"

"I wouldn't let them."

"Exactly!" I said. "You wouldn't *let* them, but you *let* your parents. You are the one in control of how you're talked to, but you've been allowing them to cross your boundaries, time and time again."

She shook her head. "Yes, but that's because they're my parents. Of course they're different from my friends. I'll get mad but I can't imagine actually telling them off. It's so disrespectful, and I don't want to do that."

"Of course, and let's just be clear that you're not disrespecting them at all by telling them who you really are. In fact, isn't it far more disrespectful to lie to someone and then resent them behind their back?"

She agreed.

"So perhaps this isn't just a *them* issue. Would you like to try a quick visualization exercise?" She's used to doing this with me by now, so she nodded and closed her eyes. "Okay, so picture yourself sitting or standing in front of your parents, talking to them. Can you now try saying what you wanted to tell them?"

She took a deep breath and started speaking, "Mom, Dad, I've been in a relationship with someone for the past six months, but I haven't told you this before. She's a woman, and she's wonderful. She takes care of me, we're in love, and I want to marry her, and I know that's something that you might not approve of."

Even though the conversation was purely imaginary, her voice gave away her reluctance. She was pushing out the words, but the words dropped and faltered. Her arms were folded over her chest protectively.

"Okay, can you hear them responding?" I asked.

"Yes, they're unhappy," she said. Even with her eyes closed, she winced as she said this, as if bracing for an attack.

"They're unhappy. Okay, now let's zoom out, like you're watching a movie and the shot is widening to include your parents and you, all in the same frame. Can you do that?" She nodded. "Now, try to notice that you're not just looking at yourself and your parents; you're also looking at three adults. Three adults having an adult conversation with each other. Is that something you can envision?" I gave her some time to settle into this vision, but she struggled with it for a bit. For some, this is an easy thing to do, and for others, it takes a little more work.

"I can't access it. They see me as a kid, so I see myself as a kid."

"Ok, let's do a body scan. Are you feeling anything in your body? What would the feeling say if it had a voice?"

She nodded. "I feel a tightness in my stomach and my neck." She placed the tips of her fingers on the base of her throat. "The feeling says she's sorry. She feels like a little kid, and she's scared she did something wrong and is going to get punished. She's so sorry. She just wants to be good so people won't be mad at her." Tears rolled from her closed eyes and she wiped them away.

"Is there anything you want to say to that part of you?"

"Just that I'm here with her, and I've got her, and she didn't do anything wrong." She put a hand over her stomach, and another over her chest.

"Okay, so let's come back to the image. This time, let's pull away the scared version of yourself from this image and replace it with a different one. Can you remember the last time you felt independent, strong, and in control?"

"Yes, when I ran a marathon and won a medal."

"Great, can you put the image of that confident, proud version of yourself in front of your parents? Let me know when you can see her with the other two adults in the room." This time, she's able to see it. The reality is, they *are* just three adults talking. But it can be hard to see, with all the roles and obligations in our way. "Okay, let's press play. See the confident, proud version of yourself tell your parents what you want to tell them. This time, let's take a look at your mother, through your adult eyes. How does she look?"

"She's worried for me. She sees my father being angry and is worried for both him and for me. She's more understanding and accepting, and wants me to be happy. But she knows my dad is very traditional. I just want to give her a hug and let her know she doesn't need to worry about me, I can take care of myself, and Dad will be fine."

"Great, do that."

She imagined giving her mom a hug, putting her hand on her chest as she takes a deep, accepting breath.

"Now, how does your dad look? And what would your adult self say to him?"

"He's angry and upset. And disappointed. He doesn't understand and doesn't want to understand. He's stubborn." Her forehead wrinkled, then smoothed. "She'd tell him the truth, that she understands. She understands he's always had a vision for her, and who he wanted her to be with. She'd say she understands the image of his daughter is different from what she turned out to be, and that can be hard. But also that this version of her isn't bad either. She's happy, she's in love, and she's cared for by someone really special. And that's an amazing thing, and she hopes he will one day be proud of her for that. And that no matter what happens, she would always still love him. And she hopes he'll love her for who she is."

With this, she opened her eyes and gave a soft smile.

I ask, "So, how do you feel?"

"Good. I know what I need to say now," she says, with a voice of calm certainty and clarity. Then, she added a final thought: "I think everything is going to be okay."

When I checked in with Kennie later on, she was proud to say she spoke her truths to her parents. She also said that while the initial conversation was difficult, they were both eventually able to slowly come to accept her in follow-up conversations. But it took repeated attempts of Kennie standing in her own adult power, rather than falling into her old childhood patterns of giving in or self-silencing to appease them. She talked about how she had to refuse to give in to screaming matches, and remained calm and understanding each time to explain how this was the reality of who she was.

Expecting our older parents to change is a tough thing. Change can be hard. Sometimes *really* hard, because to change our roles sometimes is to lose ourselves and the things we used to feel safe.

Seeing your child as an adult might mean losing your purpose as a parent, and your role in guiding your children to make what you've been taught were "right" ways to be. And if you find out what was "right" has changed, it can pull your entire identity as a "good parent" into question.

The purpose of this exercise and this step is not meant to be a guide for how you should speak to your parents. That's up to you to decide, but by your adult self rather than your child self. Only after you can find that voice can we really start communicating.

Exercise: Three Humans

This exercise works best with your eyes closed, so read through the instructions first, then give it a try.

With your eyes closed, picture yourself in a conversation with your parents. It might be a more challenging one, like telling them about a decision that you know they won't approve of. Picture yourself saying what you want to say to them, and notice if you see any reactions from them. Maybe they're expressing concern or disapproval, maybe they're telling you what they think you should do. Whatever it is, let the little scenario begin to play out.

Now zoom out of the image, so you can see yourself in the frame of the conversation. Notice your body language and facial expressions. Then, take a moment and recognize you're not just looking at yourself and your parents. You're looking at three adults talking to each other. That's all you are in this scenario—three grown adults having an adult conversation. This might be easy or difficult to do, but either way, stay with the practice until your mind can fully recognize that it's just three adults.

Now, still zoomed out, notice if what they're saying to the image of you still seems appropriate for a grown adult to be saying to another grown adult. Your mind might come up with "but they're *not* just three adults, they're my parents, which is different"—which is fine, this is just an experiment.

Notice their body language, their tone of voice, and the words they're using. Ask yourself: "Is this what an adult should say to another adult?" And if the answer is *no*, ask: "How should an adult respectfully address being talked to in this way?"

This is a practice that can be repeated as many times as you need. If you ever find yourself wanting to revert to your childhood behaviors, take a moment and zoom out, take a breath, and ask: "Can I see the three adults?"

If you can, then start asking: "As an adult speaking to another, how would I ask for my needs to be met, while still being compassionate?"— What might your words to them be? What kind of language would you accept in return?

If they speak or do things that you once accepted as a child but no longer feel it is appropriate to accept as an adult, maybe it's time to set some boundaries.

How to Set Boundaries with Family without Pushing Them Away

This seems really counterintuitive, but setting clear boundaries with our family members actually brings us closer together, rather than further apart.

This is because no matter how much we resist communicating our needs, we will always unconsciously find ways to meet them. Maybe our parents keep commenting on our relationships. Maybe we know we could set a boundary and say, "Hey, if you don't have anything positive to say about my boyfriend, I'd rather just not talk about him at all, because I'm happy with my choices. When you keep criticizing him, it feels like you're saying my needs and happiness don't matter as much as yours." But instead, we might just opt to not tell them about our relationships at all, or we might avoid their calls.

Think about the impact of that. Instead of actually asking for what we want, we end up being emotionally avoidant. Then our parents will feel they're being kept out (because, well, they are), and as a result, they nag and pry even more. It creates a negative cycle that creates more resentment on both sides.

Another problem arises when people go into dismissiveness or passive agreement when dealing with their parents, as a self-protective mechanism. People might say, "Yes, yes, yes, fine, yes I heard you, okay," but without really listening and without any intention of following through. Or people might even outright ignore their parents. This isn't actually bringing closeness, just more closed-offness. Neither the parents nor the children are set up to win in these scenarios; they're just tolerating each other's presence.

Boundaries are like guidelines for harmonious relationships. Below, I've listed a few different ways that boundaries can be created in a guilt-free manner, as well as how to handle certain challenging situations.

BEHAVIOR AND TOPIC BOUNDARIES

We can set boundaries with *behaviors* or *topics* without creating distance from *people*.

Let's say one of your parents has a habit of making comments about your weight, and they might even be a bit toxic about it, saying that you're overweight or telling you to diet. Instead of dreading the next phone call, set a clear boundary and a *consequence*: "Hey, when you talk about my body like that, it makes me feel bad about myself, and I don't like feeling bad when I'm around you. So I'm not going to talk about food or my weight with you anymore, and if you bring it up, I'm just not going to answer, because I care about our relationship. Do you understand?"

And most important, keep your word. If they bring it up again, remind them once: "Hey, this isn't something I want to talk about," and then after that, just say, "Let's talk about something else."

Do *not* get pulled into reexplaining or justifying why you're not engaging. Remind them that you've already explained, and it ultimately doesn't matter what the reasoning was, you want this behavior to stop. If they try to push your buttons by calling you too sensitive or saying, "We just want the best for you," say, "I know you care about me and I appreciate your concern. I can take care of myself. Let's talk about something else."

Boundaries can feel a little jarring at first for those who aren't used to them, because you're introducing a new relationship dynamic. This can be particularly challenging if the person you are setting boundaries around sees the act of crossing your boundaries as an *act of closeness*. This can be similar to how a friend might badger you to tell them a secret you don't tell anyone else.

These attachments to crossing boundaries can be rewired and reassociated. This is why I always stress that when we assert our boundaries, we can still remain compassionate to the person and reassure them that they're still loved. Let them know that the boundaries are being set so that you can tell them more about the things that *do* matter to you, and that boundaries allow you to reestablish a new, stronger relationship with them.

ADVICE BOUNDARIES

My mom loves to give me advice. She reads a lot of stuff on the internet, and then she sends me countless articles and random YouTube videos on everything from how to choose the best pair of socks for a hike (neither of us hikes) to how to properly peel a radish (I've never, ever peeled a radish in my entire life).

Now, I'm grateful to have parents who are so caring, but sometimes, I'm just not looking for any advice on a certain topic. However, it doesn't change how much she still very much wants to help, especially when she shows up with a pair of hiking socks she and I both know will never get worn. Or when she insists that I eat more radishes (they're good at lowering heat!) even though I really, really don't care for radishes.

For most of our adult relationship, I've largely just nodded along and accepted advice, but I never actually told her I'm not looking for more. I'd either argue back against her points, which launches us into hour-long debates, or I'd throw my hands up and do things her way. However, sometimes the advice can get into things that are much more involved, like my relationships or my career—things that will create lasting impact in my life that I can't easily shrug off just to make her happy. I've come to realize that receiving her advice can be like receiving her radishes—she can keep piling them on my plate, but I don't have to eat any of them.

Advice, like her gifts of radishes, is about two things: the sentiment of care, and the actual gift itself. And I can receive the care without having to use the gift. Instead of doing what I used to do, which was say yes and then do whatever the hell I wanted to do anyway, I realized

I could improve our dynamic by simply acknowledging her care and intent.

This is where compassionate assertiveness comes in again. Compassionately receive the sentiment of care behind the advice, and then assert the boundary after.

Let's say, purely hypothetically, she's insisting (once again) that I need to have kids *right now*, even though that's not in my current plans. In the past, I'd argue with her about how "I don't want kids right now. I don't have time to take care of them and I have different priorities," which usually would escalate things into a bigger discussion that I don't need or want. But let's say that this time, I go straight to acknowledging the love instead.

I would start by making sure she feels heard: "I get what you're saying. You're saying that kids are really important because one day they can take care of us in our old age, and the sooner we have them, the easier they'll be to take care of. Family is important and should be prioritized. Is that what you mean?"

Then, if she says yes and is satisfied I that understand her points, I'll smile and say, "You're right, family is important, I agree and I really appreciate you caring for me. You're the best, Mom!"

If she keeps trying to pull me into a debate, at this point I can simply stand firm, repeating my decision until she realizes I'm serious about this boundary. "I'm still not planning on having kids now, and I'm not looking to change that decision. But again, I really appreciate the love."

Receive the love, leave the radishes (that is, unless you really like radishes).

CREATE SPACE

Sadly, boundaries are not merely a "set it and forget it" type of situation. People need to be reminded, sometimes repeatedly, especially if the behavior is generational.

The family roles we take on, which can even include enmeshment and codependency, are often passed down. Your parents learned it from their parents, who learned it from their parents, and so on and so forth. When you're a kid, you may have learned that some boundaries aren't allowed. But as an adult, you are allowed to change the dynamic to a healthier one that works for *you*.

However, sometimes, no amount of acknowledging care will stop people from constantly trying to step over your spoken boundaries.

In those cases, remember that you have the power to *create space*.

I once had a friend who made it very clear with her parents that she would not discuss her relationships and marriage with them, as a rule. When her mother immediately cast her boundary aside ("Aiya, we're your parents! Of course we have to ask!"), she drew a clear line and said, "Mom, I love you, and I love spending time with you, but the next time you make a comment about my relationship, I'm just going to leave because it really makes me sad."

Then, while having dinner at her parents' place one night, her mother made a snide comment about her relationship. With that, my friend stood up, said calmly and without blame, "All right, I love you, and I'll see you guys for dinner next week!" and drove home. Her mother left dozens of messages (which went ignored, as they were all about her relationship). But by the next dinner, her mother had learned not to comment about it again.

This may sound extreme, and maybe even rude. But remember that *you* are also a member of the family. You have needs that deserve to be met, and it's okay that your need for respect is *just as valid* as their need for respect.

GUILT TRIPPING

Another behavior you might not want to put up with is *guilt-tripping*.

Guilt-tripping is a form of emotionally manipulative behavior. It's not some moral fault in the person; it's usually a learned response that comes from the guilt tripper not knowing how to actually *ask* for their needs, so they use guilt or shame to get what they want. And just because someone wants to take you on a guilt trip doesn't mean you have to board the guilt train.

I've heard of parents saying things like "You never call me. One day when I'm dead you're going to wish you can call me, but it'll be too late!" or "I wish you visited more often; whenever you visit, it's always so short; I'm going to be alone in a senior home one day."

When someone is trying to guilt-trip you, don't get defensive. Guilt trippers *want* people to get defensive because then they know they have their emotional hooks in. Instead, *ignore the guilt trip* and get really direct about what's underneath: "Hey, Mom, it sounds like you miss me. I miss you too, and I do want to see you. I appreciate our times together."

Remember that guilt-tripping, emotional coercion, or threats of abandonment are often learned behavior from those who, at some point in their life, didn't feel they could just ask for what they want, and may have felt forced to resort to emotional manipulation as the only strategy to get their needs met.

And if we see a family member resorting to this technique, we can hold compassion for their experience, while also holding compassion for ourselves so that we aren't sacrificing ourselves. By holding compassion for the part of them that has a need, we can be direct in communicating to that need. Ask them: "Hey, when you bring up something like that, it makes me feel sad. Are you feeling like you're being neglected?" (You'll likely experience some defensiveness around this, but it's important to check in.)

Then skip past the guilt trip, and go right for the need and solutions: "How about this; the next time you're looking at the phone and wishing I'd call, just send me a text message and I'll try to call you as soon as I am available." Offer what you're actually able to give, and what you actually want to give from a glad heart, *not* from a sense of obligation.

For this specific example, it might mean setting up a monthly family dinner, it might be putting something in both of your schedules for a regular phone call, but it's got to be a solution that you *both* find satisfactory.

If you're dealing with someone who has a tendency to want to keep chatting for longer than you're comfortable with, you can also set time boundaries early on. This might be a quick note at the beginning of the call: "Hey, I've got something to do at 6:30 tonight, so I can talk until then, is that okay? How are you doing?" This way, when 6:30 p.m. rolls around, they don't feel you're just cutting them off, because you already told them what you're available for.

WORST-CASE SCENARIOS: DISCONNECT

Is there is someone in your family who is not able to respect your boundaries, who continuously berates, attacks, or belittles you to the point that they're outright toxic or even abusive, yet you can't leave? There is always being a "gray rock."

The Gray Rock Method is taught by a number of clinical psychologists, especially those who deal with abusive or toxic behavior. Basically, it's emotional disengagement, so the abuser is talking to an uninteresting, unassuming gray rock. This is generally reserved for those family members who simply cannot stop being toxic or abusive, who simply have not done their own work enough, so they lash out at others. If you can't leave in these situations, act like you're a gray rock. Give boring, one- to two-word answers like "yes," "no," "okay," and "uh-huh." No emotional comments, no personal details. If you must, give basic factual information in the most boring, neutral tone possible. If they're making statements that are deliberately trying to get a rise out of you, shrug or ignore it. Eventually, they'll find you so boring they'll, hopefully, move on.

And if they don't move on or if their behavior is actively harming your mental health or others you care about, there is the final line of going low or no contact.

The goal when it comes to any family dynamic is to try to bring people closer together harmoniously. But there are some people who simply cannot help themselves. They may be abusive, controlling, or toxic to the point your mental health is at risk, or god forbid, they start affecting your children. In these kinds of situations, cutting off contact is not about pushing others away but about protecting ourselves and those we love. It's also an invitation for them to return in the future, once they're able to stop themselves from causing harm.

Sometimes, *temporary distance is necessary for future closeness.*

We cannot change people. But we can change our dynamics with them, we can change how we speak to them, and finally, we can change how much we let them affect us. I know people who have had to deal with such abusive remarks and behavior, or general actions that create great discomfort or unsafety, that they simply felt they needed to create distance by not speaking to their family members, either until their mental health has improved or until their own kids are older. When it comes to outright abuse, there is no excuse, and there is no need for justification.

Tell them the behavior you're distancing from, and let them know if they change their behavior, you might consider returning. Until they acknowledge the change needed in their behavior, you can simply create distance and disengage, emotionally and physically. There is no need to feel bad about this; you're protecting yourself and those you love.

If your hope is to one day reconnect to them, you can always leave the door open by letting them know clearly what you need them to change before you're willing to reconnect. This way, they still have the opportunity to return, but it's up to them whether they can decide to make that change.

No matter what, there is *never* an excuse for accepting abusive or toxic behavior.

Journaling: Writing a Letter You'll Never Send

Once we are able to see our parents as human beings, a lot of stuff might start coming up. Things we may not have allowed ourselves to say, or feel, or even *think*, while we were in our child roles.

You might feel gratitude for seeing how difficult it was for them to have gone through what they did. You might feel some sadness over how you wish they had the emotional awareness to raise you differently. You might feel a mixture of pride, of joy, of just about anything, or nothing at all. You might even feel anger or resentment, and maybe even guilt *about* feeling anger or resentment. That's okay. It's important to remember that *having feelings* is not the same thing as acting on those feelings, and to not judge ourselves for them.

Whenever I find my mind getting noisy or if I notice I'm carrying on an ongoing conversation in my mind, I'll grab my journal and write a letter I'll never send. The point of the exercise is to clear out whatever we've been holding on to, so that we don't have to keep carrying them in our mind.

Sometimes, I'll just let whatever needs to emerge pour out. It usually starts with a prompt like "Dear Mom, something I never told you was . . ." and let the words flow.

In some cases, I'll write out the full conversation I'd imagine would take place, including what I think they'd say, and my responses. The point isn't to make the conversation accurate, but to clear the system. After that, I'd either put it away in a drawer or even tear out the page and burn it.

I often recommend writing letters we never send on a regular basis, and it's not uncommon for me to write to my own parents without ever letting them know the contents. Remember they, as humans, have also grown and changed over the years, as you have. They might not be the same people now as they were when they raised you in your youth, and you are not the same person either. Just because something needs to be said doesn't mean it needs to be heard to be helpful.

Is there a letter in you that is needing to be expressed? If so, here are some prompts to try:

Something I never told you was . . .

Something I wish you had known was . . .

Something I regret was . . .

Something I hope you never find out is . . .

Something I am grateful for is . . .

Something you taught me was . . .

Something I wish you'd taught me was . . .

In this process, the most important thing is to not edit, self-censor, or judge. The purpose of this exercise is to put your thoughts into words so we can release whatever secret feelings we may have been holding on to. Some of our writings might be surprising, others might feel guilt-inducing, and others might be downright silly when you see them on the page, but all of it is here for a purpose.

After you're done, if you feel so inclined, you can also read back over the letter and look to see if there were any of these themes:

- **Permission:** If there are parts in the letter where you realized you were seeking permission—to make a decision, to speak your mind, to follow a certain desire—can you give that permission to yourself?

- **Forgiveness:** If there are parts in the letter where you were seeking forgiveness, can you give yourself that forgiveness, first? Note that seeking forgiveness from someone else is not the same thing as seeking forgiveness from yourself. It's possible to not forgive yourself for something others have forgiven you for, and vice versa.

- **Debts and Grudges:** If there are parts in the letter where you refuse to forgive them, does it make sense to keep carrying that grudge? Or would it be better for you to let your resentment go and forgive? What debts and ledgers have you been secretly tracking with this person? Does this tracking still serve you?

If after writing out your thoughts, you feel like voicing some of the things you wrote down to the other person, you can, but I usually recommend people wait a few days to let things settle first before speaking. And before they speak, they should always ask: "What is the intention I hold in sharing this? What do I hope to happen?" Maybe it's acknowledgment, maybe it's understanding, or maybe you just need to know you've said it.

You can repeat this exercise with *anyone* in your life, and you'll likely find there are some deep and important messages you've been keeping from yourself.

Breaking the Generational Patterns

If your parents didn't speak Italian growing up, chances are, you didn't either. Obviously, because language is a skill that's passed down from generation to generation.

The same goes for understanding emotional maturity. If someone didn't grow up hearing a lot of words like "I love you" or "I'm really proud of you," they may never have had that modeling to pass those words down to their kids. It might even be because they were taught that too much praise could spoil a child, or that being too emotional as a dad makes them not manly. Who knows? To this day, whenever I hug my dad and tell him I love him, the best I've been able to get out of my dad is a warm smile and a wave with "Okay, yes, yes." Which I believe is *his* version of "I love you too."

That's enough for me, because I understand that that's how he was raised.

Generally, many Asian parents I've encountered didn't focus on addressing their children's emotional needs through words. They don't always share warm feelings, like telling their kids that they love them or are proud. Most may not have known how to teach their kids how to process difficult emotions, saying, "It's okay if you're feeling sad, Mom and Dad get sad sometimes, just like you, so let's talk about it." Talking about feelings is generally not a common trait, let alone vulnerable admissions of their own feelings. Asian communities might dismiss skills of emotional literacy as mental health topics, and can even stigmatize those seeking out emotional health. The message often is that "bad feelings" are a negative mark on the family's appearance and should be kept secret to protect the family from shame.

But in that secrecy, there often hide little demons in the shadows.

In the study "Disempowering Parenting and Mental Health among Asian American Youth," scientists examined ways that disempowering parenting can impact children and their mental health. The researchers organized their findings into "ABCDG" categories, which stands for "Abusive, Burdening, Culturally Disjointed, Disengaged, and Gender Prescriptive."

Abusive Parenting is about harsh or punitive forms of parenting styles, and uses examples like "My mom punishes me when she's angry" or "My mom makes me feel unloved if I misbehave."

Burdening Parenting is about harmony and sacrifice for the sake of the family, and uses examples like "My mother pressures me to go to a top college" or "When I get a poor grade, my mother makes me feel guilty."

Culturally Disjointed Parenting is about intergenerational cultural conflict, like "My parents expect me to behave like a proper Korean boy or girl, but I feel my parents are being too traditional" or "My parents don't want me to bring shame upon the family, but I feel that my parents are too concerned with saving face."

Disengaged Parenting refers to emotional neglect or failure of parents to validate or support their children's feelings, or being emotionally distant, like "My mom sees me as a big nuisance" or "My mom makes me feel unloved if I misbehave."

Gender Prescriptive Parenting is about gender expectations, particularly toward girls, like "My parents think that girls should not stay out late" or "My parents think that girls should not date while in high school, but boys are allowed to date as they want."

The researchers examined large-scale samples of Korean American and Filipino American families, and examined how these five disempowering parenting styles have a dramatic impact on mental health, including depressive symptoms, suicide ideation, and even, tragically, suicide attempts. They found that among the respondents who had experienced disempowering parenting styles, there was a disproportionately higher degree of depressive symptoms.

What was perhaps most heartbreaking is the statistic that nearly 17 percent of Korean American girls and 16 percent of Filipino American girls confessed to suicidal ideation, possibly due to the added gender pressures. By comparison, 7 percent of Filipino American boys and 9 percent of Korean American boys felt the same.

There's little doubt that all these parents love their children deeply and want what's best for them, but emotional literacy is a skill that must be learned in order to break these patterns.

The book *Adult Children of Emotionally Immature Parents* by Lindsay Gibson talks about the various experiences people feel when they grow up with parents who didn't learn emotional literacy skills themselves. She outlines common experiences her adult clients have had, like emotional loneliness, self-destructive patterns, and patterns such as seeking out problematic romantic relationships as a result of growing up with parents who didn't know how to handle their own emotional experiences in a healthy way—let alone teach healthy emotional expression to their kids.

In a healthy parent-child relationship, parents don't just provide for the physical needs of their children (like food or a roof over their heads), but also emotional needs like unconditional love, safety, and belonging.

I often see adults who feel they're lacking self-confidence due to parental rejection, feeling lonely or unable to form new friendships, distrusting their own instincts or decisions, trying to be a caretaker to their partners, and they spend their entire lives trying to win approval or validation from everyone they meet. And often, it's because they had emotionally immature parents who didn't demonstrate how to process their own emotions or how to be responsible for them. And just as being physically present isn't the same thing as being emotionally present, being physically mature doesn't make us emotionally mature.

I again want to emphasize that the goal here isn't to blame parents. Blame doesn't do anything to help the situation. But understanding what has been passed down allows us to decide what we want to keep—and what we're ready to shed, especially as we look to the next generation.

Gibson provides a helpful checklist to identify some signs of emotionally immature parents:

☐ My parent often overreacted to relatively minor things.

☐ My parent didn't express much empathy or emotional awareness.

☐ When it came to emotional closeness and feelings, my parent seemed uncomfortable and didn't go there.

☐ My parent was often irritated by individual differences or different points of view.

☐ When I was growing up, my parent used me as a confidant but wasn't a confidant for me.

☐ My parent often said and did things without thinking about people's feelings.

☐ I didn't get much attention or sympathy from my parent, except maybe when I was really sick.

☐ My parent was inconsistent—sometimes wise, sometimes unreasonable.

☐ If I became upset, my parent either said something superficial and unhelpful or got angry and sarcastic.

☐ Conversations mostly centered on my parent's interests.

☐ Even polite disagreement could make my parent very defensive.

☐ It was deflating to tell my parent about my successes because it didn't seem to matter.

☐ Facts and logic were no match for my parent's opinions.

☐ My parent wasn't self-reflective and rarely looked at their role in a problem.

☐ My parent tended to be a black-and-white thinker and unreceptive to new ideas.

If you grew up with emotionally immature parents, all that might mean is no one taught you the tools you needed to independently process how you feel, which is admittedly a difficult thing for everyone. After all, even therapists have therapists. Knowing why we play out

314 • BIG ASIAN ENERGY

unhealthy patterns and how to label our traumatic experiences is not enough; we need to actually heal.

Many emotionally immature parents were themselves brought up feeling emotionally lonely, and grew up with limited freedoms of emotional self-expression. As such, they may say ambiguous things like "You'll understand when you have kids of your own," because that's how they were raised and so that's the only way they ever learned. "I turned out pretty good, so there's nothing wrong with the ways that I'm teaching you" ends up becoming a bit of a mantra, but the truth is that every generation of parents gets to choose what they want to keep and what they want to pass on to the next generation.

And of the various ways emotional immaturity can get passed down, one of the big ones is emotional invalidation.

Emotional Invalidation

Have you heard any of these things in your upbringing?

- "Stop looking so sad; don't you know how good you have it?"
- "Calm down; you're always so emotional."
- "You don't have any reason to be depressed."
- "You should feel more grateful for what you have!"
- "You're being too selfish with your feelings. Just deal with it."

Which are really silly things to hear when you think about it. What am I supposed to say? *"Just stop feeling sad? Oh, thanks, I'm cured!"*

I can't turn off feeling hungry if I haven't eaten. I can't turn off feeling tired if I haven't slept enough. We can try to focus on different feelings to distract ourselves, and even repress certain emotions for a brief period of time, but they'll still be there in the shadows of our minds, and may still affect us.

If I'm feeling particularly anxious or emotionally charged, I can meditate, do box-breathing, and practice mindfulness. If I'm feeling agitated and angry, I can release some of that pent-up energy by punching a pillow or yelling into blankets. All these techniques will help with bringing back some peace into my body. But it's a myth that we can control our emotions simply by ignoring them. Feelings need to be felt and released, not guilted or shamed. Sure, we can self-medicate with distractions like social media, sex, or substances, but they're not good long-term strategies. Yet because of this misunderstanding, we talk about and even shame our feelings as if they're actions or behaviors, and we judge them as such.

While typically, I find men struggle with talking about their feelings the most, all genders are faced with laughably inconsistent rules. Women are not allowed to be angry. Men are not allowed to be sad or vulnerable. Women are shamed for being too cold or "bitchy." Men are shamed if they aren't seen to be "strong and silent," to be "rational," to be stoic and in control.

But this selective emotional judgment doesn't make any sense. We judge some feelings as good and acceptable, and others are bad and unacceptable. There seem to be "positive" feelings like hopeful, inspired, brave, or joy, and "negative" feelings like fear, frustration, or anger. Even though all of them are just natural human reactions. We don't judge ourselves for laughing when we hear a joke, for feeling grateful for a friend who stays with us through hard times, or for feeling angry when we see a family member get scammed. So why do we judge ourselves when we feel depressed, insecure, or even self-indulgent? They're feelings, not actions.

And the stories we create about how our body processes our experiences are equally baffling. Why do we judge when our tear glands produce moisture when we watch a touching movie, but not when our sweat glands produce moisture on a hot day? After all, feeling something is not an identity. We can be a generally happy person who occasionally feels sad, yet we arbitrarily label certain feelings as being invalid or abnormal. I mean, who made up these rules?

And perhaps more important, *Why do we have to follow them?*

Perhaps a part of the narrative is "emotional messiness makes other people uncomfortable," so it needs to be hidden away shamefully, like dirty underwear or the secret stash of Final Fantasy cosplay outfits that I totally don't keep buried in my closet.

Of course, context is important and who we share our emotional messiness with is also important. As a parent, you may not want to share with your young kids that you're secretly scared your company is going through layoffs or you're feeling anxious about the rising prices of real estate, but it's entirely reasonable to talk about your concerns with your close friends or colleagues.

Finding appropriate spaces where you can let go and be emotionally messy can take time and a leap of faith, because it requires people who are willing to hold that space without expressing judgment. Obviously, therapists or groups with trained facilitators would be ideal for this if you don't have that kind of relationship with your friends and family, but any space where you can speak openly and honestly about your struggles without facing judgment will work.

The important thing is to recognize that *having feelings* is not something we can control, or should control, even if social etiquette might expect us to find appropriate spaces for that expression.

This is what learning emotional maturity looks like.

When we can openly acknowledge, feel, process, and release our emotions, they stop controlling us. Repressing emotions, like trying to "ignore" the anger we feel at a snide remark from a coworker, feelings of sadness from our best friend suddenly not making time for us, or trying to *live, laugh, love* our way out of the grief while going through a breakup, doesn't always make those experiences vanish.

Often, trying to carpet over our feelings with false happiness just means it's rotting away under the floorboards for years. It could manifest itself in other ways, such as chronic physical pains in our stomach and neck or in those anxiety-soaked sleepless nights. For years, I suffered with an ulcer I carried everywhere I went—an ailment I thought I had inherited from my father—until I went through therapy and it vanished in mere weeks.

The change felt magical at first, until my therapist explained this effect was actually far less fairy tales and more human anatomy. "When you're hungry, you salivate. When you're tired, you yawn. When you're stressed, you tense up in certain areas, like holding your breath or tensing your stomach. Of course that'll cause a reaction over time."

When I expressed some naive amazement that my body was so directly linked to my mind, she smiled and reminded me: "You don't *have* a mind and a body. You *are* your mind and body."

If you're finding yourself experiencing something deeper in you bubbling up as you read this, I recommend working with a therapist to help dig deeper to see if there are any parts that still need healing. Therapy in Asian communities still tends to be a stigmatized topic, but it holds tremendous power in bringing us to our true selves.

Scariest Thing I've Ever Done

I have had two deep fears I can proudly say I've conquered. The first scariest moment of my life happened when I was "wing walking," which is a type of adventure sport that involves walking on the wings of a small plane while it does barrel rolls and loop-de-loops in the air.

For someone with a deep fear of heights, conquering this fear was a big deal. It was one of the top activities I had put on my Fear List, which included facing a long list of things that had always terrified me, including: swimming in the open ocean with sharks, learning to speak in public, and confronting my arachnophobia by holding a giant spider.

But nothing on my Fear List made me feel quite so queasy as facing my other deepest fear: *going to therapy.*

Going to therapy as an Asian person can feel really weird. Not just "I'm about to get emotionally vulnerable with a stranger" type of weird, but "My family is going to think I'm a crazy person and they will be deeply worried their friends will find out" kind of weird. Not only that, but since talk therapy often involves looking at childhood traumas, it brings up the other big fear in the room—revealing family secrets, often seen as the greatest betrayal.

As a result, therapy felt like something I needed to hide, a shameful admission of my hidden flaws that might make my friends or family see me as "weak" or "broken." Asking for help is not something Asians have an easy time doing, and there is a common social stigma among Asian communities about seeking mental support.

Mental health struggles, from depression to anxiety to serious psychiatric disorders, are usually seen as moral failings—as if a person simply needed to work harder to solve their medical issues or should be curing themselves through sheer force of will, and we're often told our emotional struggles aren't a big enough deal. But they are a big deal. The CDC found that, when broken down by race, suicide was the number one cause of death among Asian American young adults aged fifteen to twenty-four, and was the *second* leading cause for Asian Americans between the ages of thirty and thirty-four. Across all groups, suicide is listed as the tenth leading cause of death in the US.

Furthermore, a national Latino and Asian American study found Asian Americans are three times *less likely* to seek mental health services than their Caucasian counterparts. Whereas 18 percent of the general US population sought mental health services during times of need, only 8.6 percent of Asian Americans did so.

When these stats are brought up, I often see the mental gymnastics people go through to justify why *Asians are different* and thus don't need as much support. Usually, this is pointing to the financial or social success of a select few more prominent Asian people, and a label of SEE? YOU GUYS ARE JUST HEALTHIER is slapped on the issue and stuffed away in the shadows.

Dr. Geoffrey Liu, a Harvard psychiatry professor, specializes in cultural psychiatry and leads the Massachusetts General Hospital Center for Cross-Cultural Student Emotional Wellness. He spent years researching mental health resources for young Asians and Asian Americans, and he points out how the "model minority" myth further worsens this issue. "It's easy to say that the reason Asian Americans don't seek care is the way their culture stigmatizes mental illness," he says. "This stance, though, ignores the role we all play in enhancing stigma by allowing dangerous stereotypes like 'model minority' to persist. As such, not only is there the shame of letting down yourself in not being able to take care of others, there's also the added pressure that we'll be letting down our communities as we don't want others to see our own groups as weak."

And that's not all. Among many Asian people I've spoken to, I've also observed the occasional belief that psychology doesn't work, because modern psychiatry seems to be very westernized.

In the Emmy Award–winning drama *Beef*, Steven Yeun's character, Danny, encounters George, his character's nemesis, and tells him, "Western therapy doesn't work on Eastern minds." The line stood out to me, not only as a reflection of a common dismissal of therapy as being "not for Asians," but also because a lot of people aren't aware that many components of "Western therapy" actually have deep roots in Eastern philosophy.

For example, Carl Jung was known to have read and referenced the

I Ching, as well as translated versions of *The Secret of the Golden Flower*. And mindfulness-based practices that are often taught in Cognitive Behavioral Therapy or Dialectic Behavioral Therapy, which are two extremely common practices in talk therapy, have roots in Zen Buddhism. Even Freudian concepts, such as Freud's work on the ego versus the id, or the focus on reducing suffering through changing our views of the self, seem to parallel Zen Buddhism's perceptions of releasing the ego.

Many of the new trends in therapy practices in Western popular culture have roots in Asian practices. Meditation, mindfulness, breathwork, yoga, tai chi, self-compassion, and a plethora of ceremonial healing practices have roots in India, China, and other Asian countries. I even have therapist friends who recommend Japanese tea ceremonies as a form of therapeutic practice for their clients, many of whom reported tremendous improvement in their mental health when coupled with other therapy practices.

So the sentiment that Western therapy or talk therapy is an entirely Western concept is, to Asian minds, a bit misguided, in my opinion. After all, our great-grandparents may not have made weekly appointments with a psychologist, but they could have gone to temple, meditated, prayed, found community, found purpose and meaning; and from these practices they may have found an alleviation of their mental suffering.

This is why I believe Western medicine's perspective on therapy should absolutely be applicable to "Eastern minds," but perhaps with a greater understanding of Eastern medicine's philosophy of a more holistic approach, and taking into account the cultural nuances of Asian clients and patients as part of their approach.

I often recommend that Asian people find and test at least one Asian therapist in their early exploration, because sometimes we need someone who has a deeper understanding of our culture and mindset, who can offer culturally sensitive tools to fit our needs. I have been given excellent recommendations for counselors who were passionate and incredibly well trained, but I just didn't *vibe* with them. I remember meeting with a white therapist who was highly recommended, and while I absolutely loved his positivity and gushing belief in me, I couldn't bring myself to fully open up because I felt that he didn't *get me*. There was nothing wrong with him, but it just wasn't a match. Of course, having an Asian therapist doesn't guarantee a connection, and some of my Asian clients have made amazing progress with their non-Asian therapists. I've personally had effective therapy sessions with non-Asian therapists. I suspect that if therapists received training in how to be culturally sensitive with clients of a range of backgrounds, that would be the best practice for all mental health professionals—but I do think the widespread use of such training is still in progress.

If a therapist works from a Western individualist background, they may not relate to clients who were raised in a more traditionally Eastern collectivist family and perspective. While setting boundaries is healthy, sometimes I feel the suggestions for *how* to communicate boundaries with parents or family can seem a bit rough and cold for my Asian sensibilities. The way boundaries are suggested is often well-suited for individualist cultures, where a child is typically expected to move out and start their own family upon reaching adulthood, but not for a collectivist culture where extended familial ties and multigenerational homes are the norm. It takes more time, more patience, more negotiations to rebuild a healthier dynamic with our parents because their expectations are often different from those of Western families.

Our emotional biology is the same, and while the concepts of healing are all similar regardless of cultural background, the nuances and communicative styles may look very different. Healing often requires having the space and safety to finally open up, be seen, process our stuck feelings, or shift our mindsets, and most therapists are prepared to work with clients through those techniques. But some clients may find that an Asian therapist might understand the complexities of Asian family dynamics better, and might suggest ways to set healthy boundaries without cutting out family entirely.

This is an important distinction. If our Eastern cultural backgrounds have long advocated for healing as not only being about treating the symptoms of the problem but looking at the body as a holistic whole, then we might feel more at ease when our medical professionals can understand that nuance.

When I speak to my Asian friends about therapy, the image they often conjure in their mind is a stereotype of lying on a therapist's couch, vulnerably confessing their sins and bad-mouthing their parents to an interrogative quack who wants to shrink their heads. Yet just as healing the body may involve working with a dietician, a physiotherapist, or even a trainer in a gym, healing our emotional "stuckness" can come from talking things out with a counselor, a friend, or a facilitated group—the same as the act of emptying your backpack after a long and tiring journey.

Emptying the Backpack

Imagine for a moment you take a backpack with you everywhere you go. You don't remember when you started wearing one. Maybe you started when you were born, but it has always been there with you. You wake up every morning, vaguely feeling the straps grip your shoulders as you scroll through your phone with your morning tea or coffee. You wear it underneath your work or school clothes. You wear it in the evenings when lounging on the couch.

You have some vague memories about when you started putting things in it. Maybe this started when your parents handed you your first responsibilities: "Here, take care of your little brother while we're running the store." This was a big deal, so you carefully made room in your backpack for your baby brother and put him in, making sure he was safe and secure.

Aside from obligations, you've also tucked other things away for the long haul, like your parents' dreams and expectations of you. Or things you didn't have space to deal with in the moment, like that time you cracked a joke in front of your cool, new friends, but no one laughed. So you threw your shame into the backpack as well, pretending the incident never happened.

Over the years, lots of things have gone in there that you didn't have time to deal with. You put all your *shoulds* in there—You *should* go to the gym. You *should* see a dentist. You *should* save for retirement. You *should* call your mom. What's wrong with you? Don't you love her? If so, you really *should* show it.

You think about your boss's insistence on how you should come in this weekend to "give the report another polish." You wanted to tell him the report is fine and he's being an idiot, but thought better. So you begrudgingly canceled your plans for Sunday brunch and stuffed all the frustration and words you really wanted to say to him into the backpack. Because that's what a responsible person does.

You even put bits and pieces of yourself in there: parts you felt were too messy and blemished to see the light of day. Or parts that had chipped off after relationships ended—words of anger you held back, questions you wish you had the courage to ask, intrusive thoughts you didn't want to let in. One by one, they were tossed into the backpack and zipped away.

Over time, the backpack grows heavier, and while it's already bursting at the seams, you still carry it, the fraying straps now digging deeply into your shoulders and weighing heavily on your back. You can still walk fine, but sometimes you need a moment to catch your breath. You feel a little guilt because your steps have slowed and your knees keep buckling, so you throw that guilt into the backpack as well.

You tell yourself, *This shouldn't be that heavy.* After all, each piece you've put in felt manageable in the moment. You look around at other people carrying their backpacks, and their loads seem so light and easy. They look as if they really have their shit together, and you should too. So you shake off your doubts and keep trudging ahead, sweat pouring down your face, and your back bent.

Your friends may occasionally check in with you with well-intentioned reminders: *"Don't forget to self-care!"* and *"Remember to put your oxygen mask on first!"*

You take their advice and take a personal day, and you do feel more rested after a nice day off or a yoga session. But in the back of your mind, you know as soon as the unreasonably flexible yoga instructor rings that damn bell saying Savasana is over, you'll have to pick up that damn backpack again and keep walking. The respite helped, but you can still feel every ounce of the backpack's weight in every step you take.

Eventually, the weight starts taking a toll. You feel exhausted all the time. You start walking in the same ruts because change feels impossible. You snap at your loved ones for something they didn't do wrong. You feel guilty immediately, and you habitually stuff that guilt into the backpack—which weighs it down even more.

Suddenly, a friend notices you're having a hard time and asks if you want to take a break with her. You usually would say "no, thanks" with a smile, but today felt particularly hard, so the two of you sit down together. She notices your backpack and asks if you'd like to dump some stuff out so you won't have to carry so much alone.

At first, you're not sure about the invitation. But you want to honor her kindness, so you sit down for a moment, unzip the bag, and take out a few recent things—things you know are okay to show others, like your frustrations at work and annoyances with your coworkers. She smiles and clears a little bit of space on the floor as she listens.

You feel a little better and start to dump a few more things out. The fight you had with your loved ones. The pressures from your family. The realization that your parents are getting old. You apologize for some of the things that tumble out, but she just smiles and says it's fine, she's made plenty of space for you.

You continue to dump things out. You're surprised at how some of the smallest things actually were the heaviest—a casual remark about your age or an innocent question about your relationship. You notice how some of the things are clumped together, tied by invisible strings you never realized were there. Piece by piece, you pull things out, a seemingly never-ending chain that lightens the weight on your back.

You're now feeling a bit guilty for the mess you're making as you tell her you hope this isn't too much. She smiles and assures you it's not. Plus, she's not here to carry things for you but to hold space while you sort through and organize your thoughts.

So you feel reassured enough to finally pick up the backpack, turn it upside down, and let everything fall onto the floor. There's so much, it takes a moment to all tumble out—those early expectations from your childhood. Sadness. Loss. Things you never got a chance to process. Small stuff tumbles out that you haven't thought about in years, like old stories of how you should make everyone happy, or old relationship wounds. They fall out alongside old travel photos, loose change, and a half-eaten Nature Valley bar.

As you sit there sorting through the mess, you also feel this catharsis of emotions flooding your body. Maybe it's grief, maybe it's relief— you can't tell anymore. Your friend looks over at you and says what you never gave yourself the chance to acknowledge: "You've been carrying so much. And it's been so heavy."

For the first time in a while, you stretch out your arms and feel a crack in your back, but it feels good. Your head's not strained from the weight anymore and you look up for the first time. You start realizing some of the stuff you've been carrying wasn't really yours to begin with, like expectations and pressures you never agreed to accept. Some have lessons inscribed on them, while others were just useless mental trash you could have let go of years ago.

Your friend helps you by asking questions as you examine the objects: "Is your brother still in your bag? Why not let him walk his own path? He's not a baby kangaroo, you know?" So you open up and let him out, begrudgingly. You realize you have gotten so used to the weight, your backpack actually feels a little empty now that he's gone. While a part of you takes a moment to grieve, you also feel pride and love in seeing him stand up and walk away on his own. He was never yours to carry forever, after all.

Suddenly, you feel clear. You take a deep breath and realize you know *exactly what to do next*. You've always known the answers all along, but your neck was so strained and your back so tired, you never had the chance to look up and see the obvious paths in front of you.

You turn to your friend and thank her, apologetic at having handed her some of your burdens, until she lovingly reminds you not to put her into your backpack! You laugh and nod, seeing the pattern.

You pack up all the pieces you realize are important to carry—your goals, your aspirations, your core values. You let go of the pieces that no longer serve you—your *shoulds*, the guilt, the past versions of you that you're ready to leave behind.

To me, this is what therapy is like.

The *shoulds* we give ourselves are about *shame*. And the more *shoulds* we carry, the more likely there's a deep sense of shame that we haven't let go of.

Therapy is not necessarily always about fixing something broken within ourselves, because we're not broken. Sometimes therapy can just be a space someone holds for you as you empty your backpack and find your footing again.

Therapists might also give you tools to better manage the grip of the straps, to clear away mental garbage, or to stop yourself from adding more unnecessary weight as you prepare for your next big summit.

What Dumping Out Your Backpack Can Look Like

When I first attended therapy, I was hesitant for two reasons:

1. Are my problems even big enough for therapy?
2. What does therapy even look like?

For a long time, I've felt that unless I was literally on fire, receiving any kind of support or simply a compliment, was guilt-inducing. After all, who am I to deserve help when others have had it worse?

Who am I to burden people with my *insignificant* problems, to hear me whine and moan, when somewhere out there might be others more deserving, like some abandoned, impoverished orphan who struggled against all odds to fight for social justice in the third world?

Sure, John, there are billions of people who face real adversity with a smile every day, but you need more help than they do because you couldn't just suck it up like everyone else?

I found myself carrying these thoughts of self-judgment as I walked through the door of my therapist's office.

As I sat down on the couch, between hanging signs that read BREATHE and ACCEPTANCE and smelling a faint fog of burnt sage, I couldn't help but feel out of place. Even sitting there, under the kind gaze and unconditional acceptance that comes with professional training, I felt that I was about to start admitting some moral failure.

I was weighed down by secret fears that my family would find out I was talking to a therapist. Even worse, I feared that I would somehow be betraying them by talking about them. What would my therapist think of my family? How can I talk about my innermost thoughts without seeming like I'm giving up my family's secrets?

My therapist, a grandmotherly white woman with horn-rimmed librarian glasses, started by giving me the head-slightly-tilted-to-the-side look. I wondered if all therapists were required to strike this listening pose.

"Where should we begin?"

I sat in silence for about a minute, trying to think of why I was there. I searched my brain for the right answer—any one of the myriad reasons I had come up with over the past few weeks . . . but came up blank. *Error 404—Trauma Not Found.* Finally, I confessed I didn't know why I was there. I was fine. I wanted to apologize for wasting her time, for not having come prepared with a deep enough problem to be solved. I wondered what I was doing there and if I should just stop wasting everyone's time and leave. I was fine, and I should figure things out for myself first before going to therapy, even though that makes absolutely zero sense.

I told her how, in my mind, I already knew all the things that were wrong with me, and believe me, I was an expert at diagnosing my own bullshit. I had read a few books on healing and tried to use all the therapy-speak words—patterns of caretaking, emotional avoidance, deflection, enmeshment, and whatever therapy word-of-the-day had populated my social media feed. But the truth was, self-diagnosing and *knowing* the problems were very, very different from actually *healing* them, and sometimes, I was just using that information to procrastinate facing the issues.

I told her I felt stuck. Like there was *something* underneath the shiny, polished surface, like glimpses of a tempest brewing beneath a thick layer of ice. As she pressed deeper, I told her I felt disconnected, a bit depressed, and isolated despite all the people around me. As if someone had unplugged the cable between my brain and my body, and I was just a robot going through the motions of what it meant to be human.

At the end of our first session, she asked how I felt. I told her honestly I felt more confused walking out than I did walking in, to which she smiled and said, "Good, that could be a sign of progress."

The first session didn't wow me, but I believed in persistence and consistency. I knew that healing takes time and repeated efforts. And also, I had prepaid for a package so there was no way I would not get my money's worth.

Over the next few sessions, our conversations dived deeper and further than my original self-diagnosis presented:

- I was a yes-person and struggled with crippling guilt whenever I let people down.
- I felt it was my job to take care of everyone around me.
- I habitually deflected every serious conversation about myself with humor, or by asking questions about the other person so we could take the attention away from myself.
- I constantly felt the need to overachieve, as though I was being secretly watched and graded. And if I couldn't live up to perfection, then I needed to demonstrate how hard I tried and how much I sacrificed before stopping or I'd feel like I was being lazy.

But I admitted to her I still felt emotionally stuck. I felt blocked, like there was a thick wall of ice between me and the rage and sadness I could sense beneath, present but out of reach. I could say all the right things about gratitude or surrender or vulnerability, but the truth was, every time I approached opening up, I kept bumping against a wall that pushed me back—a wall of shame and self-judgment that prevented me from actually looking at what's inside.

It took me months before my therapist could get me even to talk about how I felt in a way that wasn't either dismissive or apologetic. Literally, she had to constantly correct me in how I was talking about myself. I was disconnected from my feelings, and I spoke like a scientist observing the emotional habits of a distant species (in David Attenborough's voice):

"Yes, when I think back to that time, I perhaps do notice there is a bit of anger simmering underneath, which is fascinating since—"

My therapist would interrupt me with the patience of a teacher witnessing a student making the same mistake on the same test for the twelfth time: "You mean you feel angry?"

"Sure, I'm observing a curious hint of anger here, but—"

"Okay, let's try saying 'I FEEL ANGRY.'"

I paused, observing that my desire to be a straight-A therapy student was fighting with my deep reluctance to actually say the words. "*I feel angry.*"—I pushed the words unwillingly through gritted teeth.

"Okay, can you sit with that? Is it okay to feel angry?"

"Sure, people are allowed to feel anger in times like this."

"Okay. But are *you* allowed to feel angry?"

". . . No. There's no justification for me to feel angry. So I shouldn't be allowed to feel angry."

"Why do you need a reason? Can it be okay that you're just feeling the way that you do, right now?"

I sat in the heavy simplicity of that question. My mind was trying to argue back, or to find some clever analogy or sarcastic joke to take attention away from the enormity of the moment. "Yes. It can be okay. I feel angry." As I pushed the words out, they seemed to invite more behind them.

"I feel angry that I have to do this. That I couldn't fix myself. I'm angry that I failed. I'm angry at myself because I'm someone who should be able to support others, but I still don't have my own shit figured out. I'm angry I let myself repeat this pattern—I'm so angry I've been here on this stupid couch repeating the same stupid things because I couldn't fix my own problems and—" I was interrupted as my therapist handed me a box of Kleenex. Her act of kindness confused me for a second, until I realized tears had been rolling down my face without my even noticing it.

I pressed on regardless. "I'm not just angry, but I think I'm sad. I'm sad I can't be enough. I'm sad I can't always do it right. I'm just . . . I'm just . . . sad. And I'm sorry." As the words *I'm sorry* come through, I could feel a rumble in my chest and a tightening in my throat. My breath comes forth in staccato, four truncated beats each inhale and exhale.

The floodgates open and my words no longer sound like words, just repeated mumbles of "I'm sorry, I'm sorry, I'm sorry" that land in the stack of Kleenex I'm absolutely ruining with tears. I bury my face in the Kleenex, partly out of embarrassment and partly trying to clean myself up. Internally, I feel ashamed I'm such a mess, while trying to remind myself that if there's one person in the city whom I can totally be a mess in front of, it's probably my therapist.

She doesn't ask me any more questions at this point and just lets me fall apart for a while on my own. After a few minutes, I feel both empty and oddly full. A tranquility sets in the room as I finally look up and meet her gaze for the first time since I began crying.

"Sorry for making a mess," I said, looking around at the balled-up soiled tissues littering the floor and couch around me.

She smiles and says, "It's quite all right. You're allowed to be messy here. Your mess is okay."

The words landed and I put my right hand over my heart, which felt comforting and calming all at once. We sat there as I felt myself settle, like watching the glittering pieces in a snow globe drift and collect at the bottom.

Beneath the mess was anger. Beneath the anger was sadness. Beneath the sadness was shame. And beneath the shame was freedom.

The Courage of Emotional Messiness

Sometimes, the way to healing starts from having the courage to acknowledge what we feel and to sit in the uncomfortable messiness of our emotions, so we can release those emotional experiences. And you can't face those experiences without getting emotionally messy and vulnerable, which are two things many of us have been conditioned to avoid at all costs.

Western therapy focuses on the impacts of childhood traumas and family dynamics, and opening up about those experiences can be challenging for Asian Americans. We're not talking solely about our *own* internal struggles, for we have to talk about our parents' issues as well, which breaks the value of filial piety. It can feel like a betrayal.

It isn't only about avoiding messiness for ourselves, but the fact that our messiness betrays the messiness of our parents, their secrets, and their status in society. Even in the therapy container, I was unconsciously striving to be the perfect client, putting on yet another facade of "healing" but really still avoiding actual *feeling*—because *feeling* is *shameful*.

In Mandarin, there is the phrase "eating bitterness" (吃苦), which literally means to swallow the bitter feelings and struggles we experience in order to cope with challenges we face. We usually use this term under the guise of admiration—*Look at that mother working so hard for her kids she simply swallows down everything, from social injustices, to cruel acts of fate, to her own feelings of grief and sadness. She's so virtuous and we should all strive to be like her.*

This thinking makes sense, and I can see how this mindset could be helpful in my grandparents' generation. Granny was facing a freaking revolution and mass starvation while trying to bring her four kids from a war-torn China to the tiny island of Taiwan. Swallowing her bitterness wasn't just about being virtuous, but *survival for her kids.*

I can also see this value in my parents' generation. The immigrant's stress of having to adapt to an entirely new country, culture, language, and even basic things like grocery shopping, since there aren't markets here that sell the food they have cooked their entire lives. There wasn't time or space for them to take a deep breath and process.

From them, my generation learned these patterns of swallowing our feelings in order to survive, even if we aren't facing invading armies or imminent starvation, because that was *just how it was done*. We also learned about our family's judgments of those who didn't swallow their bitterness, who didn't hide their sadness, homesickness, or anger against those who treated them unfairly. These judgments may have been for others, who were labeled weak or lazy, and sometimes, these judgments might have landed on ourselves.

The shame story is: *If my grandparents who were going through war could "just deal with it" and repress their feelings to hold their suffering quietly in isolation, am I weak for wanting help?*

Some Asian Americans were raised to think that opening up emotionally makes us weak, messy, irrational (and rationality is king), selfish, and useless. These are horrible ideas to attach to the universal and fundamental human experience of having feelings. And these self-judgments can become a massive obstacle for people who need to share their struggles with a therapist or even with friends.

But the process of accepting our emotional messiness, of talking things out, of emptying the backpack, is necessary. Therapy might make you feel vulnerable, but it's actually empowering and clarifying.

How to Seek Therapy

The first thing to remember about therapy is that it is confidential.

Your therapist is not allowed to reveal anything you tell them in sessions. They are not allowed to reveal who you are, what you do, or how often you've seen them—even if your workplace is paying for it. They are not allowed to talk about anything you have discussed in the sessions—unless you are outright threatening to harm yourself or others, or if they have been compelled to do so by law. And even then, they are trained to make sure that this is only for extreme situations, and only if it's absolutely necessary.

The second thing to remember is that a therapist is not there to judge you, attack you, or tell you how to live your life. And if you meet one who does, you can find another one.

Trying to find a therapist is kind of like dating. The first person you meet might not be the perfect match for you, but that doesn't mean you stop trying.

The process can be daunting. Making the decision to work with a therapist is already a huge deal. Many people think of working with a therapist as a last resort. It's seen as the thing you do when you've exhausted all other options. It might be when your relationship is on the line or recently ended, when you're starting to feel physical symptoms like stress headaches or stomach ulcers, or when you've been feeling so low that you've lost track of what makes you happy.

If you have a friend or someone you know who has a recommendation, that's often the easiest place to start. But realize that just because a particular therapist is a good match for someone else doesn't mean it's a good match for you.

You might go in and find their style is a bit too cold and clinical for you. You might feel they're just analyzing you and trying to assign a diagnosis rather than asking you questions that help you come to your own realizations. And maybe that's not what you need right now.

The purpose is almost always to help you overcome struggles like anxiety, stress, and unpleasant emotional states, but some will go further to identify unhealthy patterns in relationships, unhealthy thought patterns, and roadblocks. Some will help you replace unhealthy coping mechanisms with better tools.

But how do you know who would be a good fit?

Making the choice to find a therapist already requires a leap of faith and courage to begin with, but even after someone makes that choice, they're often faced with a much more daunting task: Where do you begin to look for one?

Tips for Finding a Therapist (Who's a Good Match for You)

STEP 1: START WITH WHAT YOU WANT TO WORK ON.

Are you dealing with relationship issues? Are you feeling anxious, depressed, or angry and you're not sure why? Do you notice you tend to go to certain coping mechanisms or self-medication like drinking, substances, or distractions like social media? Do you find yourself going to these distractions as a way to avoid feeling certain things? Whatever your specific need, you can look for someone who specializes in that area.

STEP 2: SEEK SOURCES AND RECOMMENDATIONS.

Therapy can be cost-prohibitive, and the fact that not everyone has equal access to it is, in my opinion, an issue. But there are resources that can help that are often unadvertised or unknown, so look around first to see if there are those covered by insurance or programs. Some therapists can provide sliding scale payments based on need, and there are even some free options available to the public. It would also be a good idea to check with your employer to find out if they offer EAPs, which can provide free and confidential therapy services. In these situations, your employer won't know who accessed the services, and your sessions should be confidential.

Also, there are multiple Asian-specific websites like Asians for Mental Health or Yellow Chair Collective that specialize in listing therapists who are Asian or regularly work with those who are Asian.

STEP 3: BOOK A DISCOVERY OR INTAKE MEETING.

On your first meeting, your therapist or provider might have questions about what issues you're experiencing. Don't worry if you're not one hundred percent sure; they can help you figure things out. You have the right to ask them any questions about their background, training, and experience working with Asian clients or clients with your specific needs. All questions are welcome. Sometimes, it can take a couple of meetings before you feel comfortable to open up, but it's up to both of you to build a trusting relationship where you can be fully open and comfortable.

STEP 4: TRUST YOUR GUT.

How did you feel when you first met with a particular therapist? Did you like them? The question seems counterintuitive for many Asian people because we're so used to trusting those who are highly educated medical professionals, but the truth is, no one knows you as well as you do. If you don't believe they're a match for you, either because you feel their methodology is unhelpful or because something feels off, it's not worth forcing yourself to stay with them. Do not worry about offending them if you decide to go elsewhere—they are more than capable of handling rejection (and if they're not, they're probably not the therapist for you anyway!).

STEP 5: DON'T RUSH YOUR PROCESS.

Sometimes, people can approach therapy with a lot of pressure on both themselves and the therapist. There's a feeling that because the time can add up, there's additional guilt around "I'm not improving fast enough." Sometimes a breakthrough is the result of knocking on the same door a number of times before it's ready to open. Attempting to break the door down by sledgehammering ourselves or trying to force an outcome makes things even more difficult to get to where we want to be.

STEP 6: BE HONEST WITH YOURSELF.

As a recovering Achiever, I found in my first few months of therapy that I had a really strong desire to "do it right," which sometimes meant I was reflexively saying what I thought the therapist wanted to hear. (This was also demonstrated in *Beef*, where Ali Wong's character attended a couple's therapy session trying to say all the right things, pointing fingers at her parents, while she was secretly hiding all her true feelings and the drama that was playing out in the rest of the show.) Perfectionism has no place in therapy, and you can only get out of it what you're willing to put in.

STEP 7: YOU DON'T HAVE TO STAY IN IT FOREVER.

If you're feeling like you've gotten what you needed out of a therapy relationship and are ready to move on to something else, let your therapist know. Sometimes it's possible to want to stay in the therapy space and keep processing and processing every little thing we go through, but that's not always necessary. If you're no longer feeling it's serving you, feel free to make a change or end the sessions as you see fit. Ask your therapist if that's something they recommend, and they should let you know their honest opinion on where you are at.

Making the decision to seek help can feel extremely overwhelming, especially if we're already at the cusp of dealing with the stresses of life that led us to seek therapy to begin with. Sometimes, the thought of finding a therapist, making the appointment, showing up, opening up, and maybe even forcing ourselves to actually get out of bed and doing it every week can seem insurmountable.

But it gets better.

Instead of trying to do everything at once, realize that you can take baby steps, over time, and give yourself recognition for each one. Emailing that friend who was gushing about how great her therapist was and asking for a phone number might seem small, but it can also be a huge accomplishment in taking charge of your life, and it's worthy of acknowledgment.

After all, you deserve to be happy and healthy.

You are worthy of being supported.

Resources

Over the years, I've tried a number of different healing tools and found them all helpful for different things. Some are like Band-Aids, helpful for stopping little cuts and bruises, like interrupting unhealthy thought patterns before they worsen or fester. Others open you up and go deep, uncovering early wounds that never got attention or healing. All were helpful, but at different stages and for different purposes.

Below are only a few I've tried and had success with. There are many more, and there will always be debates about which ones are considered most valid, but personally, I just care about whether or not the approach works for me. Perhaps some might work for you as well.

COGNITIVE BEHAVIORAL THERAPY (CBT)

CBT is a science-based modality that is commonly prescribed. It doesn't focus on your childhood or talk about your past, but instead focuses on setting goals in your life and using mindset tools to help you get around mental blocks.

I really like this for more "logic-focused" individuals because it's comparatively easy to learn and understand. You identify ways your mind lies to you—such as creating all-or-nothing scenarios like "If I don't get married by this year, it means no one wants me anymore and I'm not lovable"—and point out how it's an absolute lie.

These are called Cognitive Distortions, because our mind has a tendency to take reality and distort it into all sorts of untrue meanings, like looking through funhouse mirrors that stretch or compress your shape.

A few cognitive distortions include:

- **Overgeneralizations:** When we jump to "always" or "never" after a single event, like "People never accept my invitations; it must mean they don't want to spend time with me," after only one or two attempts to invite others.

- **Discounting the positive:** Ignoring or invalidating positive events, and hyperfocusing on the negative. A common example of this is if we get ten compliments after a presentation and one neutral or negative comment, and we immediately believe the negative comment must be true and the compliments were false.

- **Mind Reading or Fortune-Telling:** Assuming someone is thinking something that hasn't been communicated or confirmed. Such as if we send an email and someone doesn't respond right away, we believe it's because they aren't interested, when it might be they're busy or even wanting to take time to give a more thoughtful response.

- **Magnification:** Taking something relatively small, such as making a mistake on a project or a social faux pas, and jumping to "People are going to think terribly of me" or "I failed," when in reality it's likely no one even noticed.

I found learning CBT to be extremely helpful for stopping bad thinking habits in their tracks and for developing tools and frameworks to challenge them so we find the truth. However, it can have limitations for some folks as it can also be used to dismiss personal experiences as distortions (for example, calling experiences of racism a cognitive distortion), when they are in fact valid.

Similar to CBT is Dialectical Behavioral Therapy (DBT), which is also quite common today and a modification of CBT. It's divided into four stages of treatment to put clients into a position of control, with a focus on mindfulness, emotional regulation, and in-the-moment coaching.

PARTS WORK AND IFS

IFS, or Internal Family Systems, is an evidence-based psychotherapy practice that identifies various subpersonalities within us. It sees the mind as a family of different "parts" of who we are, including "managers" (protective parts that try to control people's surroundings), "exiles" (parts that hold fear, hurt, or shame from early experiences), and "firefighters" (parts that try to fix situations by pushing us into things like self-medicating or binge eating).

My favorite analogy I've heard for parts work is being a bus on the road. Most of the time, the bus is being driven by our smart, rational, adult selves, making mature decisions based on reason and logic. In the back of the bus, we carry a group of various passengers, each of whom represents a different version of us with learned behaviors for coping with problems.

Sometimes, when we encounter a situation that threatens what we want (such as a partner threatening to leave a relationship), one of those parts will jump into the driver's seat and take control. IFS is particularly effective at identifying and speaking to each of your parts so that they don't keep jumping in and fighting you for your life.

SELF-REPARENTING THERAPY

Similar to parts work, this is a form of therapy where you talk to yourself. Think of this practice as seeing a representation of yourself as a child and talking to them as if you're their new parent. This helps you change unhealthy inner dialogue (learned from your parents or care-givers) into healthier dialogue.

When my therapist first introduced me to inner-child work, I felt stupid. She had me bring a picture of myself as a child (I chose a picture of me from when I was six) and had me have a conversation with him.

She'd have me ask him questions as though I was talking to an ac-tual child, asking him how he feels and what he thinks, then to vocalize what "he" would be saying as a six-year-old.

I felt both ridiculously self-conscious and self-judgmental when I started. Not only am I talking to myself, I'm talking to myself like a six-year-old. It took a lot of coaching to get through this at first.

But once I started, I noticed something—a lot of what my "inner child" was saying were things I was unconsciously feeling but struggled to vocalize. By creating this avatar, I suddenly was able to give myself permission to be honest with myself on how I really felt about how oth-ers were treating me.

When I started writing out this self-dialogue, I realized how mean I was actually being to myself. It never occurred to me that I'm not only speaking to myself, but also listening. I started writing down all the thoughts I was habitually subvocalizing to my unconscious, and I was shocked by how much outright toxicity there was.

It took a few months but the change for me was absolutely life-altering. I felt ten times more confident. I slept better. I stopped feeling guilt and stopped wanting to people-please. My relationships improved massively because I could fully and openly communicate—not only di-rectly and honestly but also empathetically. I was better at my job and I was just *happier*.

OTHER THERAPEUTIC PRACTICES

There are so many other modalities of therapeutic practices out there that can be added to this list. Some are more traditional, Western, or clinical forms of psychoanalysis, while others are more about mental wellness, which may feel easier for people from Eastern backgrounds that treat the body, mind, and spirit as a holistic whole.

Examples might include somatic therapy, which looks at how our body can manifest physical ailments from emotional impacts. Or mindfulness and loving-kindness compassion practices, which stem from Buddhist traditions.

As part of my own exploration, I've tried everything from silent meditation retreats, to emotional freedom technique (EFT) workshops that had me tapping my forehead over and over again, to psychodrama practices that had me play out past relationship conversations while beating the hell out of a mannequin in front of a cheering crowd (super fun).

Usually, I found workshops to be effective for making sharp breakthroughs, but best accompanied by working with a therapist with a plan for healing over time. As always, if you're ever uncertain, make sure you are getting support from qualified medical professionals before taking a leap into the unknown.

Resource Links

BOOKS ON ASIAN AMERICAN MENTAL HEALTH

Where I Belong by Soo Jin Lee, LMFT, and Linda Yoon, LCSW

Permission to Come Home by Jenny T. Wang, PhD

The Voices We Carry by J. S. Park

ASIAN AMERICAN MENTAL HEALTH RESOURCE LINKS

Resource	Link	Description
Asian American Psychological Association	aapaonline.org	Focuses on improving the mental health of Asian American communities through research, education, policy, and practice. Offers fact sheets on mental health concerns, anti-bullying information, and Asian American LGBTQIA+ resources.
Asian Mental Health Collective	asianmhc.org/apisaa	Aims to destigmatize mental health within Asian communities by offering the APISAA therapist directory for finding therapists who specialize in serving Asian American, South Asian American, and Pacific Islander communities in most states and Washington, DC.
National Asian American Pacific Islander Mental Health Association	naapimha.org/aanhpi-service-providers	Provides a comprehensive list of state-level programs and resources tailored to meet the mental health needs of Asian Americans, Pacific Islanders, and Native Hawaiians. Offers general mental health resources as well.

Resource	Link	Description
South Asian Mental Health Initiative & Network	samhin.org	A nonprofit organization dedicated to addressing the mental health needs of the South Asian community in the US. Provides a list of mental health providers specialized for the South Asian community, searchable by languages spoken, location, and service type.
National Alliance on Mental Illness	nami.org/Your-Journey /Identity-and-Cultural -Dimensions/Asian-American -and-Pacific-Islander	Offers resources specifically for Asian Americans and Pacific Islanders, tackling barriers such as stigma, language barriers, and the lack of culturally competent providers. Includes seminars in Chinese, Korean, and Vietnamese, and links to culturally sensitive support groups.
National Queer Asian Pacific Islander Alliance	nqapia.org	Promotes education, leadership development, collaboration, and visibility to challenge racism and anti-LGBTQIA+ bias among AAPI organizations. Provides a directory of Asian and Pacific Islander therapists.
Yellow Chair Collective	yellowchaircollective.com	A psychotherapy group focusing on the Asian American community's unique challenges, addressing intersectional identity and intergenerational trauma.

Resource	Link	Description
Asian Mental Health Project	asianmentalhealthproject.com	Strives to educate and empower Asian communities around mental health, offering resources and support systems.
Asian Counseling and Referral Service (ACRS)	acrs.org	ACRS promotes social justice and the well-being and empowerment of Asian Americans and Pacific Islanders and other underserved communities—including immigrants, refugees, and American-born—by developing; providing; and advocating for innovative, effective, and efficient community-based multilingual and multicultural services.
The Asian American Health Initiative (AAHI)	aahiinfo.org	Dedicated to improving the health and wellness of Asian American communities through outreach, education, and advocacy.
Instagram accounts for Asian American mental health	@ItsJiYounKim, @AsiansDoTherapy, @AsianMentalHealthCollective, @AsianMentalHealthProject, @AsiansForMentalHealth, @BrownGirlTherapy, @HieuPham.LCSW, @ProjectLotUsOrg, @SouthAsianTherapists, @TheMindHealthSpot	

Be the Author of Your Own Story

Sometimes, the hardest thing we can ever do is be ourselves.

If you've gotten this far, it's likely you've been considering making some changes in your life, and are looking for answers on how and where to go. Whatever you're currently going through in your relationships, your work, or even your own sense of purpose in life, the most beautiful thing about life is we can always pivot, rebrand, or just start a new path. But the prospect of change, especially when we're upleveling into who we truly are, can feel intimidating.

When people are considering a new beginning, they'll often ask if they're too late, if their past mistakes were too significant to overcome, if they're too old, too young, too inexperienced, or if they're fooling themselves because others will judge them for wanting to make a change.

During the writing process, I thought about whether the book might ruffle some feathers.

The visual of proud, confident, and empowered Asians clashes with preexisting stereotypes of who Asians are "supposed to be" in society: model minorities who keep their heads down, know their place, and do not create waves. A lot of people may not be happy to see us as leaders, as changemakers, because it doesn't fit the character they want us to play to suit *their* narratives. For them, the idea of docile and deferential Asian communities stepping into their power will seem threatening, especially if others have long benefited from putting us in the model minority box.

They may try to invalidate, belittle, or minimize our ambitions and reinventions alike, because change is almost always hard to accept. It's not just about how we're seen by others but how we view ourselves as well. Which is why I like the metaphor that our life is a book we get to write in, every day.

Right now, perhaps it feels as if you've been rewriting the same stories, living out the same patterns, and you feel stuck and too bored and unsatisfied to keep going. Maybe you want to start a new chapter, and you keep looking at the past chapters, wishing you had done something different.

In the past, your pages may have been cowritten by your parents. Perhaps they added pages in there from their own lives and their visions for you. Perhaps some pages were written by people who were once important in your life, and you felt the need to carry on their expectations of you even as you continued writing on your own.

Writing a new chapter can be easier said than done, especially if you've only been conditioned to believe there's one right way for the story to unfold. And when the narrative doesn't go the way you want, it's easy to think there's something wrong with you. But there's nothing *wrong*, because your story is not meant to read like everyone else's.

For many of us, our parents grew up writing very different books, in different languages, with different characters, and even in different genres. Perhaps theirs was a heartwarming immigrant story about finding survival in a new land, but yours is an exciting memoir of adventure, healing, and self-discovery. Maybe there's romance, maybe there's mystery, maybe there's even a touch of drama. But you won't know what kind of book it is until you've written it.

And most important, check in with yourself on two things along the way:

Who am I unconsciously allowing to influence my writing?

Who are the critics I'm most worried about?

Whenever I get asked: "How do I stop caring about what other people think?," my answer is always: "You don't, but you can choose whose opinions deserve weight." We're social creatures, and we're always going to care about what others think, and that's not a bad thing. Compassion and consideration are what make us great in our collective communities, but we can choose whose opinions should matter to us, and how *much* they matter.

Perhaps you're thinking about your family, your boss, or a close friend who you know will always have your back because they tell the hardest truths directly to your face. These are people whose reviews could be taken into consideration, so long as you trust their wisdom (an anonymous quote I love is: *Never take criticism from people you wouldn't also take advice from*). So maybe there are those whose advice you take with a grain of salt, as a small data point to keep in mind, but not enough to change your story for. Either way, I can almost guarantee you the reviews that matter are not going to be coming from anonymous strangers from the internet.

And of course, you may experience writer's block made of impostor syndrome, self-criticism, and self-doubt. Perhaps you just don't know where your story is supposed to go. Or you have an idea of where you'd like it to end, but you just don't know how to get there. And the more you see others enthusiastically scribbling in their books and publishing picture-perfect chapters—new careers, marriages, travel, celebrations—the more your writer's block can feel insurmountable.

And so some people sit and wait—for inspiration, for permission, for someone to just come and save them from the *wallowing black hole of existential despair.*

But here's the thing—no one is coming to save us. The only way you can get through writer's block is to keep writing, even when you don't know exactly where it will lead. Like any other writer, go explore, research, try new things, or even find a new café to write in, but *keep writing through the self-doubt and trust that you can edit later.*

You might get judged. You might hear criticism. Or you might get the most incredible praise you've ever received. The truth is, none of it matters that much, because in time, everything fades anyway. We get to reinvent ourselves every time we show up. The only thing that matters is whether you feel you're creating something that's aligned with your values or your sense of purpose.

Whenever someone tells me, "I don't know what my purpose is," my answer is usually "If you don't know, then *your purpose is to find your purpose.*" Your purpose does not always come from cryptic wisdom that appears in your dreams or on a spiritual journey. Your purpose can be what gives you the greatest sense of fulfillment and meaning, or what brings you joy in the moment.

Remember, you're the one writing the book, which means you're creating all the rules, characters, and plot points that come with it. Which means if you don't like how the chapter is ending so far, then you just keep writing until you create something you're satisfied with.

Inspiration and motivation are generated from actions, not the other way around. We create our motivation by doing things when we don't feel like doing them, and the ideas follow. No amount of motivational YouTube videos, preparations, overthinking will ever replace the simple truth that *doing comes before feeling.*

Say the things you've been hesitant to say. Do the things you've been waiting for permission to do. Do them while feeing messy. Do them while feeling scared. Do them imperfectly, but *do the things you've been hesitant to do*—and trust you can always start again, and again, and again.

And even if you wrote your book for yourself and not others, your book may still be read by others as a future instruction manual: *"This is how they fought their beast and won."* Your book may reach millions, or it may simply change the life of one person who came across it when they needed it the most, and wouldn't that still be worth it?

You are the author of your story, and in it, you can choose what lessons from your past you would like to pass on and what lessons you feel are no longer helpful for the next generation. But if there's one thing I hope you'll include in your story, it would be kindness.

In the film *Everything Everywhere All At Once*, one of the main characters, Waymond, shared a powerful message at the climax. He starts by saying, "You tell me that it's a cruel world . . . and we're all just running around in circles. I know that . . . I know that you've all been fighting because you're scared and confused. I'm confused, too. All day, I don't know what the heck is going on, but somehow, it feels like it's all my fault."

Then he goes on to say, "When I choose to see the good side in things, I'm not being naive. It is strategic and necessary. It's how I've learned to survive through everything. I don't know. The only thing I do know . . . is that we have to be kind. Please, be kind. Especially when we don't know what's going on."

When I first heard this speech, it moved me so deeply and profoundly because of how true his words were. No matter who we are, we're *all* fighting an invisible battle. And so many of us feel alone and isolated.

We're not defined by the color of our skin or the parenting we grew up with. We are all truly unified by the fact that we're all human beings. Imperfect, messy, confused, amazing, needy, loving, and occasionally irrational creatures trying desperately to gain some sense of control or understanding in the great cosmic mystery that's life.

When we can truly be who we are, and accept ourselves and others without conditions or judgment, life is better. We are better. And the only way to acceptance *must* come from kindness.

I hope you are outrageously kind to others, even if you're not sure they deserve it. I hope you are outrageously kind to yourself, even if you're not sure if *you* deserve it. Because deserving has nothing to do with compassion or love or kindness. It's not payment. It's a gift. And it's a gift that gives as much to you as it does to everyone around you.

Everything we do has the potential of positive impact, far beyond what we can ever know, and could echo through history until our collective stories become an anthology for the next generation.

To paraphrase Gandhi, *We need to be the change we wish to see in the world.* To create communities, brotherhoods and sisterhoods and siblinghoods, of like-minded individuals who have our backs as much as we have theirs. We deserve to be seen, be heard, and be recognized. Just as we need to fight to ensure those around us also are seen, heard, and recognized.

By reading this, you are already a part of a movement of conscious change. And by doing the work, you are setting an example for others to follow in your bravery.

My hope is that if any part of this book resonated with you, or you think will resonate with someone you know, you will share the passage with them. Even if they're not ready to see it, the message is that they are not isolated or alone. There will always be waves of change coming, and they are unstoppable. But for every upward action, we know there will be an equal and opposite reaction, where challenges against our community will come up just as fast, as they historically have.

To create the world we want to live in, we need changemakers, thought leaders, ceiling breakers, and rebels among us who are willing to break the status quo. People who are willing to stand up, speak up, and unapologetically rise and say:

We might choose to work hard, we might always stay humble, but *we are not keeping our heads down anymore.*

ACKNOWLEDGMENTS

I'd been wanting to write this book for about three years before I finally got to actually *writing.* By then, there had been a small mountain of Post-it notes with barely legible scribbles of ideas collected on my walls and desk. There were ideas from late-night conversations, and notes on suggested readings from friends eager to lend a hand in the project. Along the way of ideation, I have received help from so many incredible people, and I've worked to thank them all individually. In addition to those who have already been thanked, I want to share some shout-outs to the coolest folks ever:

First, all the love to my incredible agent Johanna Castillo at Writers House, who saw the potential of this book, even before I truly understood what it was going to be about, and championed it every step of the way.

Speaking of champions, my deep gratitude to my editor Emi Ikkanda at Tiny Reparations Books at Penguin Random House. Emi, you are a bona fide champion of Asian and minority voices, and one of the best editors I've ever met. I still don't know how you read so fast and yet can still generate so many incredible ideas. I want to download your brain.

I also want to thank Ev Wong, my writing coach, who helped me through every single page of this book. There is no way this could have been done without you, and all your suggestions, edits, changes, and ideas along the way. This feels like a co-creation, and your contributions have been invaluable.

Speaking of being there every step of the way—thank you to Amy Meraki, my partner, my life buddy, and my beloved. You helped me discover what true, unconditional love feels like, and getting to play and dance and explore and be all versions of ourselves with each other.

Patty Langlais, who is not only a brilliant therapist but also a truly wonderful teacher. You helped me come up with so many ideas and made so many brilliant suggestions that truly brought my book to life. The seven patterns couldn't have happened without your help, and your wisdom is immeasurable.

To my sister—you've always been the greatest inspiration in my life, as well as the person I most looked up to. Thank you for everything, and then thank you some more; you deserve all the love and happiness in the world and I'm deeply grateful we came out of the same womb. And of course, Rey, who has stood shoulder to shoulder with me through so many dark nights and shining mornings.

Thank you to Colin Pal, cofounder and co-facilitator of the Waking Dragons Asian Group, as well as my Asian crew at the Waking Dragons. Colin, your wisdom and energy have been absolutely foundational. And to the group: getting to see you kings, as a group of Asian men who are all courageous enough to do the inner work, is what keeps me going.

To Ji-Youn Kim, my friend and the person I know who fights most fervently for those who have been robbed of their voices, and the one who is most dedicated to healing them, thank you for always challenging me to greater depths of compassion, and for sharing your wisdom.

To the incredible training team at Integral Coaching Canada (ICC), who not only gave me the skills to be a better coach, but also how to see myself with greater clarity and truth.

To Peter Shallard, who helped come up with the podcast name *Big Asian Energy* over a fireside chat, and insisted that it was a better title than *The Rebel Cry of the Tiger Child*. Good god, what a mess that would have been.

Thank you also to Emilee Evans, my accountability rock star who somehow managed to help me stay productive every single week.

To all my instructors, coaches, trainers, facilitators who have taught me so much over the years—thank you. I'm a big believer that one can never truly create in isolation, and I have been inspired by countless people along the way.

And finally, to so many people who contributed ideas, inspiration, and just being such champions to the mission: Olivia Keane, James Mel, Juno Parlange, Toper Ravadilla, Mark Manson, Dan Go, Amy Yip, Aisen Li, Eric Wong, Danny Tseng, Andrew Chau, Jerry Won, Vicky Tsai, Sheleana Aiyana, and my sister from another mother—Renee Chen. Thank you for your help, advice, love, and encouragements along the way.

NOTES

CHAPTER 1: ASIAN CONFIDENCE HITS DIFFERENT

13 **Humility or modesty:** Sarah Kulkofsky and Qi Wang, "The Role of Modesty in the East Asian Self and Implications for Cognition," in *Focus on Cognitive Psychology Research*, edited by Michael A. Vanshevsky (Hauppauge, NY: Nova Science Publishers, 2006), 1–23, https://www.researchgate.net/publication /342064767.

17 **Asia currently covers some 4.7 billion:** Wikipedia contributors, "Asia," Wikipedia, March 18, 2024, https://en.wikipedia.org/wiki/Asia.

19 **Values get passed down:** Lorine Erika Saito, "The Complexity of Generational Status and Ethnic Identity of Japanese Americans," *Family Journal* 29, no. 2 (December 20, 2020): 213–19, https://doi.org/10.1177/106648072097 7510.

25 **"High competence, low warmth":** Susan T. Fiske, "Stereotype Content: Warmth and Competence Endure," *Current Directions in Psychological Science* 27, no. 2 (February 28, 2018): 67–73, https://doi.org/10.1177/09637214177 38825.

28 **"Appear 'Less Asian'":** Amy Qin, "Applying to College, and Trying to Appear 'Less Asian,'" *New York Times*, June 20, 2023, https://www.nytimes.com /2022/12/02/us/asian-american-college-applications.html.

28 **Princeton review test prep:** Princeton Review, *Cracking College Admissions*, edited by John Katzman and Staff of the Princeton Review, 2nd ed. (The Princeton Review, 2004).

28 **One Washington State:** Louis Casiano, "Washington School District Doesn't Include Asian Kids in 'Students of Color' Category," *Fox News*, November 17, 2020, https://www.foxnews.com/us/asian-color-category-washington.

30 **Bain & Company:** Pam Yee and Karthik Venkataraman, "New Research from Bain & Company Shows a Critical Need for Greater Workplace Inclusivity among Asian American Workers," Bain & Company press release, May 5,

2022, https://www.bain.com/about/media-center/press-releases/2022 /asian-americans-crack-the-bamboo-ceiling/.

30 **The AAAIM (Association of Asian American Investment Managers) con-ducted a study:** "Good Workers—Not Leaders: Unconscious Biases That Stall AAPI Advancement," report, Association of Asian American Investment Managers and Backstop Solutions Group, September 13, 2021, https://aaaim.org /wp-content/uploads/2021/09/21-09_BSG-AAAIM-Report-v2.pdf.

CHAPTER 2: MEET THE SEVEN PATTERNS

34 **Named Phra Phuttha Maha Suwan Patimakorn:** "The Golden Buddha Image," *Teayeon Wordpress*, April 23, 2009, https://teayeon.wordpress.com /phra-maha-mondop/about/.

CHAPTER 3: TAMING THE ACHIEVEMENT MONSTER

57 **When a group of psychologists at the University of Texas:** Kevin Cokley et al., "An Examination of the Impact of Minority Status Stress and Impostor Feelings on the Mental Health of Diverse Ethnic Minority College Students," *Journal of Multicultural Counseling and Development* 41, no. 2 (April 1, 2013): 82–95, https://doi.org/10.1002/j.2161-1912.2013.00029.x.

57 *Asian American students experienced the highest rates of impostor syndrome:* Meifen Wei et al., "Impostor Feelings and Psychological Distress among Asian Americans: Interpersonal Shame and Self-Compassion," *Counseling Psychologist* 48, no. 3 (January 26, 2020): 432–58, https://doi.org/10 .1177/0011000019891992.

58 *Why Is There a Higher Rate of Impostor Syndrome among BIPOC:* Afran Ahmed et al., "Why Is There a Higher Rate of Impostor Syndrome among BIPOC?," Zenodo (CERN European Organization for Nuclear Research), December 8, 2020, https://doi.org/10.5281/zenodo.4310477.

63 **Men would apply to positions when they met only 60 percent of the qualifications:** Tara Sophia Mohr, "Why Women Don't Apply for Jobs Unless They're 100% Qualified," *Harvard Business Review*, August 25, 2014, https:// hbr.org/2014/08/why-women-dont-apply-for-jobs-unless-theyre-100 -qualified.

65 **MIT commencement speech:** Mark Rober, "Address to MIT Class of 2023," June 1, 2023, https://www.youtube.com/watch?v=0FGlsuTnt_U.

66 **Psychologist Carol Dweck wrote:** Carol S. Dweck, *Mindset: The New Psychology of Success* (New York: Random House Publishing Group, 2007).

71 **In the book *Play*, Dr. Stuart Brown:** Stuart Brown and Christopher Vaughan, *Play: How It Shapes the Brain, Opens the Imagination, and Invigorates the Soul*, rev. ed. (Melbourne & London: Scribe Publications Pty Limited, 2010), https://books.google.ie/books?id=mom5XhWs2rMC.

71 **Emotional systems:** "Scientific Disciplines Researching Play," National Institute for Play, accessed March 22, 2024, https://www.nifplay.org/play-science/scientific-disciplines-researching-play/.

CHAPTER 4: BREAKING FREE FROM "NOT GOOD ENOUGH"

78 **Americans from East Asian backgrounds:** Cassie Werber, "East and West Have Opposite Views of Personal Success, according to Psychologists," *Quartz*, July 20, 2022, https://qz.com/1025291/east-and-west-have-opposite-views-of-personal-success-according-to-psychologists.

80 **Almost all participants were comparing:** Muqaddas Jan, Sanobia Anwwer Soomro, and Nawaz Ahmad, "Impact of Social Media on Self-Esteem," *European Scientific Journal* (ESJ), 13, no. 23 (August 31, 2017): 329, https://doi.org/10.19044/esj.2017.v13n23p329.

81 ***Excellent Sheep*:** William Deresiewicz, *Excellent Sheep: The Miseducation of the American Elite and the Way to a Meaningful Life* (New York: Simon & Schuster, 2014).

86 **Respective traits:** Shimi Kang, MD, "How the Tiger, Dolphin, and Jellyfish Parents Differ: A Brief Comparison of Parenting Styles," *Psychology Today*, May 18, 2014, https://www.psychologytoday.com/us/blog/the-dolphin-way/201405/how-the-tiger-dolphin-and-jellyfish-parents-differ.

90 **One experiment Pink quoted:** Edward L. Deci, Richard Koestner, and Richard M. Ryan, "Extrinsic Rewards and Intrinsic Motivation in Education: Reconsidered Once Again," *Review of Educational Research* 71, no. 1 (March 1, 2001): 1–27, https://doi.org/10.3102/00346543071001001.

CHAPTER 5: SETTING YOURSELF ON FIRE TO KEEP OTHERS WARM

115 **I find many Fixers:** Lindsay C. Gibson, *Adult Children of Emotionally Immature Parents: How to Heal from Distant, Rejecting, or Self-Involved Parents* (Oakland, CA: New Harbinger Publications, 2015).

CHAPTER 6: HIDING YOUR REAL SELF

171 **In her book *The Power of Saying No*:** Sally Strong, "Think You're Good at Saying No? Actually, You Could Probably Use a Few Pointers," University of

Houston, UH Newsroom, September 2, 2023, https://uh.edu/news-events /stories/2023/june-2023/05012023-patrick-empowered-no.php.

171 **"Boundaries are like":** Matt Abrahams, "The Power of No: How Boundaries Help Us Live More Empowered Lives," Stanford Graduate School of Business, Insights, February 20, 2023, https://www.gsb.stanford.edu/insights/power -no-how-boundaries-help-us-live-more-empowered-lives.

CHAPTER 7: COMMUNICATING ASSERTIVENESS

180 **Chinese journalist:** Erin Meyer, *The Culture Map: Breaking Through the Invisible Boundaries of Global Business* (New York: PublicAffairs, 2014), https:// books.google.com.ph/books?id=IMsiBQAAQBAJ.

181 **"Read between the lines":** Meyer, *The Culture Map.*

183 *See things differently:* Hannah Faye Chua, Julie E. Boland, and Richard E. Nisbett, "Cultural Variation in Eye Movements during Scene Perception," *Proceedings of the National Academy of Sciences of the United States of America* 102, no. 35 (August 22, 2005): 12629–33, https://doi.org/10.1073/pnas.050616 2102.

183 **Individualistic societies:** David Robson, "How East and West think in profoundly different ways," BBC, February 24, 2022, https://www.bbc.com/future /article/20170118-how-east-and-west-think-in-profoundly-different-ways.

184 **Less likely to take on an extreme stance:** Rui Wang et al., "Cultural Differences: Why Do Asians Avoid Extreme Responses?," *Survey Practice* 1, no. 3 (October 1, 2008): 1–7, https://doi.org/10.29115/sp-2008-0011.

186 **Four main types of communication:** "Understanding Your Communication Style," Princeton University, UMatter, accessed March 20, 2024, https:// umatter.princeton.edu/respect/tools/communication-styles.

197 **Degrees of mitigation:** Judith Orasanu and Ute Fischer, "Cultural Diversity and Crew Communication," paper presented at the 50th International Astronautic Congress, October 1999 (Reston, VA: American Institute of Aeronautics and Astronautics, AIAA, 1999).

209 **Maintain eye contact with elders:** Shota Uono and Jari K. Hietanen, "Eye Contact Perception in the West and East: A Cross-Cultural Study," *PLoS ONE* 10, no. 2 (February 25, 2015), https://doi.org/10.1371/journal.pone.0118094.

209 **Direct eye contact:** Michael Argyle and Janet B. Dean, "Eye-Contact, Distance and Affiliation," *Sociometry* 28, no. 3 (September 1, 1965): 289, https:// doi.org/10.2307/2786027.

210 *Definitive Book:* Allan and Barbara Pease, *The Definitive Book of Body Language,* Illustrated Edition (London: Orion, 2017).

210 *Power of Eye Contact*: Michael Ellsberg, *The Power of Eye Contact: Your Secret for Success in Business, Love, and Life* (New York: HarperCollins, 2010).

211 **Study on eye contact:** Judee K. Burgoon et al., "Effects of Gaze on Hiring, Credibility, Attraction and Relational Message Interpretation," *Journal of Nonverbal Behavior* 9, no. 3 (September 1985): 133–46, https://doi.org/10.1007/bf01000735.

CHAPTER 8: COMPASSIONATE ASSERTIVENESS

229 *Compassionate Leadership*: Rasmus Hougaard and Jacqueline Carter, *Compassionate Leadership: How to Do Hard Things in a Human Way* (Cambridge, MA: Harvard Business Review Press, 2022).

234 **Macaque monkeys:** Temma Ehrenfeld, "Reflections on Mirror Neurons," APS–Association for Psychological Science, February 27, 2011, https://www.psychologicalscience.org/observer/reflections-on-mirror-neurons.

234 **In 2013, a group of researchers:** Ewa Kacewicz et al., "Pronoun Use Reflects Standings in Social Hierarchies," *Journal of Language and Social Psychology* 33, no. 2 (September 19, 2013): 125–43, https://doi.org/10.1177/0261927x13502654.

239 *Culture Code*: Daniel Coyle, *The Culture Code: The Secrets of Highly Successful Groups* (New York: Random House, 2018).

PART 3: BIG ASIAN COMMUNITY

245 **STAATUS Index:** Niala Boodhoo, "Asian Americans Least Likely to Feel They Belong in U.S., Study Finds," *Axios,* May 7, 2023, https://www.axios.com/2023/05/07/asian-americans-belonging-us-hate-discrimination.

CHAPTER 9: BARRIERS TO BELONGING

249 **Asians brought diseases:** Wikipedia contributors, "Chinese Exclusion Act," Wikipedia, February 22, 2024, https://en.wikipedia.org/wiki/Chinese_Exclusion_Act.

250 **"One drop of Japanese blood":** "Executive Order 9066: Resulting in Japanese-American Incarceration (1942)," National Archives, Milestone Documents, January 24, 2022, https://www.archives.gov/milestone-documents/executive-order-9066.

251 **Transpacific alliance:** Adrian De Leon, "The Long History of Racism against Asian Americans in the U.S.," *PBS News Hour,* April 9, 2020, https://www.pbs.org/newshour/nation/the-long-history-of-racism-against-asian-americans-in-the-u-s.

252 **"Foreign-looking names":** Dina Gerdeman, "Minorities Who 'Whiten' Job Resumes Get More Interviews," Harvard Business School, Working Knowledge, March 20, 2004, https://hbswk.hbs.edu/item/minorities-who-whiten-job-resumes-get-more-interviews?cid=spmailing-25757313-.

254 **This feeling of "Sorry, Wrong Asian":** Jeff Yang, "I'm Jeff Yang, Not Jeff Chang! The Everyday Horror of Having to Say 'Sorry, Wrong Asian,'" *The Guardian*, April 20, 2022, https://www.theguardian.com/lifeandstyle/2022/apr/19/ali-wong-randall-park-sorry-wrong-asian-mistake.

256 **Multiracial Asian American:** Neil G. Ruiz, Luis Noe-Bustamante, and Sono Shah, "Asian Americans and Life in America," Pew Research Center, May 8, 2023, https://www.pewresearch.org/2023/05/08/asian-americans-and-life-in-america/.

258 **Model minority stereotype:** Viet Thanh Nguyen, "Asian Americans Are Still Caught in the Trap of the 'Model Minority' Stereotype. And It Creates Inequality for All," *TIME,* June 26, 2020, https://time.com/5859206/anti-asian-racism-america/.

261 **Employee Led Resource Groups:** Kimmy Yam, "Asian Americans Most Likely to Join Employee Diversity Groups but Don't Feel Supported, Report Says," *NBC News*, March 23, 2023, https://www.nbcnews.com/news/asian-america/asian-americans-likely-join-employee-diversity-groups-dont-feel-suppor-rcna76209.

262 **People to climb the ladder:** Buck Gee, "Asian Americans Are the Least Likely Group in the U.S. to Be Promoted to Management," *Harvard Business Review*, May 31, 2021, https://hbr.org/2018/05/asian-americans-are-the-least-likely-group-in-the-u-s-to-be-promoted-to-management.

262 **"Interchangeably Asian":** Yang, "I'm Jeff Yang."

263 **"I think my husband":** *Ali Wong: Baby Cobra,* video directed by Jay Karas, aired on Netflix May 5, 2016, https://www.netflix.com/ph-en/title/80101493.

264 **Subtle Asian Traits group:** Samira Sadeque, "In This Facebook Group, South Asians Are Being Told They're 'Not Asian,'" *Daily Dot,* May 20, 2021, https://www.dailydot.com/irl/subtle-asian-traits-south-asians/.

265 **Asian food:** Krystal Jagoo, "South Asians Are Asians, Too," *verywell mind,* May 17, 2022, https://www.verywellmind.com/south-asians-are-asian-too-5271761.

267 **Nadra Kareem:** Nadra Kareem Nittle, "What Is the Definition of Internalized Racism?," *ThoughtCo*, March 1, 2021, https://www.thoughtco.com/what-is-internalized-racism-2834958.

271 **Though a reimagining of *Romeo and Juliet*, friend-zoning Romeo:** Jason Lim, "Why Couldn't Jet Li Kiss Aaliyah?," *Korea Times*, April 29, 2016, https://www.koreatimes.co.kr/www/opinion/2020/03/638_203706.html.

271 **"As members of inferior":** Peter Chua and Diane C. Fujino, "Negotiating New Asian American Masculinities: Attitudes and Gender Expectations," *Journal of Men's Studies* 7, no. 3 (1999): 391–413, https://scholarworks.sjsu.edu/cgi/viewcontent.cgi?article=1003&context=sociology_pub.

271 **Asian man:** Grace Kao, Kelly Stamper Balistreri, and Kara Joyner, "Asian American Men in Romantic Dating Markets," *Contexts* 17, no. 4 (November 2018): 48–53, https://doi.org/10.1177/1536504218812869.

271 **Non-Asian women said:** Kelly Stamper Balistreri, Kara Joyner, and Grace Kao, "Relationship Involvement among Young Adults: Are Asian American Men an Exceptional Case?," *Population Research and Policy Review* 34, no. 5 (May 23, 2015): 709–32, https://doi.org/10.1007/s11113-015-9361-1.

272 **Asian men received:** Ken-Hou Lin and Jennifer Hickes Lundquist, "Mate Selection in Cyberspace: The Intersection of Race, Gender, and Education," *American Journal of Sociology* 119, no. 1 (July 1, 2013): 183–215, https://doi.org/10.1086/673129.

CHAPTER 10: OWNING OUR BELONGING

279 **Frederick Douglass:** Frederick Douglass, "(1867) Frederick Douglass Describes the 'Composite Nation,'" *Blackpast*, January 28, 2007, https://www.blackpast.org/african-american-history/1867-frederick-douglass-describes-composite-nation/.

280 **"Build bridges of understanding":** "Yuri Kochiyama," National Park Service, April 3, 2024, https://www.nps.gov/people/yuri-kochiyama.htm.

281 **Fred Korematsu:** Korematsu Institute and Karen Korematsu, "Fred Korematsu's Story," Fred T. Korematsu Institute, June 19, 2021, https://korematsuinstitute.org/freds-story/.

CHAPTER 11: BIG ASIAN FAMILY

288 **Living with a parent:** Laura Lippman and Renee Ryberg, "What Sets Families in Asia Apart," *Child Trends*, March 4, 2013, https://www.childtrends.org/publications/what-sets-families-in-asia-apart.

288 **Multigenerational households:** D'vera Cohn and Jeffrey Passel, "Record 64 Million Americans Live in Multigenerational Households," Pew Research Center, April 5, 2018, https://www.pewresearch.org/short-reads/2018/04/05/a-record-64-million-americans-live-in-multigenerational-households/.

290 **Therapist Sam Louie in *Psychology Today*:** Sam Louie, "How Some Asian Adults Perceive Parental Lecturing," *Psychology Today*, June 22, 2021, https://www.psychologytoday.com/us/blog/minority-report/202106/how-some-asian-adults-perceive-parental-lecturing.

310 **"Disempowering Parenting and Mental Health among Asian American Youth: Immigration and Ethnicity":** Yoonsun Choi, Mina Lee, Jeanette Park Lee, Michael Park, Soo Young Lee, and Hyeouk Hahm, "Disempowering Parenting and Mental Health among Asian American Youth: Immigration and Ethnicity," *Journal of Applied Developmental Psychology* 66 (January–February 2020): 101077, 10.1016/j.appdev.2019.101077.

312 **Gibson provides:** Lindsay C. Gibson, *Adult Children of Emotionally Immature Parents: How to Heal from Distant, Rejecting, or Self-Involved Parents* (Oakland, CA: New Harbinger Publications, 2015).

CHAPTER 12: SCARIEST THING I'VE EVER DONE

320 **Suicide was the number one:** Amelia Noor-Oshiro, "Asian American Young Adults Are the Only Racial Group with Suicide as Their Leading Cause of Death, So Why Is No One Talking about This?" *The Conversation*, April 23, 2021, https://theconversation.com/asian-american-young-adults-are-the-only-racial-group-with-suicide-as-their-leading-cause-of-death-so-why-is-no-one-talking-about-this-158030.

320 **Asian Americans are three times *less likely*:** Koko Nishi, "Mental Health among Asian-Americans," American Psychological Association, May 1, 2012, https://www.apa.org/pi/oema/resources/ethnicity-health/asian-american/article-mental-health.

320 **Mental health services:** "Why Asian Americans Don't Seek Help for Mental Illness," McLean Hospital, May 2, 2023, https://www.mcleanhospital.org/essential/why-asian-americans-dont-seek-help-mental-illness.

321 **Dr. Geoffrey Liu, a Harvard psychiatry professor:** Sam Louie, "How Some Asian Adults Perceive Parental Lecturing," *Psychology Today,* June 22, 2021, https://www.psychologytoday.com/us/blog/minority-report/202106/how-some-asian-adults-perceive-parental-lecturing.

ABOUT THE AUTHOR

John Wang is a speaker, leadership coach to the Asian American community, and host of the *Big Asian Energy* show. John is the founder of Mastery Academy and has coached Asian American clients from Google, Apple, American Express, Goldman Sachs, and other Fortune 500 companies. His videos have reached over 25 million views on TikTok. When he's not writing, John loves to travel (Osaka is his favorite city to visit at the moment). His favorite boba is brown sugar boba with milk and red bean.